Against the Death Penalty

⋮

Against the Death Penalty

⋮

WRITINGS FROM THE FIRST ABOLITIONISTS—GIUSEPPE PELLI AND CESARE BECCARIA

Texts translated and with historical commentary by Peter Garnsey

PRINCETON UNIVERSITY PRESS

Princeton & Oxford

Published by Princeton University Press
41 William Street, Princeton, New Jersey 08540
99 Banbury Road, Oxford OX2 6JX

press.princeton.edu

All Rights Reserved
First paperback printing, 2024
Paperback ISBN 9780691211947
The Library of Congress has cataloged the cloth edition as follows:

Names: Pelli Bencivenni, Giuseppe, 1729-1808, Contro la pena di morte. English. | Beccaria, Cesare, marchese di, 1738-1794. Works. Selections. English. | Garnsey, Peter, translator, writer of added commentary.

Title: Against the death penalty : writings from the first abolitionists—Giuseppe Pelli and Ceasare Beccaria / texts translated with commentary by Peter Garnsey.

Description: Princeton : Princeton University Press, [2020] | Includes bibliographical references and index.

Identifiers: LCCN 2020012463 (print) | LCCN 2020012464 (ebook) | ISBN 9780691209883 (hardcover ; alk. paper) | ISBN 9780691211374 (ebook)

Subjects: LCSH: Capital punishment—Early works to 1800. | Punishment—Early works to 1800.

Classification: LCC HV8698 .A43 2020 (print) | LCC HV8698 (ebook) | DDC 364.66—dc23

LC record available at https://lccn.loc.gov/2020012463
LC ebook record available at https://lccn.loc.gov/2020012464

British Library Cataloging-in-Publication Data is available

Editorial: Rob Tempio and Matt Rohal
Production Editorial: Ellen Foos
Text and Jacket/Cover Design: Pamela L. Schnitter
Production: Jacqueline Poirier
Publicity: Alyssa Sanford and Amy Stewart
Copyeditor: Francis Eaves

This book has been composed in Arno Pro

CONTENTS

PREFACE

Penal systems have been on my mind for longer than I care to think. I began research as a student of Roman criminal law in its social context. That these interests were not short-lived and ephemeral I owe largely to David Daube of Oxford and Berkeley, and John Crook of Cambridge. During the short but fruitful time I spent in Berkeley, I began reading in the area of comparative law. John Noonan was midwife to an early paper comparing Roman and British criminal law, though he accepted it for publication only on condition that I doubled its original length. These interests have not gone away over the decades in which my susceptibility to different academic influences and explorations has taken me in other directions.

One of these other areas of interest has been the history of political thought, or intellectual history. On my arrival in Cambridge from Berkeley, Moses Finley bequeathed to me (it seemed I had no choice in the matter) his lecture series on Greek political thought. This gave me an entrée into the group of historians of political thought under the chairmanship of Quentin Skinner and including the heavyweight quartet of John Dunn, Raymond Geuss, Istvan Hont and Richard Tuck (among others). There followed work on the ideology of slavery and on the (not unconnected) debate over property among philosophers, jurists and theologians from classical antiquity to the late nineteenth century.

A sidestep took me into the way in which property crimes were punished in the early modern era, and in no time I was involved in study of the development of imprisonment as a punishment (and to some extent that of other penalties, notably convict transportation), and in the history of the concept of penal servitude. In retrospect, I can see that capital punishment lay just around the corner. But in the first instance, it was the penalty that Beccaria of Milan proposed as a substitute for death in his pioneering *On Crimes and*

Punishments (original publication 1764, definitive edition 1766), and the way he conceptualised it as a form of slavery, rather than his attack on the death penalty as such, that caught me in his net. The next and final step was unforeseen and unexpected. I became aware of the existence of a treatise that predated Beccaria's work by three years, *Against the Death Penalty* (1761) by Giuseppe Pelli of Florence. Because Pelli was concerned centrally with the death penalty, I shifted my focus to capital punishment. I was not leaving Beccaria behind, because his most radical proposal was that the death penalty should be abolished. Meanwhile the opportunity opened up of comparing and contrasting the approaches to this subject of two thinkers who were contemporaries and near neighbours, yet ignorant of each other's existence and intellectual activities.

It is a pleasure to be able to acknowledge the generous and invaluable assistance I have received from a number of quarters in the course of writing this book and preparing it for publication. The Cambridge University Library, as a host of scholars have discovered before me, gives wonderful service in providing access to the arcane texts in its collection and in securing others which it does not possess. I am also extremely grateful to officials of the Biblioteca Nazionale Centrale of Florence for permitting me to consult selected manuscripts of Pelli.

Under the heading of intellectual influences, my catalogue begins with names already listed above, among whom I would single out Raymond Geuss, who has read the whole of the present work and has made many timely and perceptive comments and constructive criticisms. I am deeply indebted to Philippe Audegean, who as editor of the editio princeps of 2014, followed by a French edition in 2016, and as author of a number of papers on Pelli, dominates this new field of scholarship. From the first, he has encouraged me in my project, and read all my work with a critical eye—in the process picking up a number of errors and infelicities. Renato Pasta discovered the existence of the Pelli manuscript and made it available to scholars, together with the diaries of Pelli, and has composed a number of seminal articles on the author; he has been similarly greatly supportive.

On Beccaria—on whom both Audegean and Pasta have written extensively and with authority, in company with a number of other scholars—I have benefited greatly from the masterly study of Sophus Reinert on the Academy of Fisticuffs, of which Beccaria was a member, and which served as the incubator of his treatise. Sophus kindly sent me a draft of his book prior to publication. Aglaia McLintock has generously shared with me her expert knowledge of the Roman and post-Roman doctrine of slavery as a judicial penalty. I received useful feedback, with particular relevance to Beccaria and the reception of his thought, from participants in two seminars: A Jesus College symposium on 'Incarceration and Imprisonment' (2016), and a seminar of the Cambridge Italian Research Network on 'Crime and Punishment' (2017).

Colleagues and friends who have given me advice, assistance and encouragement include Anthony Bowen, John Cornwell, Matthew Dyson, Michael Edwards, Nicholas Guyatt, Marguerite Hirt, Lucy Hosker, Joanna Innes, Mary Laven, Arnaldo Marcone, Renaud Morieux, Lea Niccolai, Wilfrid Prest, Pasquale Rosafio, Philip Schofield, Gerard Smadja, Findlay Stark and Benjamin Straumann. I owe a special debt to Marina Montenegro for her invaluable assistance in unravelling the often contorted periods of Giuseppe Pelli. Finally, my thanks go to Rob Tempio and Matt Rohal for taking on this project, and to Ellen Foos and Francis Eaves for facilitating the production process.

Against the Death Penalty

⋮

Introduction

In 1968–69, the Archivio di Stato di Firenze acquired from the archives of the Pelli-Fabbroni family two large collections of documents composed by the last Pelli, Giuseppe Bencivenni Pelli (1729–1808). Around two decades later, at the end of the 1980s, the draft of an unfinished dissertation *Against the Death Penalty* came to light among the documents.[1] The manuscript was introduced to the world of scholarship (in 1990) by Renato Pasta, who had unearthed and identified it, and by Philippe Audegean, who produced the first edition, complete with a substantial introduction to the text and its contents, in Italian (2014) and then in French (2016).[2]

Pelli was a minor aristocrat from Florence who pursued a career within the Austrian Habsburg administration in the Grand Duchy of Tuscany. His most prominent post, and the one that gave him the greatest satisfaction, was that of director of the Uffizi Gallery (1775–93). According to his own testimony, he wrote *Against the Death Penalty* between 24 November 1760 and 6 January 1761.[3] It was published more than 250 years later. He never completed it. It remains in the form of an advanced draft, tapering off toward the end, and finishing with a number of fragments, some of them substantial. It is an extended treatment of a subject which had not previously been discussed from a critical standpoint and in a comprehensive way. As far as we know, it is the first systematic attack on the death penalty in history.

It is known precisely when he began to write and stopped writing, because he tells us in his *Efemeridi*, the enormous diary that he compiled, day-in, day-out, over almost half a century, from 1759. A question that I set out to answer, with the aid of the *Efemeridi*, is how he came to write the dissertation in the first place, and why he gave up the project.

Against the Death Penalty was composed approximately three years before the publication, in July 1764, of *On Crimes and Punishments*, by an anonymous author, who was later revealed to be Cesare Beccaria Bonesana (1738–94). Beccaria was also a member of the minor nobility, but of Milan, who worked for the Austrian administration in Lombardy. Before the discovery of Pelli's work, it was assumed that Beccaria's work contained the first serious attack on the death penalty.

Previously, abolition had had its advocates, such as the English radical Gerrard Winstanley in 1649, writing from a religious perspective, and the Quaker John Bellers, in 1699, who employed arguments from utility.[4] The list lengthens somewhat if we include thinkers such as Thomas More and Blaise Pascal, who were critical of the death penalty without being outright abolitionists.[5] In this category one might also place two anonymous English pamphleteers, Solon Secundus (1695) and A Student in Politics (1754). Both protested against the plethora of public executions and pressed for an alternative punishment, which they called imprisonment and hard labour, or slavery, but they contemplated reduction of the use of the death penalty rather than total abolition.[6] Another potential 'candidate', a Sicilian, Tommaso Natale (1733–1819), whose treatise on penalties has much in common with that of Beccaria, also fails the test, on two counts: first, his work was published in 1772—his claim to have completed an early version in 1759 is not accepted by scholars—and second, he wished to retain the death penalty for particularly serious crimes.[7]

Pelli targeted the death penalty exclusively, whereas Beccaria's work was an attack on the whole system of criminal law operating in his time. The latter's critique of the death penalty occupies only one chapter (28) out of his forty-seven. It is by far the longest, however: it can be assumed to have contained all that he wanted to say on the subject, and his arguments are significant and weighty. The abolition of the death penalty is also the most radical of his proposals for reform, and it attracted the most attention and controversy. There is every reason to attempt a comparison between the two treatments of the subject.

The treatments are strikingly different. This is in itself remarkable. Here we have two men, living in neighbouring regions of the Austrian Habsburg empire, writing at more or less the same time, each ignorant of the existence of the other, each under the impression that he was the first to venture into these dangerous waters, and approaching the same subject in contrasting ways. Pelli's work reads rather like a juristic treatise, though his humanity shows through, and he knows how to appeal to the emotions. Beccaria's treatise is a manifesto: it is passionate, highly rhetorical, and it pulls no punches. In sum, what we have before us is a rare opportunity to study and compare two works on the same highly controversial subject in a highly critical vein, written entirely independently of each other and more or less contemporaneously.

I offer translations of the relevant texts—in the case of Pelli's manuscript, the first English translation. Next, I explore the historical and intellectual contexts in which Pelli and Beccaria lived and wrote, and I attempt to understand their personalities and mentalities. This is an especially rewarding pursuit in the case of Pelli, thanks largely to the existence and nature of his diaries (*Efemeridi*). They are a goldmine, full of fascinating detail about his character, beliefs and interests, and the social and cultural life of Florence in the middle and second half of the eighteenth century.[8] I then set out to assess the two writers' arguments against the death penalty, pointing to significant differences and similarities, and attempting to identify the sources that inspired or influenced them.

In terms of argumentation, in summary, Pelli lines up in the main with the Dutch and German natural law philosophers and jurists of the past, joining the debate which had been in progress since the early seventeenth century on the State of Nature, the transition into civil society via the Social Contract, and the ends and justification of punishment. He made a move, however, that none of these thinkers had contemplated or dared to make, in denying the necessity, utility and justice of the death penalty.

Whereas Pelli's outlook is firmly Catholic, as shown among other things by the dominance in his discourse of the notion of original sin, which in his view underlies both criminal behaviour and the penal law that has been enacted to suppress it, Beccaria follows the secularist tendencies of the French Enlightenment philosophers in making a clean break between sin and crime, divine and human justice. His trademark doctrine, which stemmed from a utilitarian interpretation of the Social Contract, is that the penal system must essentially be directed at avoiding public harm and promoting private good, or as he famously stated, 'the greatest happiness shared among the greatest number'. Pelli arrives, nevertheless, though by a different route, at something very similar to this utilitarian and minimalist view of the criminal justice system.

My final chapter is necessarily centred on Beccaria, in as much as it is an essay on the impact of his work on selected later thinkers and politicians, with special reference to his alternative, or surrogate, penalty, namely forced labour. It is a crucial element of Beccaria's argument that the death penalty is less efficacious than forced labour as a deterrent (and the essential end of punishment, in his account, is deterrence). I am especially interested in the way Beccaria conceptualised his substitute penalty as slavery, and the way this was received in Britain and America, where his work was especially closely read and was extremely influential. The key figures in my enquiry are Jeremy Bentham and Thomas Jefferson.

Pelli left an incomplete draft of a thoughtful and searching critique of the death penalty;[9] Beccaria published a finished product which many regard as the most significant tract of modern (and early modern) times on the reform of the criminal law,[10] and which contained a highly effective attack on the death penalty. The former work was buried without trace for two and half centuries; the latter launched a movement of reform which has not yet run its course. A comparison between Pelli and Beccaria can only go so far, and is of limited utility. The same applies to the hypothetical question of what would have happened, what difference it would have made, if Pelli had published a full, polished treatise before Beccaria; and of how Beccaria would have reacted in such a circumstance. A more profitable line of enquiry might be to assess each of the two treatises as products of their times—rather than as definitive statements on the issue in question, which they are not[11]—and, in the case of Beccaria's work, in terms of the impact that it had in the short term and the long. Modern penal law was born with Beccaria: there was a 'Beccaria moment'.[12]

GIUSEPPE BENCIVENNI PELLI (1729–1808)

⋮

Texts

⋮

Giuseppe Pelli: *Outline of a Disquisition on the Death Penalty*[1]

TO THE READER

The discourse that I have conceived and composed will doubtless be regarded by many as a display of ingenuity to advocate before the public a falsity or a paradox. Our century has seen others such, that are vested with an air of verisimilitude and have had to be combated in diverse ways. In truth we should be amazed at pronouncements on the evils that issue from the sciences and from the culture of the mind, the praise of the savage life,[2] and the supposedly persuasive demonstration, so visible among us, that we have an obligation to ridicule the divine law and the law of good government. Future centuries, unless they are excessively blind, will abhor them and wonder at them in equal measure, especially because they have arisen in the full light of solid knowledge. For these works have shown that there can appear, together with human knowledge, certain strokes of ignorance. What is more, they have the unfortunate feature of being adorned with eloquence, and thus have lodged in the minds of people who would have been the best equipped to promote truths that are beneficial to the whole world.

I might perhaps merit inclusion in the number of those fine spirits, although devoid of the gifts which are so admired in them, were not the disparity between our aims and conclusions a vindication of my sentiments. I do not deny a justice of purpose in M. Rousseau and the anonymous author of the discourse which prefaces the reprint of the Satires of our Menzini.[3] Nor am I unaware that the former as well as the latter were convinced that they were procuring happiness for men—the former in counselling them to prefer ignorance to knowledge and to place brutishness above culture, and to abandon the city and retreat to the horrors of the forest and the empty seashores; and in the case of the latter, how to unearth the hidden defects in men so as to turn them against others. But would not the world be infested by a host of new evils should their projects be taken up? If, on the other hand, magistrates and rulers resolved to abolish the death penalty for criminal offences, societies would undoubtedly see an increase in the numbers of men, and the vices of private individuals would no longer be a plague upon the public peace.

In my *Discourse* the reasons for this will be made manifest. Here it is sufficient for me, rather than to mount a defence of my proposal, to convince the reader that it is in no way the fruit of fanciful speculation or bizarre imaginings. Rather it issues from that all-encompassing love to which the Ancients gave the name of piety, and from that reasonableness that has removed a multitude of abuses, while holding those that remain to be equally deplorable as those of the past; like them, they deprive the human race of that happiness to which it might aspire.

I am not animated by a spirit of censure, nor of disapproval of our customs or our laws. My complaint, rather, is directed at the blindness of those who have believed that the death of the vicious would extinguish vice. Furthermore, I attribute to the general corruption of the human heart that cruelty which is apparent even in the considered ordinances of venerable lawgivers. That germ within of capricious anger, which is betrayed in hating to death an accused man whose offence is fresh in the memory, is a product of the malice which is deeply rooted in us. The sight of this same criminal on the point of paying the penalty for his misdeeds, surrounded by the horrors of death and torn apart by the remorse of his conscience, troubles the heart of every man; and the satisfaction experienced should he obtain grace, is equal to that attending his agonised suffering under the first impulse of boiling anger. This second sentiment, though no less characteristic of us than the first, is certainly more just and more reasonable, and if I undertake to show this while arguing against the death penalty, I believe I am paying due tribute to humanity, and am vesting myself with a role which should never be renounced. Certainly if I have succeeded in saving the life of one of my fellow men at any moment of my life, I will be happier than if I have signed the death warrant of anyone, however villainous he may be, because I will have answered the call of mercy rather than followed the dictates of rigorous justice.

Perhaps my project will achieve nothing? And so? Should I for fear of using my pen to no effect, spare my breath and not counsel men to show greater humanity? Private individuals have no authority to reform the world, but they are permitted to enlighten it. And just as the powerful are obliged to perform their duty of promoting the happiness of those under them, in the same way individuals are under an obligation to indicate the means by which, in one way or another, that end can be attained.

But consider a scoundrel who has trodden beneath his feet the laws of humanity and society, a villain who has spurned the power of heaven and of the great who rule over the earth, one who in giving free rein to his passion has sacrificed—to his anger, to his thirst for revenge, to his supposed need, and to the thoughtless expression of a forbidden or brutal pleasure—the life, property, marital fidelity and virtue of his fellow citizens or of his superiors, who has failed to keep faith, who has shattered the bonds of blood and of friendship, who has, in a word, contrived to make himself the enemy of all: is sparing the life of such a one an act of humanity? There are those not amenable to be persuaded of this, men of robust temperaments who think their sentiments just because they know their own courage and strength. Such men combine abominating vice in others with believing that they are themselves secure from the danger of succumbing to it; this, however, without examining whether they are not nurturing the seeds of vice within. Anyone considering man as he is, subject to all the storms of passions great and small, driven by a blind *amour propre*, by self-interest and by pleasure, vulnerable to the temptations of sin, infinitely changeable in his thoughts and resolutions, scant in self-knowledge, the victim of injuries inflicted by perverse fortune or the malice of others, seduced by the appearance of the good and oblivious of the consequences of the bad, will understand that everyone is susceptible to committing the blackest of crimes if he is not protected by a superior force, and should therefore show compassion as much for evil acts as for the involuntary afflictions of poverty and sickness.

If it is not for man himself to judge man, only the particular Being who has the privilege of governing imperfect individuals may assume the responsibility for condemning and punishing in others what could not be discovered or chastised in Himself. Only the dubious hope of impunity can convince us of the propriety of making someone pay with the utmost rigour the penalty for a crime which we ourselves might be susceptible to committing some day or other.

You may conclude therefore that my proposition is worthy of a man, and further, if it be acknowledged that it is supported by reason, as I flatter myself to believe strongly is the case, then what is proposed in these pages will merit being put into practice. If on the other hand my line of argument will turn out to be without firm foundation, at least I will be able to console myself for having gone astray in a good cause; and I will continue to desire that the efforts of others in their projects be consistently directed at useful rather than harmful ends, as are for the most part the labours of those whom fortune has enabled to live in the tranquillity of a private chamber.

Disquisition on the Death Penalty as Established for Crimes

CHAPTER 1. INTRODUCTION

Humanity and compassion are the sentiments most worthy of a man, if only he would not disdain to compare his own weakness with that of others. Only a heart that is so totally engrossed in itself that it regards others purely as objects of contempt and fit for the venting of its own passions can view without emotion and with dry eyes the spectacle of men suffering. Perhaps some people believe that our century is worthy of praise for the philosophical spirit that has spread even as far as nations which until a short time ago were considered the most barbarous; also for having introduced among men that gentleness which is so vaunted, and which at the time of our ancestors was given the name of cowardice. But there are facts which will belie such a supposition. Even in the happiest days of the sciences and literature in the time of the Greeks and Romans, and in the fortunate century of Leo X which saw a resurgence of knowledge after so much barbarity, the world witnessed the tragic death of a Socrates, the most admirable man to have been born in the dark days of paganism; while Rome saw the extermination of fellow citizens, brought on by the ambitions of those who sought to reign over it. Consider also the evil plots woven against the greatest protector that humane letters, in flight from the Orient, had found, on the seat of the Prince of the Apostles.[4] The obvious conclusion to be drawn is that, in general, knowledge is not sufficient in itself to vanquish the detestable precepts of cruelty.

It has seemed to some that the Gospel, with its radiant message of peace, gentleness, universal benevolence and love even for enemies, all of which are distinctive features of that mentality which I have outlined, has markedly diminished that spirit of wrath and vengeance in our Europe which in other times motivated murderous heroes and enlightened legislators.[5] The peoples of the New World, however, probably did not harbour such thoughts as they gazed on the Spaniards, when, grasping this venerable volume that embodied their beliefs, they brought ruin and destruction to their lands together with its precepts of love.

A learned Frenchman in his immortal work 'The Spirit of the Laws' and in his promotion of the sublime science of legislation conveyed the message to the world that men should be governed according to those principles of gentleness which alone enable happiness to flourish. This message is also for all men an unequivocal commandment of that religion which marks us out as sons of a God incarnate. Nevertheless, additional initiatives need to be taken in order to introduce into societies and into the judgements of law courts and councils that amiability which was missing from the ancient laws because of the unhappiness of the times in which they were written.

If in these pages I am setting out to prove, with a full range of moral arguments, that death, the established punishment for many offences, is a penalty both excessive and unnecessary, not only am I providing justification for the glorious indulgence of Elisabeth, that most powerful empress of Russia,[6] in abstaining from daubing herself in the blood of criminals, but I am also proposing to instruct anyone who has the sovereign right to dictate the laws that they should respect the lives of men to a greater extent than has been done up till now.

The subject that I have chosen will have for many an air of singularity striking enough to evoke disdain. But in the event that neither my reasonings, nor the series of demonstrations that I advance in a methodical and rigorous manner, are sufficient to carry my proposition and to lead to the reform of an abuse which has been authorised far too often and is too archaic and too standard, I will certainly have the satisfaction of having sought to benefit my fellow men; and I will be happy in the thought that, although only a private individual, I have envisaged a way of saving the lives of so many whom human frailty, need, the onrush of anger, or the blindness of intellect, are leading to the gallows.

It has always been easier for men in power to satisfy the thirst of their ambition with the blood of creatures who possess reason than by exercising clemency to win the glory attached to saviours of the human race—a title that pagans were accustomed to confer most often on their gods. In the same way, it will be easier for me to set out the many proofs that there are of the validity of my argument, and in consequence perhaps to clarify the perception of others, than to induce in those who rule the nations the desire to follow the example of one sovereign woman, who for her unique achievement in instituting a practice that is most in line with the laws of nature and the Gospel, will remain forever immortal in the memory of her subjects.

CHAPTER 2. DIVISION OF PUNISHMENTS

All men are constrained by an inner necessity to perform their duties. Some of these duties arise from the very nature of men and the resulting relations that are established among them, while others follow from specific human conventions. These conventions in turn are grounded in written or unwritten laws, or in agreements voluntarily made by particular individuals. To do what they are obliged to do, or what others have the right to claim or to exact from them, requires nothing more than the deep-rooted knowledge of what they owe to themselves and to others. Depravity of the heart, however, has brought it about that these same laws have to constrain men with the fear of punishment in the event of non-observance, and that men are compelled, in order to secure mutual good faith, to bind themselves through certain promises to the imposition of a punishment in the event of their non-fulfilment. This is the origin of the very familiar distinction among punishments whereby they may be divided into *civil* and *conventional*.[7] It is not at all my purpose to address myself to the punishments of another life. They have different bases and ends from those which serve, as a rule, to set down what we should believe of punishments that are natural and external.

CHAPTER 3. PUNISHMENTS DEFINED

A punishment is *an evil that is suffered, in conformity with the positive laws, by those who transgress what these laws prescribe.*

This definition, which departs slightly from that of Hugo Grotius for punishments (*De iure belli et pacis* II, ch. 20, § 1), is undoubtedly the best, although it applies only to civil punishments. One can say of *conventional* punishment that it designates *all sanctions to which someone binds himself spontaneously in the event of the non-fulfilment of a promise made to another.* This includes cases such as the annulment of a contract where this is part of the provisions of the contract, the payment of fines or in reparation for the loss suffered by the other party to the contract, or, finally, in moderate corporal punishment (in cases where the non-fulfilment of the promise is considered to be sufficiently serious). In the charters of old not a few such punishments are laid down or threatened by individuals and private citizens: to cite only one, in the *Donationum Belgicarum* (II, ch. 29) of Aubert le Mire there is an instrument of Baldwin, *comes Hannoniae*, of 1089, in which it is stated: 'Anyone who has presumed to flout the decree of confirmation is ordered to submit to the severity of judgement, and to suffer a fine of 100 pounds if he is a free man, or if unfree the loss of his eyes.' (Heineccius, *Elementa juris germanici*, II, ch. 10, § 299 in note)

CHAPTER 4. DEMONSTRATION OF THE CORRECTNESS
OF THE FIRST OF THESE DEFINITIONS

In the preface to his *History of the Successors of Alexander*, M. Rollin complains that he has been unable to depict human nature except with traits that dishonour it, and has not seen how to introduce agreeable items into a narrative which has nothing to relate but a uniform series of vices and wickednesses. For this reason it follows that, in order to preserve the bonds of society, and to strike terror into those who should dare to harm their fellow men with criminal acts, it was necessary to impose, together with laws, punishments for those who transgress them.

Moreover it is certain that there was no means of achieving this end except by the imposition on miscreants of physical suffering, for there is nothing that we by nature dread more than this. In effect, it seems that nothing which fails to inflict pain is worthy of the name of punishment; and that it is fitting that fear of the evil that can follow from an action is greater than hope for the benefits it may bring. Legislators, however, ought to know how to create punishments that reinforce that end. There is no other way of explaining why a penalty that is heavy for one kind of person would be extremely light for another. That which is incapable of producing a sense of revulsion in the soul cannot serve as a punishment for any crime, because no one would hold back from committing an offence for fear of the evil consequences.

Punishments are so necessary to the laws that it is commonly held that they are an essential part of them, and that laws cannot be proper laws if they do not carry the threat of punishment. Grotius, followed by others, defined punishment as 'an evil of suffering imposed on account of the evil of an action'. It has been pointed out, however, that this definition does not distinguish between punishment and private vengeance, which is also an evil done to another for having fallen short in respect of some obligation owed to us, although there is a wide gap between these two things. It is necessary therefore to state that punishment is an evil that is suffered in consequence of the law, because the law is precisely that which regulates actions that are free, indifferent and external to man, and obliges him to act in a manner which is most conducive to the well-being of the society. It is all the more essential that vendetta be absolutely prohibited, and be reduced in consequence to the class of injuries.

He who corrected Grotius deemed it necessary to add that punishment is an evil that a higher authority has another suffer for a wicked deed he has committed. But in the first place, it has been amply demonstrated that every law must presuppose a sovereign invested with an authority that gives him the capability of binding his inferiors. Therefore my definition differs little from this second definition, which is that of Heineccius. I am saying substantially the same thing, in that I am persuaded that there can be no law without a higher authority, or without someone in whom the capacity resides to promulgate law.[8]

Secondly, when I say that punishment is an evil threatened by the laws, and that the laws impose suffering on us for having committed an action contrary to them, or for not having fulfilled some obligation imposed upon us by them, I exclude the despotic power of a strong man who might decide capriciously to impose on us punishments for free actions where we were unaware of a correct course, or of someone who is not vested with any supreme and legitimate authority over us.

Charles XII was the superior and original sovereign of the unfortunate Patkul, but the brutal death that he made him suffer was not punishment, but injury or revenge. Patkul after all had broken no law in drawing to Charles's attention in such a pointed way the oppression his fellow citizens were suffering in Livonia. Nor had he acted against the law in fleeing from Sweden to avoid the imprisonment that was being prepared for him. Furthermore, Patkul had been invested with the office of ambassador by Peter the Great, and this must also have released him from any legal subjugation he might have had to the king of Sweden.[9]

Equally, the celebrated Cristina, after leaving the same throne, committed a veritable assassination on the person of Monaldeschi, despite all that so many jurists, including the great Leibniz, have had to say on the subject. This whole affair, as a modern writer (d'Alembert[10]) has put it, is a sad monument to the adulation of monarchs by men of letters, whatever wrongs this unhappy courtier might have committed against his patroness.

In a word, if the laws do not indicate what one should do, or what one should never do, in any situation, how can we be punished legitimately, since we are under no obligation to know the will of the sovereign if it is not public, well known, permanent and, so to say, deposited in the laws? Also, the chastisement that we suffer at the hands of a parent, patron or husband is an evil to which we are subjected by a superior for some shortcoming. But the authority of such people comes directly from the laws of nature, which although unwritten, are engraved in us by their author. There is a precise distinction between such chastisement and the punishment which owes its origin to the pronouncement of the laws and must be exercised by way of formal jurisdiction.[11]

Punishment presupposes, finally, some offence, that is, some action contrary to the laws, whereas an evil suffered without a preceding offence cannot be given the name of a punishment. Therefore, death or the desolation wreaked by warfare cannot be deemed punishment, unless perhaps for crimes committed against the Creator. Neither do reparation or compensation for damage merit the name of punishment. They derive from another principle, though they may be due because of a misdeed. Any offence which harms another becomes deserving of punishment and reparation: of punishment because of violation of the laws, of reparation because of the need to compensate the injured party, although sometimes in the law codes of nations these two things, which are quite distinct and separate, have been confused.

CHAPTER 5. IN WHICH THE DEFINITION OF CONVENTIONAL PUNISHMENTS IS ESTABLISHED

The punishments of which we have spoken are civil punishments. Before we go any further, it must be said of conventional punishments that they have a special place in the State of Nature and among people who are free and without reciprocal, external obligations other than those imposed by the external laws of the Creator and for the preservation of the human race.

Certainly there can be no punishment in the hypothetical State of Nature in which there are no written laws, no conventions and no ruler, because there is no external obligation requiring certain specific actions, supposing that, as some people think, in the State of Nature we were very like animals in the forest. It is only the responsibility of a mother to care for her offspring until they become capable of looking after their own sustenance by themselves that gives her the authority to chastise her children in order to make them better disciplined and obedient. On the other hand, not even in this state do humans have unbridled power to act purely as they wish, but rather an injured party has only the right to seek compensation, not to punish an aggressor. Moreover, someone in a position to repel an injury by defending himself is not in his act of self-defence chastising the aggressor, but assuring his own safety.

Certainly there is in this state no other norm governing free actions than that which, through the agency of right reason, the Sovereign and author of all things has revealed to us in one way or another. It follows naturally from this that such awareness of our duties does not constrain us externally with the threat of punishment, but only imposes a requirement on us internally to do certain things on which our own preservation and that of others depends.

There are the written laws, and, according to the jurists, tacit pacts, which threaten us with punishment in case of transgression. Now, even in a state of unrestricted liberty we might impose obligations on ourselves; while in a hypothetical society, in as much as there are actions that are free and very much dependent on our will, we would have the total right to regulate them in a form such as would please anybody or be beneficial in a more specific manner. That is why, given that our corruption always leaves some room for doubts about our promises, we can reasonably constrain ourselves to fulfil them by means of some stronger bond, which can always be designated by the name punishment. The people are entirely free to regulate their interests with no other laws than those of nature. Thus the treaties and alliances between nations, which the need for security prompts them to negotiate among themselves, are so many conventional laws to which they submit themselves voluntarily in order to give the contracting parties a stronger pledge of their good faith and sincerity.

In other times, the oath appeared to men to carry the obligation of a promise, but these days it is well known that it only gives a promise a new force. As Cicero wrote (*Pro Q. Roscio Comoedo*), 'it is not the verbal pact on which the oath is based that rouses the wrath and fury of the immortal gods, but the treachery and wickedness that underlie the plots of one man against another'. For this reason, guarantees, cautions, hypothecs and finally hostages were introduced in order to protect us against treachery and prevent us from being required to depend on the good faith of those with whom we make contracts. The loss of hypothecs, the retention of hostages and other such sanctions are a kind of punishment suffered by those who break their promises.

And since in the State of Nature there is nothing to render a promise secure, in this state conventional punishments would have been more universally practised, as they are in a certain sense even at present among the nations that strike alliances or make some kind of treaty among themselves. It remains the case, however, that even in the civil state I can make a contract to give satisfaction in some matter under pain of punishment in the event that I renege on my obligation. Such a punishment can take the form not only of some action which does me some harm, but also of the cancellation of the obligation that the other party had made with respect to me. I said that the restitution of a loss was not a true civil punishment. This is true also in the case of pacts: when I bind myself to make good the loss to the party to whom I have failed to give satisfaction in accordance with the duty I have accepted, this is not a punishment, but a legitimate consequence of my obligation, which involved, albeit tacitly, reparation for the loss.

CHAPTER 6. CONVENTIONAL PUNISHMENTS CAN NEVER EXTEND TO THE DEATH PENALTY

With these principles in place, I may now move on to demonstrate my thesis. It will be straightforward to establish in accordance with the evidence, speaking first of conventional punishments, that they can never at any time be extended to encompass the death penalty. In truth, it would be necessary for me to be the master of my own life, in order to be able to cede the right that I have over it to another, and to bind myself to an obligation to lose it should I renege on a promise. The arguments employed by Hegesias of Cyrene (Valerius Maximus, 8, ch. 9 inf.), drawing on a pathetic picture of the evils that besiege human life and poison the most sweet pleasures that existence can provide, might have been so compelling that a Ptolemy who was new to the throne was forced to prohibit their declamation. The principles that in perfect tranquillity illuminate our minds, however, and the attachment that nature itself inspires in men of sound intellect, prevent us from thinking that we can deprive ourselves of a gift of which we are not so much possessors as trustees. Bearing this in mind, I do not know of any historical examples of persons who imposed on themselves so constricting a bond. I believe, therefore, that no more than a few words will suffice for my thesis to win universal acceptance. If we were to bind ourselves to lose our life for having failed to meet some contracted obligation, should we also perhaps forego the right of self-defence against an aggressor? For even in the civil state, we can be compelled only by force to suffer the punishment that we have merited. 'Drag the condemned whither they will not willingly go,' said Quintilian in *Declamationes* XI, having established that 'there is no punishment which is welcome'.[12] And what advantage would accrue to someone who had sworn a pact under terms so barbarous? Given that every obligation is dissolved with death, a person who required another to pay the extreme penalty for non-compliance would have no prospect of attaining that benefit which the contract had led him to hope for. When the Carthaginians deprived Attilius Regulus[13] of his life so cruelly because he refused to persuade the Romans to make peace and as a result they failed to obtain a peace that they had every reason to desire, they were in reality doing him an injustice.

CHAPTER 7. AS TO WHAT IS THE MOST JUST
PUNISHMENT IN THE STATE OF NATURE

In the State of Nature, as we have indicated, men have some obligations, but if they do not fulfil them, it is not permitted that they be punished.

Grotius, in setting out the grounds for a just war, finds a place among them for punishment (II, ch. 1, § 2 and ch. 20, § 38). He has been followed in this by many, and as with not a few other doctrines that are to be found in his work, it tends to flatter the barbaric desire of men of power to flood the whole earth with human blood. Even Vattel (3, ch. 3, § 41), notwithstanding the fact that his whole work glows with equity together with gentleness, includes punishment among the reasons that justify war, after asserting that the basic justification is injury received or threatened.

But a single sentence of Caius Pontius, general of the Samnites (Livy, 9 beg.), belies and refutes the general opinion: 'A war is just for those for whom it is necessary.' In fact, the necessity of making war is reducible to the sole case of defence, taken in its literal sense. President de Montesquieu (9, ch. 2) showed better judgement when he wrote that the life of states is like that of men. Just as men have the right to kill only in the case of natural defence, so states are entitled to make war only for their own preservation.

It is true that Vattel[14] was of the opinion that only the injured party has the right to punish the man who injured him. If, however, it were necessary to admit that in the State of Nature every injury could be justly repelled by the injured party, imagine the horrible warfare that would erupt every day among men, given their innate wickedness. Who in the State of Nature would be responsible for deciding what counted as a genuine injury as opposed to one that appeared to be such in the eyes of someone over-sensitive or prone to anger? At least it must be agreed that for punishments to be licit, the damage done to the injured party must be sufficient to warrant that he compel the man who injured him to give him recompense for his loss. Similarly, a people will have the right to take up arms to compel another nation to give satisfaction. In this case, such a war will never count as chastisement of an offender by the offended, but as a means of securing a just repayment for damage suffered. And in fact, how can it be that a free person has the right to punish another free person for the sole aim of correcting or chastising him?

We said that punishment is relative to the laws, so that if one lives in a state in which there are only a few natural laws and obligations and these are valid only in an internal tribunal, the impunity of crimes would raise the fear of chaos should there be no punishments. Warfare aside, there exists nonetheless a way of providing for our security and defending ourselves without attacking others or attempting to undermine their liberty.

The State of Nature can be thought of in two ways. By the first, one supposes that men wander through the forests without a leader, without a family, and live totally like the animals that inhabit the woods. According to the second, there are diverse peoples released from any dependence on one another and in fact free. In the former state, a man who is injured by another may defend himself and if he has sufficient force, he can compel the other to give compensation for the loss in so far as reparation is possible. In the event that it is not feasible, in accordance with the principle that the stronger prevails, there are two possibilities: either he must acquiesce in suffering the evil, or he must associate himself with his fellow men, in order to be able to resist in the case of a new offence or to compel the injuring party to make up the loss. And thus, following the example of this first society, others will have to organise themselves in order to be its equal in terms of power. These various societies are always in a position of independence among themselves, because only the individuals who constitute them have made contracts through pacts of reciprocal obligation, without making any arrangements for those who have not wanted to associate with them.

In the second State of Nature, so to speak, injuries can be done by one society to another society, by an individual who is a member of one society to a society with which he has no connection, by a member of one society to another member of the same society and, finally, by a member of one society to a member of another society.

In the first case, since the different societies must be assumed to have had the same juridical system to regulate matters between them as had existed between individual men before any society had been constituted, men would be required to act exactly as they were able to act before the establishment of alliances, in the event that one was injured by another. In the second and fourth cases, as a man who injures another has no right to be defended, it will be expedient that the other members of that society to which he belongs deliver him to the discretion of the injured party; that is, supposing the pacts of the association in question are not like those of pirates and thieves, and that there is no embarrassment for them if the man is compelled by brute force to pay recompense.

In the third case only can one suppose that there are written laws which provide for the security of the members of the same society or those who compose it. But if there are no such laws, and if one must envisage prescribing the punishment which is the most equitable for the contravention of pacts and other contracted obligations, then that punishment would consist of expulsion of the delinquent or removing from him the advantages which the society is providing for him. Here, then, we have come upon the punishment that is the most natural of all and derives from, and follows legitimately from, the very essence of crimes.

CHAPTER 8. THE MOST NATURAL WAY TO PUNISH A DELINQUENT IS TO EXPEL HIM FROM SOCIETY

It is certain that every society is established for the good of all who compose it, and that each member has a duty to work toward the happiness of the rest and to come to their aid without neglecting his responsibility to himself. That men should be bound to serve the caprices of an individual or of the few, that their labour and their liberty besides should be sacrificed to a patron who has no right to them other than the prejudice and the weakness of his inferiors, that their life and possessions should be at the mercy of a sovereign's nod, finally, that the most fearful, miserable and foolish of them should be at the disposal of those who in combination with their superior talent have greater resources to trick, surprise and dominate: these are the principles of a barbarous despotism such as will bring ruin and unhappiness to the human race. They are also all too common, though they should never properly spread beyond the deserts of Hindustan.

The interests of those in power can differ widely from those of the public, and this might imply the existence of laws which are at odds with the good of the latter. The best constitutions of government will always however be those which, by combining the safeguarding of individuals and the maintenance of social order, succeed in establishing a reciprocal harmony of duties directed at the common happiness.

At least it must be agreed that for punishments to be licit, the damage done to the injured party must be sufficient to warrant that he compel the man who injured him to give him recompense for his loss. Similarly, a people will have the right to take up arms to compel another nation to give satisfaction. In this case, such a war will never count as chastisement of an offender by the offended, but as a means of securing a just repayment for damage suffered. And in fact, how can it be that a free person has the right to punish another free person for the sole aim of correcting or chastising him?

What other, more reasonable, satisfaction can be obtained from a guilty person? By depriving him of the means by which he might have enjoyed a happy life, one does to him what he had in mind to do to others when he disobeyed the laws which were the foundation of his own security. Chastisement of such a kind has been in use from time immemorial, since exile and what the Christians have called excommunication were penalties that deprived delinquents of the communal life and permanent residence within those societies in which they had offended. No extensive research or deep learning is necessary to establish that exile and excommunication in one manner or another have been absolutely standard punishments among almost all peoples.

CHAPTER 9. THE ENDS OF PUNISHMENT

By demonstrating what are the ends of punishment and showing that these ends are perfectly achieved by means of those punishments specified in the preceding section, I will proceed to demonstrate that the death penalty, introduced in the same spirit, does not conduce to these ends. This will serve as the first and most direct proof of my thesis.

There are those who have claimed that one of the ends of punishment is the satisfaction that is due to divine justice.[15] But if that were so, then all the vices of men, not their crimes or breaches of the laws, would be deserving of physical punishment by the magistrates. There are in addition punishments for actions which would have been merely indifferent if the lawgiver had not expressed his will to penalise them. It is said that in such cases it is disobedience that is chastised, but there are much more pernicious vices than this that appear in numerous circumstances, where transgressing the will of the sovereign is prejudicial only to his private interests.

Revenge cannot be an end of punishment either, though it might be sweet pleasure in a barbarous heart. It is always pointless, inhumane and vile, and issues from a blind passion that makes no distinction between the objects at which it unleashes itself.

There can be no more than three legitimate ends of punishment, as in fact after Grotius all the other jurists assert.[16] The first end is to reform the criminal, the second to guarantee security and the last to provide an example to others. Without these ends, there would be no place for punishment for a specific period of time in the case of any transgression; reparation for loss incurred by an evil action would stand alone as the only obligation to which a delinquent could be bound.

That reform is a most legitimate end of punishment is proven by the advantage that accrues not only to the chastised but also to society. The fact is that men are evil. Thus it is necessary to ensure that at least their criminality does not permit them to live happily, so that they learn that only by performing their duties can they enjoy the good that they desire. The more virtuous the members of a state, the greater is its peace. That is why a society composed of scoundrels would not survive, or would do so only in a state of confusion and disorder. If a criminal who has committed an offence is separated from the society, he is given space to reflect on the damage that has been inflicted on him through his crime, in the loss of those benefits that accrued to him through residing within that body. In the meantime the body itself is freed from an infected member until such time as he returns to his duties and comes back to his senses.

Satisfaction resembles vengeance to some extent, but since it is taken by the public with the sole aim of putting a check on evil rather than revelling in the suffering of another, it is not at all at odds with the laws of humanity, as long as it does not go beyond the just limits required for the purposes of security. It has been written that satisfaction has to be taken in order to ensure that we do not suffer injury in the future at the hands of those who have harmed us previously, or of others who might be motivated to harm us because the first offenders had gone unpunished. This at least is the verdict of Grotius

(II, ch. 20, § 8, 1). From this doctrine it is deduced quite legitimately that satisfaction was not contrary to right reason in the State of Nature, whereas in the civil state it had been outlawed. This was because the laws and magistrates who apply them supplement in a certain way what otherwise we would be permitted to do on our own authority. Therefore on some occasions either the laws leave us this liberty, or, when they cannot be fully enforced, as on the sea, they permit us to use it. But this assertion is hardly compatible with either justice or truth; the evil that one does to an enemy in the State of Nature, the campaigns that one wages against pirates with the aim of compelling them to do their duty in one way or another, the power conceded to some peoples to pursue those who have done them harm, these are not punishments. For punishments presuppose a higher authority and a law, and a private individual cannot as such inflict harm even on guilty persons. He can, however, force them to explain the evil they have done in the presence of those who are vested with public authority. The real end of satisfaction, which relates to its true essence, is attained also through distancing delinquents from the society, for by this means they are rendered unable to cause further injury, while they are led to a full understanding of the nature of their crime. Furthermore, the exile that a condemned man suffers, and the disasters to which he is subjected outside the ancestral walls and at a distance from all the advantageous combinations which, in the union of those among whom we were born, raised and brought up, serve to sustain us and give us pleasure: all this serves without doubt as an example to others. In a word, by dissuading men from shunning their duties, security is enhanced.

CHAPTER 10. THE ENDS OF PUNISHMENT ARE NOT ACHIEVED BY INFLICTING THE DEATH PENALTY ON CRIMINALS

'Death banishes any fear that a miscreant will offend anew; it serves as a terrible example to anyone who nourishes such thoughts; and it restrains and corrects those who might have considered harming some member of the society which he who suffers such a punishment is deprived of forever.' This is the language of prevention and cruelty, dressed up in what could only be the garment of sweet talk. The penalty in question does not in fact serve the prescribed ends of punishment, missing their spirit. It is clear that a man who is put to death is not corrected. It is also clear that the example of execution has thus far not put an end to crimes in the world. Nor has it dissuaded certain criminal minds from polluting the public happiness with execrable evils.

Thus to succeed in preventing some weak person, moved more by lack of courage than by choice, from committing a crime, is considered less worthwhile than removing a single individual from the earth. The horrendous punishment of the impious François Ravaillac did not dissuade the wicked Damiens from turning a furious right hand against the revered Louis XV. And the slaughtering of Damiens, so fresh in the memory, did not for one moment hold back the conspirators of Lisbon from carrying out their criminal plots and ambitious designs against Joseph I, with their attempt on his life in a barbarous act.[17] Such examples abound in the historical accounts of those centuries in which the lives of sovereigns were more exposed to the fickleness of their subjects, as they do in the records of those nations that liked to make a show of spilling blood while avenging tyranny or smoothing the path to the throne of a new tyrant. It was in vain that the blood of so many was shed, if through the tortures and the punishments that they suffered they did not succeed in teaching a mortal how to respect the laws.

The death penalty is not required by public vengeance either, and because every government, as Providence dictates, should provide for the greater good with the lowest level of evil that can be achieved, it is certain that the government should do its utmost to safeguard the security of others without excessively unbridled rigour, and without pointlessly applying punishments which are unnecessary. For this reason the law of Dracon (Plutarch, *Solon*[18]) was barbarous for punishing idleness with death, while in the cause of stimulating industry it deprived of life those who might have been induced to become industrious. This was not the only law which led a Greek (Demades) to say that Dracon had written his laws in blood, but he perhaps was taking a leaf out of the book of the Egyptians, who according to Herodotus (in Euterpe) used to punish as guilty of a public crime those who did not take on some form of employment to provide for their subsistence.[19]

Indeed it has been permitted among some peoples to take it upon themselves to exact satisfaction for offences committed, whether by challenging to a duel someone who has in one way or another caused one provocation, as among the peoples of the north, or by putting a delinquent to death after a certain time has passed since the lodging of a complaint before a judge, as among the Muscovites (if what Grotius asserts is true, II, ch. 20, § 8, 5). Such actions have unquestionably served as an invitation to a kind of continuous warfare among those who have been assembled under one and the same authority for the purpose of living in peace. The Spartans actually left young

Alcandros to the mercy of Lycurgus to be punished as he wished for having put out one of his eyes with a blow from a stick. Instead of punishing Alcandros as he might have done in a fit of anger, Lycurgus devoted himself to instructing him with gentle and virtuous sentiments, and then appeared before a public assembly, where he proclaimed, 'Citizens, here is the man you consigned to me. I have revenged myself on him by seeing to it that owing to me he has become an honest man' (Stobaeus, *Sermones* 17; Plutarch, *Lycurgus*[20]). One may permit men of such virtue to revenge injuries, but Lycurguses are few and far between.

CHAPTER 11. AGAINST THE DEATH PENALTY: SECOND PROOF

It may be supposed that men once lived in a State of Nature and outside of any society, and that having become aware of their unhappy situation were of a mind to provide for their security and their comfort by uniting together. This being so, it is quite certain that the bonds of their union must have been pacts or conventions tacitly or explicitly established, and with the understanding that such conventions would be maintained by the supposed consensus in the generations which followed those who first contracted such bonds amongst themselves. I will not enter into a discussion about the content of the basic conventions enacted by these people, but in any case it is beyond doubt that they must have agreed that they could be forcibly constrained to fulfil their contracted obligations; they would not otherwise have found anyone willing to trust in their word alone. It is this pact, moreover, that gives legitimacy to the exaction of punishment, and that arms the public authority against those who are impudent enough to disobey the laws—the public authority having been granted the power to make these laws in the first place for the common advantage. But when men, as one supposes, came together to found the first civil society, they had beyond doubt certain duties that were essential for their existence actual or possible, and these duties constituted the code of nature which still to this day remains the basis of all other obligations.

The first law imposed on them as created beings is that they acknowledge the First Being who drew them out of nothing. The second law follows in quick succession: it obliges them as living beings to seek self-preservation. Coming only in third place, and deriving from their status as beings living with others like them, is the duty to profess for those others a perfect benevolence. The first of the aforementioned laws supposes that man is endowed with reason, but the second he shares with animals. Thus Ulpian, without understanding the former law, had the whole natural law consist in the latter, defining it as 'what nature has taught all animals'. In fact that instinct of the senses and appetites which warns us to flee that which can harm us and to pursue that which can serve to satisfy our simple physical needs, is equally characteristic of man and of every other animal, which is as unyielding as we are in procuring for itself its own preservation, in so far as the forces with which it is endowed permit it. There is a very precise corollary to this hypothesis, if I am not mistaken: men did not intend to tie themselves down to certain duties which, once embraced, would have obliged them to pay with their lives in the event of their violation. In fact, they could not tie themselves down in this way, because such a convention was diametrically opposed to the law of nature which imposed on men the duty to promote their own preservation. And since this is so, how could men found a society with the end of gaining for themselves a greater security than they had enjoyed in the State of Nature, and at the same time give up that right which they possessed to defend themselves, and surrender into the power of another their own life, which they themselves lacked the authority to dispose? It is true that they divested themselves of the power to give retribution for injuries, to enforce promises, to have full ownership over their rights and, finally, to exact what was theirs from others, but in doing so they had no intention of ridding themselves of every natural defence and of losing the ability to resist an aggressor who had suddenly threatened their life. Thus no guilt is incurred by anyone in any society if in the pursuit of this end he kills another who has attacked him with force. As the jurist Ulpian wrote, 'we are entitled to repel with weapons anyone who comes at us with weapons' (3, § 9ff, *de vi, et vi arm*).[21] Oedipus in Sophocles used such a defence in justifying his murder of his own father who had moved to assail him: 'Tell me one thing in answer to my question . . .' (Heineccius, *Iuris naturae et gentium*, p. 149[22]). My reasoning is so sure, that although it is universally taught that every criminal must submit to punishment for his crime, in line with the tacit convention that is supposed to have been introduced when societies were first established, it nevertheless holds true that the guilty man is not required to inflict the punishment on himself, because he cannot be forced to neglect to defend himself or to ignore the command that he preserve himself, nor can one imagine that he might have willingly subjected himself to such a sanction. Thus in Athens, although it was the practice for the condemned to make a declaration as to what punishment their crimes deserved, this was not required of those who merited the ultimate punishment (Cicero, *De oratore* 1[23]). It was for no other end that nature provided us with the instinct to know with certainty how to secure our own preservation, although we have needed to employ reason in order to discover the duties that bind us to others: it is clear that our existence depends in a certain manner on our survival, without which every other bond would be null and void and which no one is better placed than ourselves to promote in any circumstance.

CHAPTER 12. AGAINST THE DEATH PENALTY: THIRD PROOF

Cicero (*Consolatio*),[24] the most eloquent consul to have been accompanied by the Roman fasces, the orator who rose to the heights through the power and elegance of his words, narrates that Dicaearchus the Peripatetic composed a book on death in which he claimed that 'many more have been extinguished by the brutality and cruelty of men than by all other kinds of calamity'.[25] I do not know if this philosopher counted the death penalty, a common punishment set by men for not a few crimes, among the effects of the cruelty of men to their fellows. I do know that it would not have been difficult for him to show that this penalty, extremely barbarous since it promotes neither private advantage nor the public interest, sacrifices many individuals who might otherwise have survived to the benefit of the society of which they were members. It is true that given the circumstances in which the human race found itself, it was not possible to continue to practise the expedient of punishing the guilty by expelling them from their respective societies without correspondingly filling with criminals those places that were nearest at hand. But this does not justify applying the most violent means of securing freedom from them by depriving them of their life and therefore of all human association. I do not in fact believe that anyone can be persuaded that such a punishment will turn out to be in some way advantageous to the criminal, since he is being deprived entirely of the means to correct his actions— something which should however be accorded to all those who have fallen into some misdeed—nor that it is of any benefit to any other private individual. My security demands that I live without fear of one who has once harmed me, but it is indifferent as to the manner in which the public authority brings this about. The spirit of revenge can only prompt me to thirst after the blood of the man who has plotted against my life and my tranquillity, but humanity and religion inspire me to pardon him, while at the same time natural law leads me to take steps to deprive him of the capacity to harm me again. What if the injured party has lost his life? Do those who survive him have the right to obtain the pointless satisfaction of extinguishing another citizen? Can they find in the death of the perpetrator an effective way of drying the tears shed in the loss of the father, spouse or friend, and recompense for the loss that this wretched man has inflicted on them by reducing them to the unhappy state of orphans, widows, inconsolables? One can say the same of all the other crimes which inflict harm on private individuals and never find in the execution of the criminal the necessary remedy.

But nor does society ever have an interest in ridding itself of a citizen, unless it is more inclined to follow the laws of revenge than those of equity and utility. What crime is there in effect which will lead a public to derive a beneficial satisfaction in the death of the man who committed it? The strange law of Solon which in Athens (Diogenes Laertius, Solon[26]) prescribed the death penalty for magistrates caught under the influence of alcohol, and the execution of Otanes, the Persian judge whom Cambyses had flayed alive as a warning to the son whom he chose to take over the office of the father, not to follow his example:[27] these incidents display a useless barbarity. One could chastise a magistrate for allowing himself to be overwhelmed by wine and to be put in a position where he falls short in administering justice, and one should punish a judge guilty of putting base profit before his duty. But in the first case a failing which could be corrected in a thousand ways, and in the second an offence for which prevention of its recurrence in the future would have been sufficient, were too harshly punished: by removing from the world a man who could be an excellent judge—if one passes over the odd slippage into intemperance—or at least a worthy practitioner in another employment in which he would not have been tempted to sell justice.

Would it not be a thousand times more profitable to make use of criminals for public works, so that the sight of their misery at labour would serve as an ever-present example to others, than to sacrifice on the gallows a delinquent, who would provide only a spectacle of a moment for anyone who derives pleasure from witnessing the depressing tragedy of his sufferings? It is not a rare occurrence that the laws, in order to punish someone who has killed a citizen, removes another from society, creating a new and pointless void as recompense for the first, when the latter could be filled in some other way. The duke of Alba certainly did not quash rebellion with the death of the count of Egmont and the count of Horn in the Low Countries,[28] nor did he restore the jurisdiction of Philip II over these territories. On the contrary, the ashes of Jan Hus actually gave the heretics cause to ratchet up the hatred that they nurtured against the Catholics.[29]

So true is it that even in the case of the most serious of crimes, withholding death is sometimes better than shedding the blood of the criminals, which gives miscreants an opening to excuse and justify their designs. This is not a lesson to suggest to a tyrant, who, in fear of all the consequences of that grim despotism that he is resolved to consolidate, believes that he is secure in his throne if he removes with iron all those who can cause him fear.

CHAPTER 13. AGAINST THE DEATH PENALTY: FOURTH PROOF

We have now prepared the ground for a new and comprehensive demonstration of my thesis, which is based on the observation that the most imperfect government is that in which the death penalty is most commonly enforced. It does not take much to prove that the government in which total power rests in the variable and transitory will of one man, sustained by force and fear, and ruling the people like vile slaves, is a system of law completely contrary to nature. The reason is that the rights that are exercised by one man over the rest are reciprocal, and therefore entirely opposed to and incompatible with the slavery of despotism. Nevertheless, even in a state of this kind, principles are in place for preserving it as far as possible, although those principles are as barbarous as their effects. It is without doubt one of those principles that severity must always reign beside the throne in order to keep subjects in a state of fear. This inseparable companion of all tyrants counsels merciless punishment of all those actions which threaten to break the shackles of slavery, and the chastisement of their perpetrators, with no other end in view than to deprive of life all those who might cause harm, extinguishing courage and snuffing out every spark of ambition.

Thus it is that in despotic regimes many crimes severely punished elsewhere are tolerated without any attention paid to them, while under a monarchy or a republic many other offences which under a despotism are judged to merit the most inhuman punishment do not incriminate a citizen. The smallest act of disobedience, the most shadowy suspicions, the insignificant offences, the most vague words, the most natural complaints: all these are punished with loss of life by a sovereign who maintains his authority in proportion to the level of fear which his peoples hold for him, itself proportionate to the fear of his subjects that he nourishes in his own heart. If, furthermore, under

a despotic government, punishments ought to be and are in effect more severe than in any other order, then it is legitimate to believe that the most barbarous punishments are not the most natural, because they serve to prop up
the most repugnant of states into which humanity has fallen through its own
weakness. And if the death penalty transparently serves to fuel fear of tyrants,
then it cannot be the punishment most appropriate in societies where moderation reigns.

If you read into the history of all the nations, that most pitiful spectacle of
human miseries, you will observe in the history of tyrants, who in all times
have found the means to maintain their rule at the expense of humanity, a
barbarity and a supreme readiness to punish offences with the death penalty.
Appian of Alexandria and Tacitus will inform you as to the way the Triumvirs
conducted themselves in Rome, in addition to those emperors under whom
tyranny and despotism reigned supreme—without any need to evoke the
historians of Asia and of all those countries ruled by such a government. I
pass in haste over this subject, sparing myself a detailed account of cruelty
and wickedness and sparing others a narrative of horrors, especially as there
is no shortage of other proofs that the death penalty–which is applied even
where benevolence, respect and honour prevail—is excessive.

CHAPTER 14. AGAINST THE DEATH PENALTY: FIFTH PROOF

It is astonishing, when one looks through the law codes of those nations
which we rather too readily call barbarian, to find that they punished crimes
with pecuniary penalties not with blood (*Spirit of the Laws* 28, ch. 36),
whereas more civilised peoples have carried severity to the point of punishing with death even the less heinous offences. The principle that the punishment should be in just proportion to the crime cannot be disputed, because it
is more necessary to prevent a relatively serious offence than a minor one that
is less harmful to society.[30] In fact, if a less serious offence is as harshly punished as one more serious, a criminal will inevitably choose to commit the
latter, if he harbours greater hope of concealing it or of gaining greater benefit
and advantage. In the case of all those crimes which are punished with death,
however, and where the punishment is enhanced by the application of additional desecration of the corpse, or of punishment of a different order, they
all receive equal punishment. This is because an offender has no greater fear
of the rope than the axe, nor does he tremble at the prospect that his body
will be fuel for the flames or be cut into pieces, a spectacle for passers-by.

Thus loss of life will only be a punishment for a single crime, never for a number of crimes of different kinds: it cannot be in some way diminished or enhanced so as to punish proportionately crimes of different kinds or of diverse levels of malice or carrying varying consequences.

It is so clear as to require no proof, that all societies have an interest in punishing some crimes with greater severity than others. In fact, maintaining the security of the lives of subjects and even more so of the life of the sovereign, defending the constitution against any attempts to disturb it by the introduction of novelties, suppressing crimes that bring shame to humanity, these are matters that those responsible for establishing the laws in any government should hold dear. If then under moderate governments milder punishments suffice for the prevention of crimes, why do legislators everywhere not make it their business to establish these punishments, rather than fill their codes with threats of death? In so doing, they would be able through punishment to bring greater security and in consequence less harm to humanity and to various societies. Those who have witnessed an increase in army desertions and who have thought this could be prevented by the indiscriminate use of the death penalty—against those who, for a handful of coins, go to confront such a fate—have made a big mistake. The argument that people ought to be governed with a certain prudential benevolence rather than extreme rigour must be convincing. It is equally clear that, as President de Montesquieu has written, the failure to punish, and laziness, rather than moderation in punishment, are responsible for all the excesses and the slackness that are observable in the customs of some peoples.[31]

Finally, in a word, everything that a law calls a punishment is effectively a punishment.[32] Principles of this kind tend to act as life insurance for the citizenry and contribute to the suppression of vice in each and every society. Thus it is not right for the more moderate governments, which are by definition those most active in permitting happiness to flourish among men, to operate the same methods as tyrants do to maintain a constitution which is monstrous and against nature. The criminal laws of the Romans were much harsher under the kings because their government was tantamount to a military and despotic regime. As the constitution changed, so did the laws, to the point that it was not permitted that any citizen be condemned to death. Hence Livy was right to say that no people was more enamoured of moderation in punishment.[33] Then Sulla—as a modern commentator has noted—confounded tyranny, anarchy and liberty, apparently having in mind nothing less than a multiplication of the number of crimes, with the end in view of setting traps for the lives of his fellow citizens. All things considered, were more crimes committed in the first and last periods of Rome, or in that in between? For clarification, one must read the history of this the mightiest of powers.

CHAPTER 15. AGAINST THE DEATH PENALTY:
SIXTH PROOF OR ARGUMENT

Before responding to the many objections that will be raised against my construction by those who, influenced by a practice that is employed all too generally and too commonly, will try to find arguments to justify something that should rather be deplored, I put the question whether it is right that a man in one polity should lose his life for an action that in another political system would not have been punished at all. The crafty Cartouche, who was justly punished but with a penalty that was hardly equitable, would in Sparta not only have suffered no punishment at all, but would have been revered (Aulus Gellius 11.18).[34] As to the many who have been put to death for adultery,[35] how they would wonder at the mildness of our laws (in the feudal fiefdom of Turricchi, bishop of Fiesole, the penalty set for adultery is fifty lire if accompanied by violence and twenty-five lire if voluntary), and even more so at our customs in this regard?

I am not saying that justice is a sea that is stormy and ever-fluctuating and that crossing a river or a mountain turns up new crimes, or that time, place and circumstances render actions criminal that in the absence of laws would be absolutely indifferent, or that finally honesty and goodness find their source solely in the opinion and authority of the legislator. These are maxims that can scarcely be heard from the mouth of a Spinozist or a confessed Pyrrhonist without anger, because they cloud over every natural light in the heart of man, and accustom . . . [folio 56 missing] . . . and inhuman. And how should this not be the case if justice is invariable everywhere, if its principles suggest the same ideas among all those who are prepared to give heed to them, and if what is appropriate in one place or in one set of circumstances should apply in all, apart from some few issues necessarily left for the consideration of sages? My book does not convey instruction that is contrary to public safety or to the peace of states or to the rules of justice and decorum.

Let us now go briefly through all the crimes, in particular those against the dictates of nature, and let us see if the death penalty is appropriate for them.

We will then be able to judge whether I have been right to make myself the advocate and defender of humanity in order to free the world of a prejudice. Let us then add a new and more specific argument to demonstrate what we are proposing.

CHAPTER 16. ENUMERATION OF CRIMES AND EXAMINATION OF THE PENALTY OF DEATH AS IT IS CUSTOMARILY APPLIED TO THEM

Gratitude toward the Creator is, beyond dispute, because of its importance, the first among the natural laws. Therefore anyone who falls short in this regard in some way deserves to be punished. Blasphemy, heresy, idolatry and so on are crimes that should not go undetected under a good government, even though intolerance has always been too grievous. Anyone who knows his God, but is still so impious as foolishly to launch a verbal attack on Him in a rash outburst of passion, is a monster of wickedness. But should he be punished with death for this? Punishment lies in the hands of the offended, and civil governments are responsible only for seeing that the offender return to his senses and for making him recognise the extreme nature of his sin. They should go no further than this, lest the public peace be disturbed and the citizens subjected to slanderous vexations. I do not address other crimes here, because the political constitutions are responsible for regulating actions in this area.[36] And when diverse religions are not suffered in a single state, our religion, the true one, does not preach the use of iron and fire to force people to follow its path, a path laid down with gentleness only: persecutions are opposed with forbearance, harshness with compassion, martyrdom with constancy. Our religion also teaches that minds are not won over by force, but rather by doctrine and example; and finally, that knowledge of the divine truths knows how to insinuate itself in hearts without needing to be defended or explained by cruel methods. The Church has its own time-hallowed laws which prevent unbelievers from consorting with believers, and the first Christians only took steps to distance themselves from those who did not want to listen to their preaching, or who, of wavering or weak faith, abandoned the truth to run back into the shadows. This was the teaching of Christ when he said . . . [37] The civil laws and the magistrates are obliged to maintain these practices, and by means of punishment to bring back evil men rather than losing them forever, uselessly; meanwhile charity and hope of reformation should counter despair of their repenting.

Too great a rigour adds numbers to those who are martyred in a false cause; it does not make sincere disciples of the Gospel, and examples of this are all too common.

CHAPTER 17. THE SAME SUBJECT CONTINUED

The laws that derive from the relationships of men with themselves belong to the second rank of natural law, as already stated. But of the thousands of ways in which one can fall short with these laws, suicide alone is the offence that governments are in a position to punish. In some places this offence is not punished, and among the Romans it was only in the time of the emperors that for reasons of avarice it was declared deserving of punishment, although this is the case wherever the force of the arguments of Socrates (in Plato's *Phaedo*) is recognised, and it is acknowledged that taking one's own life is an injury inflicted on oneself and on society. This offence, however, is the only one which cannot be punished with death, and it should not be punished in the case of a person who had merely tried to commit it, lest he succumb to the very problem that he wanted to avoid.

CHAPTER 18. THE SAME SUBJECT CONTINUED

Finally, the natural laws of the third class are deduced from the relationships which result from the natural laws of the first and second classes, and they inform us of our responsibilities toward the diverse beings that are with us on this earth. These are the responsibilities that more than others ought to be regulated by positive laws and constitute the bonds of society. Failure to meet them is a major source of the offences punishable by magistrates. In treating in due order a matter that is extremely wide-ranging, we will observe that one can by some action harm society as a whole or the persons who represent it, or one can harm some individual citizen with regard to his person, property or honour. Otherwise, one can contravene the requirements of the law with respect to certain things that are by their nature indifferent, such as the making of a contract of obligation, the formalisation of some contract or the disposal of goods that are under our ownership. Crimes of the first category are crimes of lèse-majesté, which are governed by the most severe laws because such crimes do most harm to the public or threaten the collapse of the constitution of the State.

GIUSEPPE PELLI: *AGAINST THE DEATH PENALTY,* FRAGMENTS

Fragment 1: Outline of a dissertation on punishments

'We are the cause of our evils'[38]

The various meanings given to the word punishment have created a great deal of misunderstanding. Thus it is necessary to define the term with precision and at the same time take issue with the definitions proposed by Grotius and others.

In my view, punishment civil or criminal might be defined as *an evil threatened by the laws against those who transgress them.*

Without legislation there can in fact be no punishment. Therefore by the law of nature no one can chastise another, and it is only on the supposition of a society, which cannot exist without some civil laws, that the necessity of punishments arises.[39] Punishments, however, would be no more necessary than rewards if everyone in fulfilling the laws did not enjoy public security, which is precisely the good that accrues to every individual from observing them.

Punishment taken in a general sense may be divided into *conventional* and *civil.* Conventional punishment arises from the pact, and is that which everyone signs up to spontaneously, while civil punishment is as we have defined it above.

Besides these two cases, the evil that one person does to another in any way is either *injury,* or *vengeance,* or *defence.*

It is true that *chastisement* too is a kind of punishment, but this also presupposes a higher authority or a law. And since this word in general refers to the means employed by parents to correct their children, it is clear that death can never be a chastisement because death does not correct anyone but destroys him.

Conventional punishment can never be extended to encompass the death penalty, because no one can renounce the rights that he has or can give them up. No one has the right to kill himself, therefore no one can give his consent to another, or permit another, to kill him in a particular case.

Under the law of nature nothing apart from defending oneself is permissible. Returning an injury is not, because otherwise vengeance would be legitimate, as would that war of everyone against everyone which Hobbes depicts, because if we could return an injury, each person would be the judge in his own case.

Under the positive law punishments are established through a tacit conventional pact, by which each person tacitly binds himself to submit to those punishments that the higher authority will judge to be suitable for transgressors of those laws that it will please him to impose for the benefit of all. Since, moreover, no one can fix death as a conventional punishment, so the death penalty cannot be considered as intended in the supposed social pact.

There are three ends of punishment: *reform, satisfaction* and *example*. The death penalty is excessive with regard to these three ends. Let us demonstrate this.

The natural punishment for all crimes would involve losing the benefits of that society in which the crime was committed. But since at present all men constitute an entire and universal society, so this penalty cannot be applied generally. This is because one cannot expel a man from the world except by killing him, and if one had to apply the death penalty for all crimes, this would be in many cases too severe a punishment.

With regard to heresy, it is worth mentioning the passage in the Gospel where Christ gives orders to preach, and if the light of the Gospel is not accepted, to depart, shake the dust off one's feet, and so on.[40]

The treatment of the adulteress can be cited as proof of gentleness and of the reform of the Mosaic Laws.[41]

Death cannot be the punishment for certain particular crimes, because these are relative to various laws.

Is it just that a robber should be condemned to death when in Sparta he would not have been punished?[42]

The pecuniary punishments of the barbarians[43] achieved recompense for damage.

Who does greater harm, a single tyrant on the throne, or a hundred criminals in chains?

The penalty of Talion is no reparation for crimes.[44]

The death penalty can be considered from the point of view of metaphysics, politics or strict law.

Every crime imposes repayment for damage, satisfaction for the injured party and satisfaction for the public authority, that is, for justice.

The punishment is the evaluation of the crime.[45]

A crime 'is every illicit action where someone crosses the limits of the faculty conceded us by nature' (Cocceji[46]).

Eustratius on Eth. Nic. VI.1 defined anger in a man as the boiling of the blood around the heart caused by the desire to drive out pain (that one is suffering).[47]

Fragment 2: Prospectus of my dissertation on the death penalty, setting out the propositions which work towards proving my conclusion, the evidence on which they are based and the corollaries that follow from them for my purpose.

Without higher authority there is no law. Without law there is no obligation, duty, responsibility and so on.

Crime is every action contrary to the law written or unwritten.

In the State of Nature, there are the laws deriving from the various relationships in which man finds himself.

In society there are the aforementioned laws and those which have been imposed by men on themselves.

The higher authority alone can compel men to fulfil their obligations and impose a punishment on whoever contravenes them.

The punishment is the valuation of the crime, or the evil that the laws threaten against those who flout them.

Every crime imposes recompense for the damage done and subjection to the punishment prescribed for it.

In the State of Nature, there are no prescribed corporal punishments for crimes for which God has reserved for Himself the right to punish.

Punishments are therefore of positive law.

Those laws cannot consist of Talion because Talion can never be applied, as it is excessive, inconclusive and so on.

The ends of punishment are two only: security of others and example.

Everything, therefore, that can bear on those two ends is certainly subject to punishment.

The greater or lesser gravity of a punishment depends on the greater or lesser frequency, malice, consequences and so on, of the crime.

Axiom I. When there are various ways of achieving the same end, the one to select is always that which is the more straightforward and less harmful.

Axiom II. That which brings no good to anyone is invariably useless.

Axiom III. That which is useless does not deserve to be employed.

Axiom IV. We should not do to others what we would not wish to be done to us.

The precept that bids us to give everyone his due requires us to give reparation for injuries which prejudice a right.

One cannot give reparation for an evil by imposing the same evil. Suffering an evil that we have done to others does not compensate the injured person, because the pain suffered is not susceptible to reparation.

To give satisfaction for a crime through the infliction of pain is a kind of vendetta.

The appetites of corrupt nature confer no right.

Fragment 3: Objections and replies

§ 1. OBJECTION AND REPLY. THE PUNISHMENT OF TALION

To provide further confirmation of our discernment, we may now respond to objections that might be made to the thesis we are defending. This will remain secure once those arguments are defeated which in the opinions of some are capable of refuting it. First of all, we are confronted with the lengthy discussions of the two Cocceji, father and son, on the punishment of Talion. They claim that it is enjoined by the law of nature against any illicit deed by which another has received an injury; and further that the ends of punishment indicated above[48] derive from the civil institution (Heinrich von Cocceji, *Commentariis in Grotius*, 2, ch. 20, § 13, beg.[49]). But such a doctrine is based on foundations so weak that it will be easy to demolish. In spite of all the erudition that can be adduced to support it, the very idea of such a punishment makes it abundantly clear that it is quite impracticable; and the consequences drawn by the aforementioned writers, of great wisdom, moreover, will convince us that they have built a construction in the air that will all too easily fall apart under its own weight.

The punishment of Talion, in their view, 'is the law under which each man suffers what he has inflicted'.[50] But how precisely can an injury which someone has received be measured so that the injurer is made to suffer as much? The same thing can be an injury relative to one person, and the Talion too light a penalty for another, as if a man of low status were to be publicly beaten for having done the same thing to another who is vested with some respectability and dignity. Quite often it is too difficult to have a criminal suffer the same evil or the same injury as he has inflicted on another. Some people cite as an example a man blind in one eye who injured an enemy of his by depriving him of his sight altogether.

In the end, such a punishment is rarely capable of upholding that equality which its advocates know so well how to boast about in their discourse. There might be a man who with one blow has deprived more than one person of life, and who could not simply by his own death make satisfaction for the injury done to each of his victims. And there might be a man who has wounded another with a weapon in circumstances such that it would be impossible to construct a case, however cleverly, against the culprit who was liable to punishment for his offence.[51] Such considerations have led people to write that it is necessary to make an assessment of the injury and that it is appropriate to punish offenders in the light of such an assessment.

§ 2. ON VENGEANCE

The doctrines of the Cocceji give too much sanction to *vengeance*, which Christians, and gentile philosophers too, have identified as a brutal sentiment, 'deriving', as Eustratius on Aristotle explains (*Eth. Nic.* 6.1) 'from a boiling of the blood around the heart moved by a desire to transfer pain onto something else'.[52] Thus it is that animals, being unable to revenge themselves on the person who has injured them, bite the instrument that was used against them and the rock that has struck them. And if it is not the spirit of vengeance which inspires the act of inflicting an evil upon someone who has done evil to others, what else can it possibly be? And how can one physical pain be satisfaction for another if not by arousing pleasure at observing someone who has done us harm being placed in similar circumstances? Seneca was right when he said (*de Ira* 2.32): 'Vengeance is an inhuman concept, and yet is taken for a just one; it differs from insult only in the order of action. Anyone returning a wrong does wrong, but with more justification'.[53]

It should be said that the same Samuel von Cocceji, in his comment on Hugo Grotius II xx § vi, acknowledged this, when in his gloss on this passage of Seneca he wrote, 'Seneca said that the word "ultio" is treated as a just word, but is also inhuman'.[54] If revenge or Talion as a punishment is inhuman, can it be put into operation without incurring the charge of cruelty, when even those who support it admit that it is inhuman, in other words, disproportionate, useless, excessive? But there is more. The same writer goes on straightaway to concede that the punishment in question is inconsistent 'with the perfection of human nature', not, however, with the law of nature. It is as if natural law were a consequence of the complete unruliness that our corrupt nature drives us into, rather than a check to recall us to our duties. Should the punishment of Talion be naturally applicable to crimes, it would in no way be dependent on the laws; and every offence that man committed against the dictates of right reason would have to be chastised independently by higher authority or by the considered judgement of someone with the resources to overpower and subdue the offender. But this runs entirely counter to what is least disputable in the literature of the law of nature and of nations.

The aforementioned Samuel von Cocceji supposes (see his § 1) that the necessary reparation due for every illicit act that has caused injury to someone is made 'in making amends for the damage done' and 'in suffering an evil equivalent to that which was done'. He should however have shown, with regard to the latter, how one can give satisfaction for an injury. Until a clear demonstration of this supposition has been given, we will be entitled to make the judgement that his whole argument is founded on a petition of principle, and that Dio the philosopher in Plutarch's *Life* was right to assert that 'in the judgement of the law, revenge is considered just in comparison with the injury done in the first place; according to nature, however, it springs from the same weakness of the mind'.[55]

Those sayings, rather, have the status of the axioms which lay down that one should not do to others what we would not want to be done to ourselves; that what might turn out not to be useful is not worth doing; that what produces no good result is always useless; and finally, that when one can obtain the same end in more than one way, it is always better to choose the way that is more secure and less harmful.

The appetites of corrupted nature confer no rights; and my physical needs would not justify aggressive behaviour toward or abuse of a woman, even if she was not subject to the will of another. There is no doubt, therefore, that the supposed principles of those who are advocates for Talion are founded on erroneous suppositions.

Heinrich von Cocceji the father correctly held that the right to punish can never be attributed to a private individual (*ad dictum* ch. prop. 10), even in the cause of obtaining satisfaction for an injury received from another. I agree; but this seems to me to rule out the punishment of Talion in its full rigour. In as much as the supreme power is that which alone has the right to punish criminals, it must also have the full weight of responsibility to investigate crimes and assess their gravity. From this it follows that it must be permitted to decide what is the just recompense and satisfaction for a crime. For if it was never permitted for the victim of an injury to inflict on the injurer the same injury in order to redress the wrong, then one cannot say that the magistrates by a tacit concession have the whole responsibility of investigating the crimes and punishing them in the way that, in the State of Nature, if not just anyone, at least the injured party could do. And whenever the authorities have the right to substitute for the rigorous punishment of Talion a punishment that they might consider more consistent with the nature of their government, how can one deny that they could replace the death penalty with some other punishment? The jurists put it well when they state that even if private vengeance is not permitted, public vengeance is. In other words, men can unburden themselves of this savage desire, and leave its execution to those magistrates who were chosen precisely to enable men to live in greater happiness and security. Lucretius's words are pertinent (5.1147ff.):

> Since each man was ready in his anger to avenge himself more cruelly than is now permitted by the just laws, men grew to view this life of violence with distaste.[56]

If the punishment of Talion had been due by the law of nature, it would seem certain that it sprang from the faculty that each man had to obtain satisfaction for the injuries he had received. Otherwise the public authority would be able to modify punishments at its pleasure, which would not be conceded by opponents of homicide and adultery. But to comprehend how wrong this is, it is enough to repeat the words of Maximus of Tyre (*Dissertation II, Whether one should answer injury with injury*):

> If a man who suffered injury should undertake to revenge himself, then the evil so to speak passes with a leap from one man to another, and injustice is followed by injustice. If it is conceded in law to him who has suffered an evil to avenge himself against the man who caused him harm, it follows that vengeance will rebound again from the latter to the former, because justice is equal between the two parties. If this is how things stand, why ever, O Jupiter, did you create for us a justice founded on injustice? Where is this evil going, and where will it end?[57]

There is no need for me to examine this sentiment. It is sufficient to my purpose to make clear into what absurdities the most serious defenders of Talion have fallen; they will never have the courage to reply to the objections directed at them by the philosopher Favorinus, in Aulus Gellius (*Attic Nights* 20.1.14–19).[58]

Heinrich von Cocceji pronounces (in a note on Grotius) that death is the true penalty of Talion for homicide and adultery. Regarding the latter, there will be a great many unjust laws, namely those which have not held that such a heavy penalty should be imposed for a fault for which too many offenders could be found and which would be too hard to defend. With respect to homicide, if death were the due punishment for any killing whatsoever, the life of a sovereign would be as dear as that of his most abject subject, and staining oneself with the blood of the former would be as serious as spilling the blood of the latter. They have taught that 'a sovereign cannot absolve in the case of homicide, adultery and other crimes which demand Talion by the law of nature', because in such cases he would be making use of a right that rests uniquely with an injured party, and because he would be going beyond the limits of the power given to him solely for the defence of those who suffer injury. But similar sentiments are completely erroneous, in so far as they presume too narrow a limitation on the rights of the public authorities, also in so far as they leave scope for private individuals to take their own revenge for injuries that they might consider to have been punished less severely than they deserved. And when could one say that those to whom it has been conceded by men to govern the various societies—under the sole condition that they maintain, in the tranquillity that is so coveted, the peoples whom one supposes to have abandoned the wild forests to live in perfect friendship—when could one say that they have reduced the right to administer justice to the defence of the oppressed alone, and have not extended it to the free choice of the punishment that is due to offenders?

I have no wish to refute the consequences for the right of war that the aforementioned jurists have deduced from their system, because there would be too much to say if I did this properly. I want only to observe that their doctrine has led them to uphold the message that it is not permitted to punish any of the crimes that can be committed against the Supreme Being, because such a right is reserved for the injured party alone (see add. to § 44[59]). If however this were the case, who after a homicide would act for the dead, who would take the side of those who lacked the courage to avenge themselves, who, finally, would stand up to the brute force of a scoundrel who with his crimes harassed the weak, given their retiring disposition and circumspection? Therefore the penalty of Talion is an entity of ideal reason which would foment a continuous war in the State of Nature and among various societies, under the pretext of punishing, without knowledge of the cause, crimes genuine and supposed. It would stand in the way of reparation for losses, by demanding an equality between punishment and injury which amounts to sheer fantasy.

§ 3. THE SAME ARGUMENT CONTINUED

The laws delivered to the Hebrews from the mouth of Moses serve as proof to those who endorse the punishment of Talion, and thus as an argument against our hypothesis. I myself will always refrain from explaining what one reads in the Sacred Scriptures with reference to certain universal rules, because we do not know the true relationships of a government over which God presided, and because the reasons which led Him to lay down certain commandments are hidden from us. Besides, the Gospel holds up teachings as different from those commandments as revenge is from pardon, and chastisement from the remission of a penalty. Thus it appears safer to make our judgements under the guidance of these teachings rather than the aforementioned commandments, even though the inner cruelty of all men means they are naturally inspired and driven towards harshness and hard-heartedness rather than gentleness and mildness.

But it is also worth reflecting on the fact that these same punishments which are seen to be laid down in all their severity in Exodus (21:23ff.), in Leviticus (24:17–20) and in Deuteronomy (19, end), were repurchased with a monetary tax which served to give satisfaction for the injury, as is noted by authoritative interpreters.[60] On the basis of these principles of jurisprudence, Cain believed that his brutal murder of his brother would have given anyone encountering him the right to deprive him of life (Genesis 4:14). The Lord however had reserved for himself the punishment of such a monstrous act (Genesis 5:15, 24), and threatened to destroy with a seven-fold punishment of Talion anyone who foolishly undertook to punish this excess—this to make it evident that in the State of Nature it is not permitted to punish the crimes of others.

The expression used here in Scripture is worthy of some attention. The death of Abel merited the death of Cain in accordance with the literal meaning of the precept (Genesis 9:6): 'Whoever sheds blood, let his blood be shed.' God, however, wanted to punish with a penalty seven times greater the man who would have made Cain pay the penalty for his crime. Thus the loss of Cain's life was not the just satisfaction owed for the harm he did to his brother, and in consequence in this case death or, let us say, the punishment of Talion, was inequitable. What does this signify, if not that in these same Scriptures such a punishment is not regarded as adequate satisfaction for all crimes without distinction, and that Talion is not a just reparation deriving from the law of nature, as those who have engaged themselves in its defence have held?

The ease with which we explain any event at all has led writers to judge that the following were punished by Heaven with such a punishment: Brutus and Cassius for having assassinated Caesar (Cassius Dio, *Hist.* 48, beg.; Suetonius, *Julius Caesar*, end); those who betrayed the emperor Gordian III (Julius Capitolinus, *Gordiani* 33); Pyrrhus for having shed the blood of Priam before the Altar (Pausanias, 14.17); Philip king of Macedonia who himself administered poison to both Aratus king of the Achaeans and the orators Eurycleides and Micion (Pausanias, *Corinth.* 2.9);[61] and more than a few others whose fate has been in one way or another attested. But the judgements of Heaven are inscrutable, and the events in question unfathomable. Therefore I cannot say whether in history the scoundrels who have escaped the punishment of Talion in this life exceed in number those who appear to have fallen victim to its severity.

Various passages in the New Testament are adduced as proof of the justice of such a punishment. Thus in Matthew we read (7:1; 26:52): 'The measure you give will be the measure you get'; and 'he who takes up the sword will perish by the sword'; also in John (Apocal. 13:10): 'If anyone is to be taken to prison, into prison he goes'; and there are various similar expressions. These do not so much establish the justice of the punishment of Talion in the strict sense as demonstrate the appropriateness of some punishment for scoundrels who have committed a crime.

§ 4. THE SAME ARGUMENT CONTINUED

It is certain that the aforementioned testimonies of the Sacred Scriptures, and those also which can be found in the gentile writers who knew of a Providence that controlled the affairs of this lower world, indicate only that God has made known His will to judge men in accordance with their actions, and to allocate chastisements in proportion to their crimes; also that the flash of that truth has penetrated even the dark shadows of idolatry. But that the Supreme Lawgiver has laid it down that Talion is the universal punishment for all crimes, that the civil authorities should punish criminals in accordance with this law and that the principal aim of this same law is to return injury rather than secure the safety, example and reform of men: these are the imaginings of those who in a prejudicial spirit examine the sacred Books for matters on issues outside their scope.

The mere fact that in many circumstances the true punishment of some offences through Talion might constitute a new crime is enough to convince us that we have an inadequate understanding of this word, and that certain phrases that one encounters are owed to its vividness. But if we went into this, the thread of our discourse would be broken, and there would always remain the riposte that however we interpret the matter, it is certain that in Scripture the death penalty is laid down for idolatry, homicide and adultery. Certainly inspection of the laws by which God governed his chosen people leads us to suppose beyond all doubt that all his commandments for them were absolutely just, but does not create any obligation on us to do what was done among the Hebrews. Regarding idolatry, Tertullian wrote (*Adv. Jud.* 3): 'The Old Law defended itself by vengeance with the sword ... the New Law laid down clemency.'[62]

Fragment 4

I will not, in order to combat his opinion,[63] present the arguments with which Donna Filippa Pugliesi (Boccaccio, 6.7)[64] persuaded the authority of Prato to alter the excessively cruel statute of that city which ordered the burning alive of any woman caught in adultery whether for love or money. And if I told you that all those few laws are unjust which establish death as the punishment for this crime, because they were issued without the consent of those whom they for the most part affect, and because it is better that somebody should make use of what is left over than to want or allow it to go to waste and spoil—for the needs of a man alone are meagre in comparison with the desires of a woman; if I said these things to you, you would think that I was treating the matter in a frivolous way, and that in the absence of more solid arguments I have clung on to those of an amiable short-story writer in order to combat the opinion of those who have undertaken to discuss in all seriousness what is no joking matter.

Fragment 5

The limitation of the power of the sovereign, that derives from his nature and the will of those who have formed it in accordance with natural principles, is such that he cannot produce unjust laws, and that any laws that are unjust do not carry a true obligation.

Laws can be unjust in terms of both ends and means, that is to say, with regard to both what they impose and the manner in which they impose it.

It is absolutely certain that all men through an inner obligation are constrained to carry out certain duties that are dependent on the natural laws and the civil laws, the latter being immutably dependent on the former. Nevertheless these same laws, by their sanction and by punishments, acquire a new degree of force through which their observance becomes the more secure. In consequence, the most accredited public jurists have held that punishment is essential and necessary in any law; thus those laws have been judged defective which have not carried some punishment for those who violate them. It is not for us to go into the reason for this at present, though it is just that we set down an accurate idea of punishment, since the various notions that some have had of the concept have produced much confusion from which false doctrines have derived.

GIUSEPPE PELLI AND CESARE BECCARIA: CORRESPONDENCE (1766–67)[65]

Letter 1: Giuseppe Pelli to Cesare Beccaria, Florence, 24 March 1766

Most illustrious sir, lord worthy of the highest reverence,
Having discovered in the Fifth Edition of the wonderful tract *On Crimes and Punishments* the true identity of its author, I cannot refrain for one moment from presenting myself to the man whom I have already admired above any other, as one who in this age has laboured with laudable zeal to illuminate the impenetrable chaos of the criminal justice system. Such praise is not due to Your most illustrious Lordship from me so much as from all those who love humanity. I am also bound to confess to you that I attempted some years previously a similar work, as friends of mine are aware, and stopped short of giv-

ing it a final polish. The reason is that I was promoted to a position in which from time to time I am obliged to give a judicial opinion on the punishment of criminals. I thought it proper not to reveal my feelings, so as not to draw attention to myself without any specific purpose in something that would have stirred up trouble, given the prejudices in which the ignorant mob is steeped. When the work of Your most illustrious Lordship appeared, however, I in the quiet privacy of my chambers was among those who applauded your generous endeavour, and I envied the credit that it was winning through the discovery of a new truth in the moral sphere of things. Though I am unknown and without merit, permit me, Your most illustrious Lordship, to present myself to you, transported by the joy of dedicating my devotion to him who has thought as I myself have reasoned, to offer you my congratulations and render you the true homage of friendly sincerity. Would that I were sufficiently grand to reward a philosopher of such distinction or had the legislative power to be able to put his teachings into practice. My status as a private citizen does not permit me to do either the one or the other; it leaves me solely with the desire to obtain the necessary sympathy for my frankness in appearing before you, and to be regarded by Your most illustrious Lordship, as the most sincere and the closest friend that you could desire. Without disavowing this frank character of mine, courtesy demands that I employ the customary words to declare myself the most devoted and affectionate servant uniquely of Your most illustrious Lordship.

Giuseppe Pelli

Letter 2: Cesare Beccaria to Giuseppe Pelli, Milan, c. 11 April 1766

Most illustrious sir, lord worthy of the highest reverence,
I am surprised and moved by the most kind letter that Your most illustrious Lordship so graciously wrote me on 24 March. I am aware that I do not merit so much, and that my good fortune is entirely due to the beneficent and generous spirit of humanity which I see shining through the marvellous letter of Your most illustrious Lordship. You have shown that you are capable of realising my honest intention, which alone covers over the defects of my little work and has earned me the favour of sensitive and enlightened souls.

I am genuinely proud to have met with the approval and admiration of Your most illustrious Lordship. If for good reasons you have not given the final touches to your own work, then that is Italy's loss, even if Tuscany has gained a minister abounding in talent and virtue. If it is possible for Your most illustrious Lordship, then divide your time between the sovereign and the public; you would be rendering service to the happiness of the human race and of the country.

Your complimentary words to me are entirely to be attributed to the interest of the subject that I have treated, and to that faintest but nonetheless genuine ray of virtue that I have ventured to shine through in my little book. Your most illustrious Lordship is much too magnanimous to be the harsh censor and to withhold your favour from the feeble efforts of a good citizen.

The letter of Your most illustrious Lordship is too splendid to fail to awake in me a strong desire for your correspondence and friendship. I will endeavour to make myself worthy of it by cultivating truth and virtue, to which your mind and heart are devoted. Assuring you of my admiration and sincere and close friendship, with my highest esteem and my deepest devotion, I remain the most faithful and affectionate servant of Your most illustrious Lordship.

Cesare Beccaria Bonesana

Letter 3: Giuseppe Pelli to Cesare Beccaria, Florence, 12 May 1766

Most illustrious sir, lord worthy of the highest reverence,
The letter that Your most illustrious Lordship with extreme generosity had the kindness to send me in reply to mine last month, in April, is too courteous to be composed by a philosopher and to be addressed to an individual who also himself has the innocent vanity to appear as such; this cannot be held against him when there are so many people who live in the world whose sole purpose in life is to chatter in line with their prejudices. I am worth little in society in comparison with you, who have the talents needed to bring it enlightenment and to confer benefit on the human race.

On discovering that your portrait was being prepared here, I took steps to be the first to acquire it and I was successful in so doing. Thus I have the pleasure of contemplating your person in effigy in my rooms, being unable to have that of enjoying the physical presence of a master and friend such as I desire Your most illustrious Lordship to be to me. It is most fortunate that the commission came into the hands of the best engraver that we have here and who is thus worthy of representing his subject. You will no doubt agree with me that the engraving is well executed, and I would be greatly in your debt if you would grant me your assurance that it is a good likeness, since in this way I will feel greater satisfaction when contemplating it.

Some articles in the periodical that is published in your city, entitled *Il Caffè*, have given me the firm conviction that they come from the hand of Your most illustrious Lordship. I have therefore immediately placed an order with a bookseller to have them delivered to me. In Milan any person of good taste must be envious of persons endowed with learning as profound as that which appears in the works that come from your pen. I lack the capacity to flatter, but I have sufficient sensibility to be greatly moved by beauty and truth. This sensibility nevertheless is not at the same level as the fortitude that is required to know how to emulate it. Were you to meet me, you would see that I am of much lower station than the person that you in your courtesy imagine me to be. If nevertheless the initial step on the journey to knowledge is to be acquainted with and to hold in the highest esteem those who possess and profess it, then I must consider myself to be of some worth, in as much as I have had the good fortune to feel myself inspired to admire Your most illustrious Lordship, to whom I have the ardent wish on every occasion to bear witness of my most sincere and deepest affection.

It behoves Your most illustrious Lordship to enrol me as a recipient of your commands. For as far as my littleness in comparison with your great merit permits, I will forever show myself, with the greatest solicitude and attentiveness, the most devoted and the most dutiful servant and friend of Your most illustrious Lordship.

Giuseppe Pelli

Letter 4: Giuseppe Pelli to Cesare Beccaria, Florence, 19 May 1767

Most illustrious lord, lord most revered master,

The lord count Verri whom I had the fortunate occasion to meet during the brief time that he spent here, has assured me that you have returned to your homeland after your journey to Paris. This news gives me a reason to appear once more before you, to offer you a small token of my friendship. My secretary has at my request translated from the French a memoir of the Economic

Society of Bern on the legislation regarding agriculture, and I have added in
haste some annotations and a preface. There as here I have cited your most
esteemed person and the authors of the *Caffè*. The booklet has been printed
in Lucca, with the date of Bern, and is in Milan with Giuseppe Galeazzi, to
whom I have written with the request that he present you with a copy in my
name. I have rendered the justice that is owed to your character not only on
this occasion, but also in one of the eulogies I deliver in the *Serie dei ritratti
degli uomini illustri toscani*, a work which is being printed under the patronage
of His Royal Highness and which the forementioned lord count Verri has
seen. To receive praise from me is of little consequence for you, since Voltaire
himself has celebrated your immortal work, but I am moved by the ambition
to let the people know that I am able to appreciate you for your work. My
honoured lord marquis, the circle of men who know how to think is very
limited. In Italy, Milan has more of them than any other city. I assured lord
count Verri of this, and now confirm it with you, for I do not know where
one could find, otherwise than in Milan, a group of friends capable of writing another *Caffè*. Certainly here I would be unable to tell you the names of
such men, as much as I love my country and feel that we are not without
men of talent. I read a booklet published last year in your city: *Delle leggi
civili reali*. The author of the work, though not the brothers Verri nor Bec-
cheria, nevertheless shows great talent, and I would very much like to know
his name. In the obscurity that is mine, I yearn to know the people who
bestow honour on our age, and to give them the homage of my praise, even
if, as far as the things of this world are concerned, my significance is that of
a link of virtually no value. Lord marquis, men are all citizens of the world,
not of one city alone. Each individual can embody more than one persona,
one of which may be the friend and admirer of those few people who, scattered over the globe, have the capacity to bring enlightenment to the human
race. I am enchained by my circumstances, but nevertheless I sometimes
imagine myself to be in the company of the d'Alemberts, the Eulers and the
other grand geniuses, and I like to consider what a noble spectacle it would
be, if they were all to be brought together in the same place to work on a new
Encyclopedia.

Most esteemed friend, I ask your pardon if my illusory wishes drive me
to bore you with my lengthy letter. You see how I am speaking freely. It is in
the same tone that I beseech you not to tire of giving service, by producing
new works. The persons who have gained enlightenment wait in expecta-

tion for them. Divide your attention between your family and your compositions. Continue to tear aside the veil of ignorance that still blinds so many people, and with that noble passion that fires you to do good to your fellow men, put your mind to the task of writing for their benefit. I await your further works with eager anticipation, and I will forever continue to declare myself the most devoted and affectionate friend and servant of Your most illustrious Lordship.

Giuseppe Pelli

Context

⋮

Tuscany

The early and formative years of Giuseppe Bencivenni Pelli (1729–1808) are to be placed in a Tuscan, an imperial and a Roman Catholic context.[1] He was born in Florence in the last years of the Medici dynasty and lived there continuously after his student days in Pisa. Florence was the wealthiest and most populous city of Tuscany. Tuscany lay within the Holy Roman Empire, but from 1569 enjoyed the semi-independent status of a Grand Duchy, initially and for the best part of two centuries under the Medici. As such, it was not governed by the Pragmatic Sanction promulgated by the emperor Charles VI in 1713, which provided that the provinces that were ruled directly by the Habsburgs would be inherited by his daughter Maria Theresa as an integrated unit (and rule them she did, from 1740 to 1780).

With the extinction of the Medici dynasty in 1737, the title of grand duke of Tuscany passed to Francis Stephen of Lorraine (the emperor Francis I), who in 1736 married Maria Theresa. He succeeded Charles as Holy Roman emperor in 1745. Francis took little personal interest in Tuscany, but set up a Regency Council for Tuscany in Vienna with ultimate authority over the Grand Duchy, and introduced a number of foreigners, many of them displaced Lorrainers from Nancy, into significant posts in the government. They held the presidency of the Regency Council in Florence—first Prince de Craon and then, for almost two decades from 1749, Comte de Richecourt—and occupied seats in the Regency Council and the Senate. The tradition of non-interventionist, indirect imperial rule appeared to be further threatened when Richecourt launched a series of reforms designed to modernise the administration and economy and to moderate the influence of the nobility and the Church.[2]

This programme of reform was stepped up under the successor of Richecourt (who retired to Nancy for reasons of health in 1757), Marshall Botta Adorno, a military man from Lombardy who had led imperial armies in a series of wars. A prime mover of reform in this period was his minister Pompeo Neri, a conspicuous representative of a new breed of Florentine nobles who pursued power and influence in the imperial service.[3] The departure of Richecourt more or less coincided with the return of Pompeo Neri to Tuscany (in 1758) after a spell in Lombardy where he had pushed through a long-delayed reform of the cadastral register of Milan (paving the way for agricultural improvements) on behalf of the Habsburgs. These were the top officials with whom Giuseppe Pelli had to deal when he was embarking on his career in the late 1750s and early 1760s. This was also the time when he was composing a draft of his treatise *Against the Death Penalty*. His diaries provide valuable information about the opportunities that were opening up for new men to work in the local and imperial administration, and about the nature of the relationship between the seat of power in Vienna and the provincial capital of Florence.

The next and more dynamic phase of reform in Tuscany, presided over by Leopold of Habsburg-Lorraine ('Pietro Leopoldo', to whom the grand dukedom passed on the death of Francis in 1765), included, and culminated in, the publication of a new code of laws which, among other things, abolished torture and the death penalty.[4] But this was in 1786. Pelli's own project of an attack on the death penalty had sometime before (in early 1761) sputtered out, unfinished, unpublished, unknown. It is possible, but quite uncertain, that Pelli had a subsidiary, advisory role in the preparation of Grand Duke Leopold's law. When the law was promulgated, he was fully occupied with the directorship of the Uffizi, a position much more to his taste and in tune with his interests than involvement with the judiciary. But he had accumulated first-hand knowledge and experience of the judicial system of Tuscany, and this received official recognition when (on 3 April 1771) he was selected as a member of a small committee established by the grand duke 'for the general reform of the system of provincial magistracies and tribunals of the Florentine State' under the chairmanship of Pompeo Neri.[5] The proceedings of this committee cannot be followed in detail; it is likely enough that the personnel changed after the death of its chairman in 1776 and following Pelli's appointment as director of the Uffizi in 1775. Further, the committee may have been charged with reform of the judicial administration and structure rather than of the penal code. In any case, it was Beccaria's treatise, published a decade earlier, that set in motion the movement for penal reform. There never was a 'Pelli moment'.

Finally, under the heading of historical context, the Church. In eighteenth-century Italy, the power of the Papacy was on the wane, but the Church was still highly influential in the society, culture and economy, not to mention the law and legal practice. An ecclesiastical career carried significant benefits, such as tax exemptions and fiscal privileges, and unsurprisingly was chosen by many. As Domenico Passionei, from the small town of Fossombrone in the Marche, a future cardinal, papal legate and Vatican librarian, wrote at the age of eighteen (in 1710) to his father:

> I hold dearest the interests of our family, and after theirs my own, and then that our posterity remember me ... The brightest boy in every family always takes the cloth in order to advance his family with him.[6]

Pelli was one of a number who bore the title 'abbate'—Pompeo Neri was another—which marked them out for a ecclesiastical career should they wish to take it up. Many did not, opting instead for secular employment. Pelli's first 'job offer', which he turned down, involved service at the court of a cardinal, which would have given him an inside track into the priesthood. He also considered becoming a monk, but decided it was not for him,[7] any more than was a clerical career.

Pelli was chosen by Pompeo Neri to assist him in revising the law on mortmain. During the long period of Spanish rule, ecclesiastical landholdings had grown considerably in Tuscany as elsewhere, with the consequence that a steadily increasing amount of property was unavailable for purchase and exempt from secular control because of entails and mortmain, the 'dead hand' of the Church. Pelli saw no contradiction between, on the one hand, the pursuit of personal piety and the upholding of Catholic theology and ritual, and, on the other, cutting into the vested interests of the contemporary Church and its hierarchies.

There was in fact greater prospect of reform of the Church from within in Italy than, say, in France, where, following the revocation of the Edict of Nantes in 1685, an absolutist state set about imposing Catholicism on its subjects. The hostile reaction of Enlightenment thinkers such as Voltaire exposed them to censorship and severe punishment.[8] South of the Alps, Pelli's earlier contemporary, the celebrated historian, jurist and priest Lodovico Antonio Muratori of Modena (1672–1750) had already demonstrated that a critical spirit—responsive to ideas from abroad—could be reconciled with religious belief and practice.[9] Pelli (it will be argued) was able to find within the religious community of Florence kindred spirits who shared his humanitarian convictions and gave him support and inspiration for his critique of the current penal system. How it was that he drew back from publicising his beliefs, whereas Beccaria, writing a few years later in Milan, did not, is a conundrum that I will attempt to resolve.

The Man

Giuseppe Bencivenni Pelli was the younger of two surviving brothers. They were orphaned early. Their four surviving sisters were placed in convents. On the death of the older brother, Giuseppe took over the family name Bencivenni. He did not marry, but in 1770 adopted Teresa Ciamagnini, aged seven. In due course she married Giovanni Fabbroni, they had a son, and the name Bencivenni lived on through the combination of the two families.[10]

The family was not well off and under Pelli's brother's mismanagement its situation worsened.[11] Pelli lacked the resources to complete his course of studies in law in Pisa.[12] It was not until he embarked on a career in administration under the auspices of the Habsburg empire in the Duchy of Tuscany that his financial situation improved, and then not straightaway.[13] He remained very sensitive about his material circumstances. Junior posts in the administration were badly paid, if paid at all, and he was constantly looking for ways of improving his position.[14]

We are extremely well informed about the personality, life, career and interests of Giuseppe Pelli, thanks in large part to the *Efemeridi*, the multivolume diary that he left behind, with almost daily entries spanning the years 1759–1808; besides, his diary begins with a hundred-page introduction charting the course of his life up till 29 August 1759.[15] Pelli saw himself as standing in a long line of autobiographical writers such as Cicero (of the Letters), Augustine and Montaigne, as well as various citizens of Florence—for diaries were something of a Florentine specialty.[16] In time Pelli would acknowledge, but without warmth, the contribution of Rousseau to the autobiographical tradition (the *Confessions* was published in 1782). Montaigne however is 'amicissimo' and his prime model: 'I read Montaigne as I go walking; in some passages I recognise myself, and that is very satisfying.'[17]

Pelli emerges in his diary as a man of letters and culture. He was a prodigious bibliophile. He cites with approval, and fellow-feeling, the observation of Montaigne that his three main interests were men, women and books, though perhaps in his case the order would have been reversed, with 'books' in pride of place. He bought books every day, so he says,[18] and read profusely to feed his many interests, which included history, biography, current affairs, antiquity and antiquarianism, religion (he was, as already noted, a pious Catholic), philosophy, law, politics, economics, agriculture, education, women and marriage, demography, medicine, botany, geology, drama, art, fiction and poetry. He was very sensitive to the weather, and presents a brief daily record of the weather in Florence over half a century and more; he even speculates about the reality of climate change.[19] He tells us about his leisure activities, which included attendance at religious and secular festivals, drama, art exhibitions, a football match (he saw a team from Florence defeating one from Bologna[20]) and, his preferred pursuit, days off in the countryside, walking and lunching with a friend or friends. He carefully chronicles his health problems: he was a self-confessed hypochondriac with a tendency to depression, and found relative peace of mind only in his later years when he had achieved recognition and fulfilment. He comes across as extremely high-minded and conservative in his social attitudes: he slips easily into moralising about the sinfulness of the human race or the weaknesses of women. Especially in his early and middle period, when he was climbing the career ladder, he describes himself as timid—a quality that has a bearing on the history of his dissertation *Against the Death Penalty.* Finally, although he read very widely, and declared that it is better to read than to write,[21] he was a prolific writer over a wide range of subjects.[22] Most of his written work—and this too is very relevant to the dissertation—remained unpublished or was for limited circulation.

Pelli's career culminated in his directorship of the Uffizi Gallery (1775–93). Previous to that (1770–75), he was principal editor of the leading literary journal of Florence, *Novelle Letterarie,* These posts enabled his long-standing passion for literature and art to flourish. I focus here on the early part of his career, when he was much less happy with his employment. These years provide the setting for the incubation, composition and abandonment of the death penalty dissertation. Of particular relevance is his appointment on 28 January 1762 as *segretario* of the Pratica Segreta di Pistoia e Pontremoli, in effect, the senior judge in the criminal courts of Pistoia and Pontremoli within the Grand Duchy of Tuscany. This was a significant promotion, which improved his financial circumstances and established him as a man of consequence in the administration and in society.[23] In addition, if we take at face value an assertion made in a letter to Beccaria (of March 1766; 'Letter 1' above), the assumption of this very post issued in a resolve to abandon his dissertation *Against the Death Penalty*. He claims that he gave up the project, leaving it unfinished and unpublished, precisely because he saw a conflict of interest between his new position and his disapproval of the death penalty.[24]

There is a problem here: there is a gap of a little more than a year between Pelli's abandonment, or suspension, of the dissertation in early January 1761 and his appointment as judge, which was formalised in February 1762. Does this discrepancy matter? It does matter, in so far as the true explanation for his stepping back from the dissertation, supposing we could discover it, might be expected to be revealing as to his character and his attitude and circumstances at the time.[25]

In any case, we have before us an intriguing historical counterfactual. What if Pelli had persevered with his project and given himself another month or two to complete it?[26] He was a fast worker and he was raring to go. His diary entry of 25 November 1760 reads as follows:

> I am interested in nothing else than in producing the above-mentioned little work which I have thought about at various times. The truth is that I find myself able to compose with a certain facility, and this gives me the urge to speed on with the work so that I keep the wind that drives me in my sails.[27]

He had clearly given a great deal of thought to the subject before he decided to put pen to paper, if he had not actually begun writing it before he says he did.

How would Pelli's work have been received had he completed it and presented it to the public in a polished form? A comparison with Beccaria is tempting, but ultimately futile. My guess is that it would have created a stir, especially in ecclesiastical circles, but would not have sent out the tsunami that followed the publication of Beccaria's work. We need to remind ourselves that Pelli envisaged writing only on the death penalty, while Beccaria was advancing a whole programme of penal reform, encompassing, among other things, torture, detention, presumption of innocence, proportionality, the supremacy of the law, the role of magistrates, testimony, proofs—and the death penalty. And that is before we take into consideration the style and presentation of the two works, the one a closely argued legal treatise, the other a spirited manifesto. We should perhaps think in terms of the two works being potentially complementary, making an impression on different, if overlapping, audiences. Beccaria's vision of a secular society based on sociability, equality and individual rights, in addition to the specific reformist principles that he was asserting, was too advanced and radical for Pelli's chosen readership, and guaranteed the survival of his reputation into the modern age. It is too much to suppose that Pelli might have received comparable homage from later epochs as a pioneer of penal reform, had monuments dedicated to him and received posthumously a plenitude of volumes in his honour.[28] The fact remains, however, that Pelli's work, even in its incomplete and unrevised form, and not that of Beccaria, was the first comprehensive attack on the death penalty.[29]

It is the case that Pelli does not emerge as a man of great stature and towering intellect, a Montaigne, a Bacon or a Montesquieu (three of his exemplary intellectual giants).[30] Nor does he claim to be one: he often cuts himself down to size and preaches the necessity and benefit of limiting one's ambitions. He was a minor aristocrat of Florence who held significant but not top positions in politics or the law in the Grand Duchy of Tuscany. Beccaria, as it happens, was of similar stature: he was for the larger part of his career an active and respected civil servant of the Habsburg empire within the province of Lombardy.

Again, the treatise *Against the Death Penalty* stands alone as Pelli's contribution (and an aborted one at that) on the subject of the reform of the criminal law. In his diaries, he grumbles from time to time about the inadequacies and injustices of the legal system, but he does not go into detail, there is no general form of criticism and he admits that he can and will do nothing to rectify the system's failings. This is a stance which he adopts regularly in the face of controversial matters.[31] In the case of Beccaria too there was virtually no follow-up to his pioneering book.[32] The French philosophers who were admiring of Beccaria looked to him to write something rather more expansive on the subject of legal reform than the mere libretto that he had produced, but their urgings fell on deaf ears. We are confronted with a demonstration of the fact that a work of small dimensions can make a big impact, if it arrives at an opportune moment.

THE LIFE-CYCLE OF *AGAINST THE DEATH PENALTY*

For a glimpse of the history of this dissertation, we can turn to Pelli's diary, the *Efemeridi*. In this enormous work, as we have already seen, he recorded his thoughts and reflections, interests, reading material, actions and a selection of events in Florence and elsewhere, over the course of half a century. I say 'for a glimpse' of the history of the dissertation because that is all we are offered. Pelli is cryptic about the conception, composition and abandonment of his death penalty treatise and about the milieu from which it arose. We can, however, do something with the morsels that he gives us.[33]

The project contemplated

I neglected to say yesterday that among some of my friends it was asserted that it would be better not to condemn to death any criminal for any crime at all but to retain him for public labours. I am also of this opinion; at one time I wanted to write a dissertation on the subject. But so as to avoid swimming against the tide, I judged it better to hold back from undertaking this task. It would certainly not be a small labour to bring into focus the matter of punishments in their true nature, and the pointlessness of taking away the life of a man for a crime when he could in a thousand ways deliver partial compensation for the harm he has done to society.[34]

Pelli had been conversing with friends unnamed about the death penalty. They disapproved of it as did he. He claims further that he earlier had in mind writing a dissertation against the death penalty. He doesn't say when it was that he thought of doing so (or whether his friends encouraged him to take up the project now). There is not a whiff of an interest in the subject in the twenty-three page summary of the first three decades of his life, apparently written, or completed, on 29 August 1759. Only a little over two weeks into the diary proper (whose start date is 1 September 1759), however, we have the above entry, which suggests that he had indeed earlier contemplated writing on the subject from a critical perspective, but stayed his hand, for two reasons. First, his message would be strongly opposed: presumably he means that the powers that be (the political, judicial and ecclesiastical authorities) would be strongly critical of it. The death sentence, carried out in one way or another but often with great cruelty, was an established feature of secular and ecclesiastical criminal justice in Italy and elsewhere in Europe. Secondly, Pelli was unsure that he could prove his case: he felt he would have his work cut out to do so. The argument, as he indicates here, would necessarily revolve around an examination of the nature and purpose of punishment. He would in addition have to convince potential critics of the uselessness of the death penalty when in his view other means of punishing criminals existed that would benefit the community. He does not say why he he had not been confident of producing persuasive arguments on these matters. In sum, Pelli had been unsure that it would be worth his while to proceed with such a project. And (we must assume) he was still unsure, and presumably for the same reasons that had carried weight with him earlier.

The project undertaken

> This morning's conversation with a friend has led me to resolve to turn my hand to the composition of a dissertation 'On the Penalty of Death', with the aim of demonstrating that it is excessive, unnecessary and perhaps unjust when applied to any crime whatever. I have spoken of this elsewhere (I, 114). I have charged myself with this work with the sole motive of bringing some benefit to my fellow men. I am desirous of taking it to a conclusion, and of publishing it, though I have no illusion that I will witness any change in the world in this matter. May God lighten my path and give me sufficient strength to bring my undertaking to a happy ending. It has one object and one only, the well-being of others.[35]

More than a year has passed. Pelli has changed his mind. Following discussion with a friend, he will write against the death penalty. He intends to argue that it is 'excessive, unnecessary and perhaps unjust'. This characterisation of the death penalty is fully compatible with that which appears in both his own treatise and that of Beccaria. Pelli's works include a number of unpublished scripts. But this one, against the death penalty, is apparently intended for general circulation. After all, Pelli has the general aim, the 'sole aim' in fact, of benefiting mankind. On the other hand, he doubts that he will be able to bring about any change in penal systems. This is an acknowledgement, echoing that of the previous text, that he anticipates that his proposal and his arguments will be strongly opposed, and that he suspects his critics will prevail, in the sense that they will block any reform of the law and judicial practice. But he no longer appears to be apprehensive about 'swimming against the current'. Pelli invokes the Deity: he trusts that God will be on his side, and this is closely associated in his mind with his purpose of benefiting the human race. Surely God will support such a venture, though how exactly He will do so is not spelled out. In helping Pelli to formulate convincing arguments, perhaps? Or just in allowing or enabling him to complete the project?

The project suspended

I have worked until now on the dissertation already referred to . . . concerning the death penalty, which has been prescribed by the laws for some crimes. I have written a substantial amount, but not to my satisfaction; I have not quite pinpointed the line of argument that will prove my thesis. I have therefore decided to put the subject aside and take it up again on another occasion, and to make a judgement in cold blood as to whether I have the arguments needed to sustain my thesis, or to conclude that I am mistaken. Indeed the product of our pen has to be allowed to mature so that we do not peddle things that might bring us dishonour.[36]

Pelli says he has written a lot ('assai')—and the internal evidence of the diary suggests that he has done so in around six weeks, which is remarkable if true—but he is going to stop in his tracks now, perhaps to resume at another time. And in fact a diary entry of 1 April 1762 (the next text quoted below) shows that more than a year later he had in mind the possibility of returning to the project and bringing it to completion. He is giving up at this moment because he does not feel that his arguments are decisive.[37] This explanation or justification is to be taken seriously. Pelli was a modest man, and may well have been unsure of his own ability to do justice to this important topic. He might have thought he would *harm* the cause of penal reform, if he put only weak arguments or arguments without persuasive force, which could easily be countered. As to the rider that if he went forward with the project his reputation might suffer, this shows that he was sensitive to the reception of his work, should it be published. But we may reasonably suspect that he was worried that he would attract criticism not so much because of the quality of his arguments, but rather because he was airing them at all.

The project reconsidered?

The reason that it seems to me that one can, in criminal cases, be quite inclined to clemency is that I am not persuaded that anyone is harmed as a consequence of the handing down of a lesser penalty. In civil cases, what one gives to one person is often taken away from another; so it is necessary to consider carefully every decision so as not unjustly to deprive anyone of what is his. But in criminal cases, that a convicted man who might deserve to be punished with death is instead condemned to imprisonment, or to exile, and so on, is not something that is prejudicial to another; the public has its revenge and public security is assured, when the delinquent is punished in some way or other. In any case, one can never know what is the true level of punishment that should be imposed for any transgression whatever, although each and every act must carry some differing grade of malice and deceit. These thoughts of mine will not perhaps carry conviction for any judge, but they are consistent with what I outlined in my Dissertation on the death penalty. *That is a work that I regularly contemplate giving the final touches to at the proper time.* I find it so completely natural to think in this way that I do not believe that I will ever walk away from making decisions in accordance with this line of argument. In fact I here and now declare that it will be infinitely difficult for me to induce myself to condemn anyone to death.[38]

More than two years have gone by since the suspension or abandonment of the dissertation *Against the Death Penalty*. Pelli is in his first month as chief judge of the criminal courts of Tuscan Pistoia and Pontremoli. In this passage, he gives a hint that he may revive his dissertation. This is wishful thinking. He is clinging to the hope that he can perform his role as a criminal judge without compromising his convictions, which he claims are still firm, about the death penalty. In support of this view, he produces an astonishing argument: that it is easier to judge criminal than civil cases, because in criminal cases leniency is never a mistake. This is backed up by the statement, reflecting his deep reading of Montaigne (who was a judge in his time) that one can never be sure at what level to pitch a punishment. The final sentence gives the game away: it will be 'infinitely difficult' for Pelli to issue a death sentence, in effect, to be a judge in criminal cases.

The judge versus the philosopher

The first crisis was not long in coming. Less than four months into his new job, his worst fears were beginning to be realised. In the first passage cited below, he is found ordering the torture of an accused man, and expressing dread at the thought that he might have to issue a death sentence in the foreseeable future. The diary entry reveals the tug-of-war that was going on between Pelli the 'philosopher'—convinced of the 'barbarity' of torture, and by implication of the death penalty too—and Pelli the judge, duty-bound to enforce the laws. The solution, he thinks, lies with a benevolent ruler who would reform the laws. He feels, however, he lacks the stature to influence such a ruler, even if he were in place.[39]

Today I had occasion to settle a criminal case by ordering the torture of the accused. In truth I am against this torment, which seems to me quite barbarous, but in the present state of our jurisprudence, an ordinary individual vested with the profession of judge cannot expect to reform it rather than adapt himself to it. In some circumstances, there is no more expedient way of arriving at the truth or clarifying the evidence—*Gloss: this is the language of ordinary criminal jurisprudence, which I am adopting as judge, not as philosopher*—where it appears that we have to observe the methods commonly applied. Still, if I were of a rank that brought me closer to the sovereign, I would propose that a person so enlightened and upright examine in all seriousness whether there is a way of prosecuting and punishing crimes without the imposition of this torment. And I do not doubt that if the matter were given some attention and serious thought, one might achieve the end of bringing some benefit to humanity—*Gloss: and we are waiting for this highly desirable reform*. But for the present one must carry out one's duties according to current practice, and limit oneself to practising such scrupulous discretion as is required to prevent one from treating abusively one's fellow men. May it please heaven that these cases be rare, and rarer still those where one is bound to sign a death sentence. But I fear that I will find myself in a situation where I have to do this.[40]

Worse was to follow in the course of Pelli's second year as criminal law judge. He managed to escape passing a death sentence on one occasion in

January 1764, but did not avoid doing so in another instance in March of the
same year:

> I am much concerned about a case of great significance involving a
> household theft committed by a maidservant at the expense of her pa-
> troness. I am glad that there is a defence that can save the life of this
> wretched person so that I am not yet in the unpleasant position of hav-
> ing to issue a sentence of death.[41]

> Yesterday I had to assent to the designated penalty of death in a court
> case in Pistoia against a certain Francesco Arcangioli, a runaway ac-
> cused of a household theft committed at the expense of cavalier Bal-
> dassar Sozzifanti, his patron, in August 1762. Cases involving accused
> persons who do not present themselves are treated differently accord-
> ing to our jurisprudential system than those where the accused are at
> hand, and in the former cases the dictates of the laws are necessarily
> strictly adhered to. I have no wish to get involved in assessing whether
> in relation to absconders we are at the limits of what is just; but I do
> say that a delinquent is worse off if he runs away than if he allows him-
> self to be detained. Although humans by nature are inclined to the for-
> mer expediency, the laws on the other hand must of necessity ac-
> knowledge a distinction between those who defend themselves and
> those who seek to escape from being subjected to punishment. I have
> some particular examples in mind. The truth is that the punishment of
> crimes is subject to all the vagaries which everything else in the world
> is subject to.[42]

The same conflict between Pelli's inner convictions and the letter of the
laws is visible here, but, unlike in the matter of torture, he does not suggest
any resolution. The statement with which he signs off the latter diary entry
above is lame, but it is not a mere platitude if it implies that Pelli will exploit
such flexibility as there is in the law to exercise clemency. All in all, however,
once his career as a criminal court judge was launched, the odds (which were
in any case not short) of his returning to his dissertation *Against the Death
Penalty* had lengthened.

Enter Beccaria

A booklet of 104 pages in quarto containing a discourse entitled *On Crimes and Punishments* by an anonymous author has appeared recently; no provenance is named but it was printed in Livorno. I have read it with close attention and found it admirable. It is true that at certain points it is most obscure and that the style is very individual, making use of mathematical terminology. All the same, it contains a great many good things, serviceable truths, praiseworthy maxims and doctrines which could produce excellent results. It chimes in with many of my ways of thinking and advances the same opinion as I do on the death penalty, although his route is different to the one I followed in the outline of the dissertation to which I have made reference elsewhere. I have heard others praise it, so I can believe that my judgement is dispassionate. My only regret is that someone else before me in Italy has published an opinion which I myself wanted to express, moved by an inner desire to make myself useful to humanity. But if this glory is not to be mine, at least I can take that glory that comes from having explored this subject in a more profound way two years before this author has done, and to have harboured the same thoughts for an even longer period, as can be seen from my *Efemeridi*.[43]

Where Pelli had hesitated and prevaricated, and as a criminal law judge was wrestling with his conscience, someone else, with a greater sense of adventure or with fewer scruples or with greater protection, took the plunge and came out with a critique of the death penalty (among other things). We might regard this as inevitable, but Pelli does not appear to have seen it coming, and it hurts. He does take a stand, as well he might: his critique of the death penalty is considerably more detailed and substantial than that of Beccaria; and he did have grounds for saying that he expressed his opinions in writing before the anonymous author—although this latter claim is hopeful rather than self-evident, for the thus-far anonymous writer might after all have followed a path similar to Pelli's, producing a draft and sitting on it for a time while he tested the waters. Pelli could not have known whether or not this was the case. Furthermore, the evidence that Pelli cites for his own earlier work on the subject of the death penalty is accessible to diary readers only—and who had access to his diary? And such evidence was thin. To prove his point, he would have had to produce his own work, and fast.

As it is, Pelli's reaction to the publication of Beccaria's work does not include an express resolution to complete and publish his own dissertation immediately, soon, or in the not too distant future. He could still have made a claim to chronological priority and to having produced a more comprehensive treatment of the subject than Beccaria had done. We are free to conclude that the same considerations which stayed his hand in 1761 and thereafter still weighed with him. The letter of praise that he wrote to Beccaria on 24 March 1766, once the latter's authorship of *On Crimes and Punishments* was revealed, does address such considerations, but in an unsatisfactory way. Here are the relevant lines:

> I am also bound to confess to you that I attempted some years previously a similar work, as friends of mine are aware, and stopped short of giving it a final polish. The reason is that I was promoted to a position in which from time to time I am obliged to give a judicial opinion on the punishment of criminals. I thought it proper not to reveal my feelings, so as not to draw attention to myself without any specific purpose in something that would have stirred up trouble, given the prejudices in which the ignorant mob is steeped.'[44]

In 1766, that is, two years after the original publication of *Crimes and Punishments* in 1764, Beccaria had dropped his anonymity and revealed himself as the author. Pelli congratulates him, while pointing out that he had earlier composed 'a similar work' but left it unfinished. He goes on to explain why he gave up the project. Pelli was within his rights in claiming chronological priority for his own composition, although he does not date it closely or cite relevant diary entries as evidence, but merely refers to unnamed friends as potential witnesses. The specific reason that he gives for giving up the project is questionable. As pointed out above, there is a gap of more than a year between the abandonment of the project and the assumption of the office to which he refers, the Segretaria della Pratica Segreta di Pistoia e Pontremoli.

Among the several references that Pelli makes to his dissertation in the *Efemeridi*, this is the only one where he brings his career explicitly into play. Yet for some time he had had his eye on an administrative career, and he had already begun to climb the ladder. We may suspect that the need for patronage for career advancement was a factor in dissuading him from going public with provocative, radical ideas, well before he walked away from the death penalty project. To discover what was going on, we need to probe into his earlier career and become better acquainted with the ambitions and temperament of the man.

But first it would be desirable to investigate his circle of friends, and ask who might have played a part in providing encouragement, advice and support, and indeed discouragement, as he progressed through the cycle leading from gestation to abandonment of his project.[45]

MILIEU

Pelli had for some time been considering writing against the death penalty when a conversation among friends brought the matter to the forefront of his mind. The friends are unnamed. Nine months later, a conversation with a friend, also unnamed, encouraged him to write, and he took up the challenge. Around six weeks later, after writing at speed a substantial amount, he renounced the project—without referring to advice or intervention from anyone.

To add to the mystery, if we are to take at face value Pelli's accounts of his country excursions (typically to a villa or an inn) with one friend or occasionally two, at such times the subject of crimes and punishments was never directly raised.[46] Yet if he confided in anybody, it would surely have been with his walking companions, who were virtually always intimates. It is striking, moreover, that while Pelli leaves in anonymity the friends who by his own account participated in his decision making, he invariably names the friends who went walking with him.

It looks as if Pelli was being protective of his friends. These were difficult if not dangerous times for critics of authority, ecclesiastical and secular. The Inquisition was far from dead, nor was the struggle for control of censorship and the sale of books over and done with. As for the target of Pelli's critique, the death penalty (as already indicated) was firmly established at the centre of the penal system, for petty as well as serious offences, and might be inflicted with monstrous barbarity. Many must have been repelled, on humanitarian and religious grounds, by its presence and promiscuous use, and some leading thinkers spoke out against cruelty in punishment.[47] But no one had put the case against the death penalty in a systematic and comprehensive way: not Montaigne, none of the succession of great natural law jurists, not Montesquieu.[48] There was no one-man crusade or group campaign against it before Pelli and Beccaria. The former bucked at the last hurdle, and the latter published anonymously and saw his work put on the list of prohibited books, savaged by critics and, in some places, burned. I see Pelli as associating with a small group of men of conscience who were pious Catholics, as he was, and who shared their progressive views in informal meetings, underground, as it were.

The worlds of Pelli and Beccaria were in some ways (not in all) significantly different. The Accademia dei Pugni to which Beccaria belonged, in Milan, played a significant role in the composition and publication of *Crimes and Punishments*.[49] This was a small, close-knit group of like-minded individuals who shared intellectual interests and reformist ideas and projects, and debated them regularly and with vigour. Over two years, they produced a literary journal, the *Caffè*, a vehicle for their considered thoughts and opinions, and in addition they composed more studied essays and dissertations which were usually published anonymously. Beccaria's treatise was one of these. Pelli, in a letter to Beccaria, speaks of this group as unique in Italy at the time, and he was surely right. He would model the *Novelle letterarie*, of which he became chief editor in 1770, on the (recently defunct) *Caffè*.

Florence had its Academies, learned societies where, typically, erudite papers were delivered on specialised topics. Pelli was involved in some of these, notably the Accademia Colombaria and the Accademia dei Georgofili. They were useful to him, at least initially, for meeting people and making contacts, but none of them became in any sense his spiritual or intellectual home, and his interest in them was intermittent, and, in the case of the Accademia Colombaria, temporary. He also occasionally records attendance at soirées held in the houses of men of prominence in the political and cultural world.[50] The diaries leave the firm impression, however, that Pelli preferred to meet with a small number of 'friends' (in addition to some acquaintances, who included women) individually, or in small groups.

Identifying friends who might have contributed to his decision making is a speculative undertaking, but it is worth the effort. The crucial period runs from September 1759 through to January 1761. The name that stands out in the diary entries in the first part of this period is abate (or padre) Giovanni Andrea Bartoli, who sometimes appears together with signor Giulio Rucellai; and in the second part of the period, Giovanni Maria Lampredi.

Bartoli receives several warm tributes from Pelli. Writing towards the end of August 1759, around two weeks before he reports on the conversation with friends about the death penalty, he refers to Bartoli as a current, confidential friend.[51] Bartoli had taught him Greek, was the dedicatee of Pelli's early work on 'Happiness' (1753), had strong literary interests (he translated Plutarch's *Lives* into Tuscan), and was a frequent walking companion. As already indicated, walking in the countryside with a friend or friends was a favourite pastime of Pelli: 'I would do this all my life if I could.'[52] One may tentatively characterise Bartoli as one of a group of pious Catholics, lay or clerical, who were quietly critical of man's inhumanity to man, such as was displayed in the law courts of contemporary Italy. Another who figures in the *Efemeridi* at this time is Marco Lastri, who is described as a confidant and a kindred spirit, and was a regular walking companion, until his accessibility to Pelli was somewhat reduced by his appointment as parish priest of Signa outside Florence. This is reported by Pelli in his diary entry for 18 September 1759; the conversation with 'friends' about the death penalty had taken place only a few days before, on 14 September.

Bartoli, interestingly, is absent from the *Efemeridi* between 17 October 1760 and 13 April 1761, a critical time in the history of Pelli's dissertation, when he decided to write, wrote fast and then stopped writing.[53] Into this gap we should insert Giovanni Maria Lampredi (1731–93).

Lampredi was also a man of religion, having studied theology and canon law and entered the priesthood, but, unlike Pelli (and Bartoli), he was highly ambitious, adventurous and self-confident. He was four years younger than Pelli and had just the start in his career that Pelli lacked. Of humble origins (his father was a baker[54]) but intellectually precocious, Lampredi gained a powerful patron in Gaetano Antinori, an extremely wealthy Florentine patrician. Antinori employed him as his personal secretary and as tutor for his son on a handsome salary, thus giving him financial security, and promoted his early entry into salons of the intellectual elite and into significant academies, including the Accademia Etrusca di Cortona and the Colombaria. Lampredi repaid his patron with a series of publications, including two on ancient Etruria (1756; 1760), both dedicated to Antinori. The independence (as distinct from the security) that he craved was achieved in March 1763,[55] on the death of his patron, followed soon afterwards by his appointment to the chair in canon law at the University of Pisa—from which he moved five years later to his real target, the chair in public law. We cannot dwell here on his later career. In the crucial early period when Pelli was in close contact with him (for they gradually drifted apart and then fell out[56]), Pelli must have envied his friend's good fortune, brilliance and self-confidence, while benefiting from his company.

Lampredi crops up for the first time in Pelli's diary in the entry of 2 October 1759. Pelli was his guest at a 'private academy' arranged by Lampredi in the house of Antinori, featuring a poetry reading with a preface delivered by cavalier Anton Filippo Adami, a new man, described as such in the diary, who had risen to high office.[57] A few weeks later, Pelli reports that he had sent comments on a book to Lampredi at his request.[58] The first of their country walks is recorded under 22 February 1760. Such excursions became more frequent from the early summer, and by the autumn Pelli says (under 29 October) that he was spending a lot of time in the company of his 'intelligent friend'. Meanwhile, at least from February 1760, Pelli was taking an active interest in Lampredi's literary projects. According to the diary (under 7 February and 22 September 1760), he persuaded Lampredi to write a life of Machiavelli and provided some assistance with it. On 18 June 1760, he acknowledged receipt of a second work on the ancient Etruscans from his 'very good friend', with the comment

> I had already read parts of it and discussed with him some things in it regarding religion, advising him as to changes or omissions. So the work is not new to me, but I have read the whole book now with the greatest of pleasure.[59]

Did Lampredi reciprocate? Lampredi was fast out of the blocks, but Pelli too was writing, at his own pace, in the course of 1760—for example his biography of Dante and, in the month of December, a dissertation *Against the Death Penalty*.

Lampredi not only knew that Pelli was writing the latter work, but was also knowledgeable about its content. This emerges in a most bizarre way. In December 1760, the two men exchanged letters concerning a city called Gelopolis ('City of Laughter'), the product of Lampredi's lively imagination. In one of the two letters that survive from their correspondence (both by the hand of Lampredi), one Fedro Hilarion (alias Lampredi), who purports to be an inhabitant of Gelopolis, invites his friend Verecundo (alias Pelli) to join the ranks of its citizens. The penal system of the city is presented by Hilarion presumably as an attractive feature, and is described as follows:

I move on to the system of penal sanctions in Gelopolis which you were asking about. You are aware that the committing of offences comes first, then punishments are sought. Just as offences are few and far between in Gelopolis at this time, so punishments are rare occurrences. We need not say anything about the more stormy passions, such as arise from the thirst for honours and gold—so there is no place for theft, murder, assassination, calumny. When some offence occurs which does not involve either things or persons or the reputation of a third party, the first time around we make use of caring, paternal admonitions, and we try to convince the mind rather than cause fright through chastisement of the body; for we know that once chastisement or the fear of punishment ceases, the motive for not going astray is also removed. In the case of offences against a third party, we try to resolve them amicably together; the offender is reprimanded in the presence of the offended party and is obliged to make recompense such as to give satisfaction to the latter. In this way we encourage the offended party to make allowances for the aggression of his fellow citizen, seeking thus to wipe out the offence and the memory thereof. In Gelopolis, exile is employed as the gravest punishment for the more serious offences. We do not see what is gained by depriving a guilty person of his life. The political end of punishment is generally accepted to be correcting the criminal, giving an example to others and providing for the security of the good. The correction of a criminal is not obtained through his death. Others can take fright equally from the sight of a man hounded out of the city in indignity together with the loss of all his goods, as from witnessing his death. The security of the good is attained in equal measure by his death and by his exile. What benefit does the offended party derive from the death of the criminal? What good is it to the city? The Romans at the height of the Republic—and in this they were attending more to the voices of Reason than to those of Despotism and Tyranny—were content to summon to justice any criminal, even for the crime of treason, and if he did not respond and fled the city in default, they were perfectly satisfied, and did not seek more from him. If their desire was to rid themselves of a villain, a disturber of the public peace, it mattered little to them whether they achieved this through death or through exile. By either means they had obtained their end. The result of their thinking along these lines is that in this happy city the blood of a citizen is never shed. We would have been unhappy if we had arrived at such extremes. Either we would have lost our reason, or the citizens would have been caught up together in the extremes of criminality.[60]

Pelli's dissertation-in-progress clearly lies behind this construction. He must have discussed the content of his work with Lampredi and requested and received feedback—following the pattern established earlier by Lampredi. Beyond this it is hard to go. It is not necessary or plausible to hold that the basic arguments of the dissertation were derived from such discussions and exchanges, or, to put the extreme case, that the dissertation was as much Lampredi's as Pelli's. It is similarly improbable that Lampredi was engaged in undermining Pelli's work with ridicule and mockery. We might have been tempted to believe this after reading what comes before: a criticism of women in general (they are 'bandits', prudently excluded from Gelopolis except for sexual exploitation) and of a supposed female companion of Verecundo in particular (an 'animal').[61] But, whatever Lampredi was up to in that section— he may simply have been having (his kind of) fun[62]—there is no hint of satire or irony in the sketch of the imaginary penal system of Gelopolis.[63] If Lampredi was making a serious point at Pelli's expense, it might have been that Pelli's reformed penal code, and specifically the abolition of the death penalty, was utterly utopian, unattainable in this world. Such a hypothesis is not to be rejected out of hand, though it is hard to see how it could be tested. A complication is that Lampredi at the time was himself writing two short books on legal subjects, which unlike Pelli's dissertation did see the light of day. They dealt with topics that were under debate at the time, but were not seriously controversial.[64] It appears that Lampredi had nothing explicit to say in print about the death penalty until the last years of his life, when he produced a substantial work on public law, in the course of which he fell short of the Beccarian abolitionist stand on the death penalty.[65]

The precise contribution that Lampredi made to Pelli's dissertation, indeed his general attitude to that work, remains a mystery. Lampredi was in close touch with Pelli in the period in which he was actively engaged in composing his dissertation, and was well informed about its content. It is likely enough that there was spirited exchange between the two on points of detail, and indeed on central arguments. This is guesswork, but I suspect that Lampredi was the unnamed friend who was party to Pelli's decision to write the dissertation, who supported him in this and perhaps even egged him on.

That was the difficult decision to make, and perhaps a man of initiative and self-assurance such as Lampredi was needed to overcome Pelli's natural timidity and irresoluteness. By the same token, Lampredi was not the person to persuade him to abandon the project. As I see it, it had come home to Pelli that his career prospects would suffer if he proceeded with it. This had for a long time held him back, but now it loomed as an unsurmountable obstacle. There may or may not have been direct intervention from members of the establishment on whose support he depended. Any one of them who was privy to his publishing plans, or who got to know about them late in the day, would surely have regarded them as foolhardy and have warned him against pursuing them.

CAREER

Pelli studied law in Pisa but left the university without taking a degree, having insufficient funds to complete his course. He says that he specialised in law because others wanted him to, rather than because he felt especially drawn to the subject or to a career as a practising lawyer.[66] When, around a decade later, he became a criminal court judge, this was not a profession that he had ever had in his sights, and he was not comfortable in practising it.

Financial constraints necessitated that he look for employment.[67] On returning to Florence from Pisa, he sought out people of importance in the community and (as we saw) frequented Academies, where he might expect to meet men of standing and intellectual interests who were potential patrons and friends. He secured introduction to the prestigious Accademia Colombaria (among other Academies) and was soon co-opted on to a sub-committee for the revision of its regulations.[68] There were some false starts in his quest for jobs: for example, friends with ecclesiastical connections pointed him towards service in the courts of cardinals, but the meagre honorarium and the 'insidious and dizzy round' of such courts did not appeal to him.[69]

Marginally more promising was the possibility of replacing a senator (who had lost his power of speech following an accident) in one of his roles, that of *assessore* of the Congregazione del Conservatorio dei Poveri di San Giovanni Battista già spedale di Bonifazio. This was a temporary post which paid very little, but he put in for it with the backing of Marchese Ferdinando Incontri, a senator and state councillor, who appears to have been a family friend.[70] He was unsuccessful, thanks to the operation of 'intrigues and cabals'.[71]

His fortunes improved soon afterwards with his appointment as an aide in the State Secretariat:

> About this time, for whatever reason, but independently, on 12 August of the same year, 1758, I was summoned by His Excellency the Lord Abate Pompeo Neri, a member of the Regency Council in Tuscany, with whom I had no contact. He proposed to nominate me as one of the nobles whom he had in mind to assign to the government in the State Secretariat with some stipend, although up to this time this was not customary. With the greatest pleasure I grasped this most auspicious opportunity for honourable advancement. Thus in September, my name was forwarded to Vienna, together with that of cavalier Giulio Mozzi, for a position in the State Secretariat, with a stipend of 100 scudi per annum.
>
> The prospects looked very good but the outcome did not match expectations, as is often the case with courts. In November a dispatch came from the Emperor admitting us into his Secretariat but without the stipend that had been hoped for and repeatedly promised by the ministry in Tuscany. The universal advice of friends was that we obviously should accept, on the terms dictated by the sovereign, notwithstanding the fact that he was not obliging us to do so. On 8 December 1758 therefore, on the day of the celebration of the Feast of the Immaculate Conception of the Virgin Mary, I together with the aforementioned cavalier Mozzi took the customary oath; the secretary of state Giovanni Antonio Tornaquinci officiated. I was given the portfolio of petitions of amortisation, as well as responsibility for sundry other matters relayed to me on a daily basis by order of the first secretaries of the Regency Council, whom Mozzi and I served as aides.

He continues,

> To recompense me in some manner for my labours, however, and to make up for the loss I suffered for not having gained the position in the form that had been proposed to me, the government was generous enough to grant me a grace-and-favour position for a year in the Magistracy of the Capitani di Parte. I took up this post on the 1 March 1759, and I now hold it together with the undersubscribed persons.[72]

Pelli's trawling for contacts had paid dividends. He had landed a patron in Pompeo Neri, who (as we saw) belonged to the inner circle of Florentine magnates serving the Austrian emperor. Pelli would soon aim higher: a visit to Marshal Botta Adorno, head of the Tuscan government and chair of the Regency Council, is recorded in October 1759. He would call on the great man to pay him homage eight times at least from early December 1759 to mid-May 1760. On 22 May, following a meeting of the Regency Council, Botta sent a dispatch to Vienna requesting a 'pensione' for Pelli.

Pelli regularly importuned officials and important persons in the search for better pay and conditions of employment. But he liked the work at the State Secretariat, so much so that when another appointment was conferred on him (the one that is most relevant to us, namely that of chief justice of the criminal courts of Pistoia and Pontremoli), he did his best to hold on to his existing job. He was finally compelled to leave it in January 1763.[73] His special responsibility, for petitions of amortisation, brought him under the direct supervision of Pompeo Neri, who was especially concerned with the revision of the law of 1751 on *mani morte*.[74] This law had brought Church and State into conflict (because the bulk of inalienable and untaxed property belonged to the Church and other religious institutions), and had produced an administrative logjam (because the Regency Council had been assigned the responsibility of making judgements in disputed cases, of which there were many). Pelli maintained an interest in this issue well after he had been forced to withdraw from active engagement with it.[75]

With his account of his selection as an aide in the State Secretariat, Pelli brings to an end his summary of the first thirty years of his life.[76] We may surmise that he viewed this (relatively humble) appointment as a major turning point in his career. There is no hint in those twenty-three pages of any particular interest in criminal justice, although (as we saw above) the diary entry of 15 September 1759 relates that he had 'earlier' (presumably in the months or years preceding September 1759) toyed with the idea of writing against the death penalty. He had judged it wise to stay his hand because of the hostile reception it would receive. There is no sign that he was already contemplating employment as a magistrate or judge within the criminal justice system, a move that would have made the airing of critical opinions on the penal system decidedly problematic.

If Pelli did not have his eye on a career as a criminal law judge, what ambitions did he nurture? He was open to offers, but had definite preferences: a desirable job would need to carry prestige, bring in a decent income, allow him time for reading and writing and various leisure activities and be tenable in Florence rather than in the imperial capital, Vienna.

On 1 August 1760 (well before he had decided to write against the death penalty), Pelli applied for the position of *assessore* of the Magistrato dell'Abbondanza di Firenze, for which one of the magistrates had put him forward.[77] His application was unsuccessful. Later in the same month, however (28 August), following a meeting of the Regency Council, he was 'graced' with appointment to the Magistrato dei Nove Conservatori della Giurisdizione e Dominio Fiorentino, for a period of six months. As he recorded, 'I really was not expecting so much, because this is one of the higher magistracies and the grant of the provision to me [sc. for his position as aide to the State Secretariat] was too fresh.'[78] This body exercised important administrative and (civil) jurisprudential functions. Pelli would now be rubbing shoulders with men of some stature, including three senators. The position also brought in a salary, and at the end of his tenure Pelli duly enters into his ledger the income that had accrued to him (the figure is missing from his text).

The next job opportunity that arrives for Pelli exposes the disadvantages of the patronage system from the point of view of the client: what if he should be pressed to apply for, or to take, a position that he does not want? Pelli is put forward, along with others, for a post on the Council of Tuscany *in Vienna*. The relevant diary entry is that of 22 September 1760. As he puts it, he undoubtedly would have thanked the city for doing him this 'honour'. His true feelings, however, are revealed in the words that follow, which were evidently not for public consumption:

> I have no reason to believe that I should expect it, because of my age and my other circumstances, but supposing it were true, I confess frankly that I would not be at all happy, because I would hate getting caught up in that dangerous whirlpool, I am not at my ease at court, I love to work in peace to improve my days and to earn enough to sustain me in proportion to my birth and my very limited desires. My resources are scarce for modern living and for the added strain on them which such a posting would bring.[79]

The emperor took his time to come to a decision, time enough (and more) for Pelli to undertake, compose and abandon his dissertation. The decision, when it arrived, in a dispatch of 26 January 1761, after five months' delay, was not in his favour.[80] Pelli expresses his relief at this, while at the same time claiming that he had been widely tipped for the post 'by the city'.

It is worth glancing at the curriculum vitae of the successful candidate, senator prior Tommaso Piccolomini, on whom Pelli passes judgement with a mixture of praise and criticism:

> In a recent dispatch, of 26 January, His illustrious Majesty has chosen as a member of his Council of Tuscany in Vienna senator count prior Tommaso Piccolomini . . . .[81] He is a talented and able individual, who performed well in his studies but is of rather strange disposition and is discourteous towards those beneath him. He was, to begin with, in the State Secretariat as I am, then he passed to the post of secretary of the Uffizio delle Tratte and of the Pratica Segreta. With this promotion any suspicion that the post in question would fall to me—and the city thought for some time that this would happen—has come to an end. I am utterly content with this, because I have no love for courts, and I have no desire to be parted for long from my solitude.[82]

Piccolomini (of Siena) had apparently begun his career in a position similar to that which Pelli was now holding in the State Secretariat, but he made it a launching pad for an impressive series of offices, involving two secretaryships and a seat in the senate of the city. One of the secretaryships was that of the Pratica Segreta (di Pistoia e Pontremoli), the very post that Pelli later claimed made it impossible for him to complete and publish his dissertation *Against the Death Penalty*. Pelli mentions the secretaryship of the Pratica Segreta here only in passing:[83] he shows no interest in the post. His attention is focused on the position in Vienna, which he did not want.

Another upwardly mobile Tuscan whose career intersected with that of Pelli and also included the secretaryship of the Pratica Segreta and a spell in Vienna was Count Vincenzo Alberti. If Pelli had won the approval of the emperor for membership of the Council of Tuscany in Vienna, he would have replaced Alberti, who had been chosen for the Council of the State and the Council of the Regency in Florence. Alberti took up these positions on 3 July 1761. Before moving to Vienna, he had held a position (unspecified) in the State Secretariat and was secretary of the Pratica [sc. Segreta)] of Pistoia and Pontremoli. This is confirmation of the boost to a career that might follow service on the emperor's Tuscan Council in Vienna—a move that Pelli had set his face against. It also suggests that the secretaryship of the Pratica Segreta was standardly a rung (one of several) in the career ladder of an ambitious administrator and politician.

Soon after he 'failed' to be co-opted on to the Council of Tuscany in Vienna, Pelli lost out on a position that he did covet—the secretaryship of the Regency Council in Florence. This post had fallen vacant after the departure for Vienna of Domenico Richard, and is first mentioned in a diary entry of 16 February 1761, that is, a little over a month after Pelli stopped writing his dissertation. In a later entry, of 23 July (see below), Pelli indicates that his name was included in the list of nominees. He expected that a newly appointed colleague of his in the State Secretariat (one Monsieur Reautan[84]) would be chosen, because he had stronger backing. He continues,

> I don't lay claim to this post, and others are more senior than me. So I will wait and see what life will bring me, as I usually do, without any complaint whatever, apart from the fact that I think that my income is too low.

When the post was eventually awarded—to cavalier Francesco Siminetti on 23 July 1761—Pelli betrayed genuine disappointment: 'As to how my presumptions about this turned out to be misdirected I would not know what to say.' Still, a rationalisation was at hand: he goes on to say that the position would have been financially disadvantageous for him and would have cut into his leisure time.

Pelli had thus missed out on his first choices, namely the secretaryships of the Council of State and the Council of Regency. Not long after, in August 1761, the role of criminal judge in the Tuscan courts of Pistoia and Pontremoli intruded into his consciousness, apparently for the first time. A glance at the careers of contemporaries would have shown him that this was one of the several posts that was worth taking up and that led somewhere. There is no sign that he was seeking this particular job, and although he secured it in the end, he made it difficult for the authorities concerned, at several levels, to appoint him.

Was he a suitable person for the post of criminal law judge? He doesn't think so; nor did Marshal Botta, who, when Pelli's candidature for this post was mooted, made it clear that he favoured another, with more pertinent qualifications.[85] Although Pelli had accumulated some experience in civil cases, especially in the sphere of property law, he was a tiro when it came to criminal law. Once appointed, we find him undertaking a 'crash course' in criminal law and the criminal justice system.[86] At the same time, he expresses anxiety that his appointment would arouse envy and hostility, and he knew that his performance would be closely monitored by rivals. We have already seen that early on in his tenure of his office as a criminal law judge he found himself embarrassed by having to administer torture and sign a death warrant.

The post in question became vacant once Piccolomini left Florence for Vienna to become a member of the Council of Tuscany there. That appointment is securely dated to 26 January. His departure, which came later but is of uncertain date, is mentioned in Pelli's diary entry of 17 August 1761. Pelli was advised to compete for the post, though not in the first instance—as mentioned above, the head of the government in Florence was supporting someone else. In any case, Pelli held back. When he did make it on to the list of candidates, he sought to impose conditions on his candidacy: namely, that he be allowed to hold on to his post in the State Secretariat and retain the salary attached. Months of tortuous negotiation followed, involving officials in both Florence and Vienna, from mid-August to December. Pelli was gradually persuaded, clearly against his will, to consent to allow his candidacy to go forward. His appointment was announced on 28 January 1762 and published in Florence on 11 February;[87] he was sworn in on 25 February. The first meeting over which he presided—he had, he says, the 'consultative and deciding' vote—took place on 3 March.

CONCLUSION

Pelli in his letter to Beccaria of 24 March 1766 disclosed that his appointment as a criminal law judge had forced him to abandon his dissertation *Against the Death Penalty*. The situation was rather more complicated than this would suggest.

Throughout the period of gestation, composition and suspension of the dissertation, Pelli had not yet taken up the role of a criminal law judge, nor is there any sign that he harboured any desire to do so in the immediate or not too distant future. The position came into his sights apparently for the first time seven to eight months after he stopped writing his dissertation. He did not seek it, he was dragooned into applying for it and he bargained for special terms in holding it—namely, the retention of his existing post with the State Secretariat, together with its salary. He did so in a way that would have been tiresome for those who were advancing or dealing with his candidature. It must have irritated the head of the Tuscan government, Marshal Botta, to have been informed by Pelli that there was a precedent for holding the two posts together, and to have been forced into giving what was the perfect response, amounting to 'I will not tolerate such scandalous (and inefficient) goings-on on my watch.'

The fact that Pelli stopped writing his treatise and put it aside does not of course necessarily mean that he was abandoning the project for good. One might suggest in his 'defence' that he only abandoned it definitively when he got the unexpected appointment—or, perhaps more realistically, when he had settled into his job.[88]

Once he had become involved in the practical business of trying and passing judgement on criminals, the odds that he would return to the dissertation were seriously reduced. He complained in his diary about inhumanity, injustice, corruption and inconsistencies in the judicial system, but felt that he could do nothing about them. The law could not be reformed, and its practitioners could not be corrected from within, and certainly not by him. He arrived at the default position of exercising as much leniency and flexibility as he could within the framework of the existing law. He administered torture and he sentenced to death where this was laid down in the law. Pelli the jurisprudent triumphed over Pelli the philosopher.

The final nail in the coffin of the aborted dissertation was the appearance of Beccaria's *Crimes and Punishments*, in 1764. It was predictable, to his credit and certainly in tune with his personality that Pelli was prepared to praise the man who had stolen a march on him, went to considerable efforts to befriend him and defended him against his critics. If he had once nurtured hopes of achieving the giddy heights of court-philosopher to Grand Duke Leopold, who abolished the death penalty and torture in his Act of Reform of 1786, he failed. It is not impossible that Pelli had some subsidiary role in advancing the reform of Leopold, though there is no proof either way. It may be a pointer that on 3 April 1771 he was selected as a member of a small committee established by the grand duke 'for the general reform of the system of provincial magistracies and tribunals of the Florentine State', under the chairmanship of Pompeo Neri.[89] This shows at least that the grand duke or his close advisors appreciated his talents and expertise. The proceedings of the committee cannot be followed in detail. One wonders if Pelli remained a member after the death of the chairman in 1776. He himself had taken over the challenging and fulfilling position of director of the Uffizi in the previous year. Further, the committee's business is likely to have been primarily administrative, namely cutting back, and bringing order and efficiency to, the overgrown and corrupt judicial system inherited from the era of the Medici. The grand duke's law, when eventually it was promulgated in 1786, did contain a series of regulations governing the structure of the judiciary, the responsibility of judges and court procedure, and whoever drafted the law would have been able to draw on the work of the committee of which Pelli was a member. It was of course Beccaria's treatise, published a decade earlier, which set in motion the movement for penal reform.[90]

To return to Pelli's letter to Beccaria, with which I began this section: my argument has been that Pelli's career ambitions in general, rather than his tenure of the secretaryship of the Pratica Segreta, were the root cause of his 'failure' to complete and publish his dissertation. His financial circumstances were such that he needed a job, and one that would pay well. In order to secure lucrative employment he had to cultivate patrons among the elite, and, equally importantly, he had to avoid the disapproval of those high officials who decided whom to promote. It was not so much the 'mob' who might be expected to react adversely to a dissertation against the death penalty (as suggested in the letter to Beccaria), as the leadership of the Church and of the State. Pelli appears to have calculated that the publication of his dissertation would seriously jeopardise his chances of obtaining respectability and financial security in Florence and Tuscany.

There is an additional factor to be taken into account. Time and time again, especially in the formative years of his career, Pelli described himself as timid.[91] This was not false modesty. He genuinely disliked courting 'the great and the good', and put a high value on his 'solitude', by which he meant a quiet life reading the books that he acquired in profusion, writing his own compositions (typically not for publication), going to the theatre, attending religious celebrations and strolling in the countryside with a few select friends, with whom he discussed literature, social morality and diverse other matters. (He rarely gives a detailed account of such conversations.) He had a tendency to back away from offering judgement or taking sides in matters that were controversial, such as the Jesuit–Jansenist dispute and its political ramifications.

In general, he was not one to 'raise a storm', 'make a fuss', *fare strepito*—a phrase he uses often to describe a characteristic in others (such as Hobbes) of whose views he was critical.

In sum, it is not surprising that a man of firm religious faith, strong moral convictions and deep humanitarian sentiment should have written a dissertation against the death penalty at a time when the brutality of the criminal law system was all too visible—although it should be noted that no one else had done so hitherto. Equally, however, it is not surprising that a man by nature reticent, who lacked the backing of a family and inherited patrons, and who was forced on to the 'job market' by his lack of financial resources, should have held back from publishing such a work. Cesare Beccaria was differently placed, in a number of significant ways.

Argument of *Against the Death Penalty*

⋮

Preliminaries

Against the Death Penalty is incomplete. The surviving manuscript consists of a preface, an 'Introduction', eighteen chapters and a number of fragments. Pelli presumably intended to integrate the more substantial of the fragments into the text in some form or other. It is reasonable to regard what we have as an advanced draft.[1] As Pelli indicates in the *Efemeridi*, when he had made the decision to publish, as with his biography of Dante, he took care to produce finished copy, with editorial assistance if he could find it.[2] On that occasion, his attempt to involve a friend in the operation failed, and he had to be his own editor. We can safely assume that he would have polished up this manuscript too, had he decided to go ahead with it. In fact, the bulk of his written work remained unpublished. Beccaria, in contrast, was a member of a close-knit group on which he could freely draw for comments, assessments and material assistance, a group presided over by a 'built-in' editor in the person of his patron and mentor Pietro Verri.

Pelli's attention is focused narrowly on the death penalty, as signalled in the title. Other aspects of the criminal law and judicial system are touched on in passing. Rather surprisingly, he has nothing to say about torture, which receives a powerful indictment from Beccaria; for a record of Pelli's hostility to torture, one has to go to an entry in his *Efemeridi*.[3] Towards the end of the main text of his dissertation, Pelli says he will produce a broad survey of crimes and the punishments appropriate to them and an additional argument against the death penalty. These promises are not fulfilled.

Pelli sets out his stall in the preface 'To the Reader' and the Introduction. He distances himself from a class of men of learning and culture who have produced showy and eloquent but ignorant works. They would have been better employed instructing people in truths that would benefit the human race; he will not add to their number. The 'panegyric of the savage life' is cited as a prime example. Pelli is referring to the *Discourses* of Rousseau 'on the Sciences and Arts' and 'on Inequality'. He goes on in the same paragraph to specify some doctrines of the same philosopher (whom he now names) of which he disapproved.[4] He had not yet seen Rousseau's *Social Contract*, which was published after he had abandoned his project and just when Beccaria was on the point of launching his.[5] The work impressed him, as he subsequently records, with the exception of Book 4 chapter 8, 'Of Civil Religion', with its forthright attack on the Catholic church.[6] Here we have an early indication of Pelli's lack of sympathy with Transalpine Enlightenment philosophers, with the exception of Montesquieu.[7] His intellectual and spiritual allegiances lay elsewhere. The natural law philosophers and jurists from Grotius on provided the main foundation and stimulation for his own ideas. Pelli reveals himself as a close reader of, among others, Grotius, Heineccius, the Cocceji father and son and Vattel. We can add to these names that of Pufendorf, who happens, however, never to be referred to in the text.[8]

Men of science and culture, if they truly wish to promote the happiness of humanity, should follow his (Pelli's) example. Moved by piety and love for the human race, he will endeavour by means of rational argumentation to persuade those in authority to abolish the death penalty. Its abolition would at once swell the manpower resources of the society and free it of the vices that infest it. The economic or utilitarian argument for abolition here mentioned will receive brief reference later in the treatise; the moral argument will dominate the work. As is confirmed by countless entries in the *Efemeridi*, Pelli was deeply pessimistic about human nature, and prone to moralising. Here he labels the punishment by execution of the 'vicious' as itself a vice, having its origins in the 'general corruption' of our hearts, our innate tendency to give way to capricious anger, cruelty and malice.[9] The message that humanity is evil runs as an obbligato through the treatise. He reminds those who advocate or approve of the harsh punishment of criminals that they too are human. Each and every one of us can sink into criminal activity if not protected by a superior force. Given that 'our hope of immunity' is 'dubious', and that the Supreme Being is the ultimate judge of men, the rational response is to be as compassionate toward criminals as toward the poor and the sick.[10]

The Introduction takes up the themes of the preface, although now a glimmer of hope is allowed to filter through the gloom. We are first informed that it comes naturally to men to feel compassion and humanity for criminals. There is an 'if only' clause: if only men were aware of their own weaknesses, they would experience such emotions. Secondly, the spread of 'knowledge' and 'the philosophical spirit' has produced a Montesquieu (not only a Rousseau), who preached the desirability of gentle government characterised by a penal system with moderate and proportionate punishments, in pursuit of human happiness. Thirdly, there is the Gospel with its message of love. Unfortunately, neither enlightened philosophy nor Christianity has extirpated cruelty. Pelli sharply condemns the destruction wrought on the New World by Spaniards carrying the Holy Book. Finally, although history has demonstrated that, even in 'the happiest days', judicial systems have been marked by cruelty (as exemplified in the death of Socrates), there is the contemporary, exceptional, counter-example of Russia under the reforming empress Elisabeth.

In identifying the message of gentleness and moderation as essentially Christian, with reference to both Montesquieu and Elisabeth, Pelli displays his credentials as a man of religion. His aspiration is clearly to sow the seed of reform within progressive circles in the Catholic church. He was well aware that the ecclesiastical authorities would smart at his attack on the death penalty. But he nurtured the hope that by showing that he was writing from within and not against the Church, he would be able to temper their opposition and save his book from public condemnation and perhaps even incineration.

In these introductory chapters, Pelli is modest and unaggressive. There are strategic reasons for this, but it is also in tune with his character to strike such a note. In the course of his treatise, he writes with passion, making frequent and effective use of the rhetorical question, and in such moments his humanitarian instincts and motives and his commitment to his cause come to the fore. But he is also insistent that his case rests on rational argumentation.

As to the arguments themselves, he declares himself prepared to countenance their rejection. There is a hint at the end of the Introduction that if shown to be wrong, he would be content to retire to 'the tranquillity of his private chamber', not in high dudgeon, but in the knowledge that he has 'gone astray in a good cause'. It is true, and intriguing, that in the main body of the text, when he is setting out his 'proofs' one by one, he regularly asserts that what he is putting on the table is self-evident and hardly open to challenge or dispute. This may be a rhetorical strategy lifted from some handbook. Or he may be appealing above the heads of the men of science and learning, whom he has already condemned for their ignorance, to the fundamental rationality and common sense of the broader readership he is addressing.

At any rate, the diary entry which announces his abandonment of his project shows that self-doubt and diffidence lay just around the corner: 'I have written a substantial amount but never to my satisfaction; I have not quite pinpointed the line of argument that will prove my thesis.' He will leave it for another occasion 'to make a judgement in cold blood as to whether I have the arguments needed to sustain my thesis or conclude that I am mistaken. The product of our pen has to be allowed to mature so that we do not peddle things that might bring us dishonour'.[11]

Pelli claims not to be moved by 'a spirit of censure or of disapproval of our customs and our laws'. Yet he goes on to acknowledge (as an abolitionist could hardly fail to do) the cruelty 'that is apparent even in the considered ordinances of venerable legislators'. He does not, however, hold current politicians or judicial officials responsible. In so far as he has human targets, they are soft: those intellectuals and cultural leaders who should be tracing the path to public happiness but have not lived up to their responsibilities. The blistering onslaught on judges, magistrates and jurists so conspicuous in Beccaria is absent in Pelli. Rather, he looks to 'magistrates and rulers' to reform the laws, having in mind the desirability of increasing manpower resources and of securing the public peace by stamping down on the vice of private individuals. It is by exposing Fallen Man as the source of the problem—good Catholic doctrine—that he thinks he can escape the opprobrium of men of power and influence. Sin is at the back of everything. It underlies crime, certainly, but it is also behind the measures taken to repress crime through laws and judicial practice.

Chapters 2–8 prepare the ground for the attack on the death penalty. Pelli picks up the thread of contractualist theory, in which he is well versed, giving special attention to the issue of the presence or absence of sanctions in the State of Nature, prior to the transition to civil society. He wants to show that punishment properly defined did not exist in the State of Nature, although constraints of various kinds did: they were necessary, otherwise 'the inherent wickedness' of men would have involved them in constant warfare with one another. He calls these sanctions 'conventional' as distinct from 'civil' (both qualifying 'punishment', a term he uses reluctantly in the case of the former), with 'civil' applying only to the positive law of political society.[12] He further insists that the conventional 'punishment' that was characteristic of the State of Nature stopped short of the death penalty. That, the ultimate sanction, is not countenanced by divine law, which governs the State of Nature through the medium of natural law.

The argument is dense and rather convoluted.[13] These early chapters, 2–8, are prime candidates for restructuring and revision, and would probably have received such treatment had Pelli taken his project a stage further. Beccaria's work (as already noted) had been subject to the scrutiny of colleagues and extensive subediting at the hands of Pietro Verri. Pelli is taking the reader through his investigative thought processes, rather than presenting him with the results of completed research.

The sequence of his thought is roughly as follows. There is an innate sense of duty among men, issuing from the laws of nature and ultimately from God, which manifests itself in relationships and agreements, norms and conventions. In the State of Nature, there exist restraints and sanctions against breaches of contracts and promises made on a voluntary basis. As with disciplinary action within the family, these rank as chastisement rather than punishment. Also excluded from the category of punishment are the consequences of warfare,[14] and compensation for injury or loss. Further, because humanity is corrupt, natural law sanctions need to be supplemented by punishment. Grotius's definition of punishment—as evil suffered on account of evil done— fails to distinguish between punishment and private vengeance (a subject to which Pelli will give a great deal of attention in the fragments). Successors to Grotius, among whom Pelli singles out Heineccius, corrected this error by adding that a 'higher authority' was needed to impose the 'evil' if it was to be classified as punishment: 'for there can be no punishment in the hypothetical State of Nature, in which there are no written laws, no conventions, and no rulers'. In sum, punishment properly defined did not exist in the State of Nature.

Conventional 'punishments', however, were very much at home in the State of Nature. People owe no obligations apart from 'those imposed by the external laws of the Creator and by the preservation the human race'. The preservation of oneself and the human race is a necessity, a duty and a right, grounded in divine command. Here, in his chapter 5, we are given a foretaste of Pelli's Second Proof against the death penalty, to be presented in chapter 11.

All the norms governing human behaviour in the State of Nature are of divine origin, and this is sufficient grounds for excluding the death penalty from conventional 'punishment'. Pelli adds for good measure—with his eyes still on the Creator—that none of us is owner or master of our own life, but only a trustee, and on these grounds we are not entitled to cede to another our right to live.[15] There is a brief aside as he searches the historical record, unsuccessfully of course, for cases where someone has deprived himself of such a 'gift'. That would be akin to giving up the right of self-defence. Nor was there any advantage to be gained by the offended party in such a sacrifice. The famous case of the Roman general Attilius Regulus is invoked: in executing him for failing to persuade the Roman senate to make peace, the Carthaginians were (so to speak) shooting themselves in the foot. They did not get the peace they desired.

Pelli's focus in this section has been on the State of Nature, but he allows himself a brief anticipation of political society, adding that 'even in the civil state, we can be compelled only by force to suffer the punishment that we have merited'. He quotes Quintilian; he might have cited Hobbes.[16]

Similarly, in advocating exile as the best way of dealing with offenders, Pelli seems to shift the scene from the State of Nature (in chapter 7, headed 'As to what is the most just punishment in the State of Nature') to civil society (in chapter 8, headed 'The most natural way to punish a delinquent is to expel him from society').[17]

The argument proceeds in this fashion. Chapter 7: men have obligations in the State of Nature, but should they fail in them, there is no *punishment*, but only reparation for losses suffered. This applies equally in relations between men and nations. As Montesquieu argued against Grotius, states can make war and people can kill, but only in self-defence. Vattel was of the opinion that only the injured party had the right to punish someone who had injured him. Given our innate wickedness, however, this would lead to total warfare in the State of Nature, where pacts of reciprocal obligation enable a measure of security to prevail. In the absence of written laws, the breach of pacts and obligations is most naturally and most appropriately dealt with by the separation of the delinquent from the society together with its benefits.

In chapter 8, the spotlight is turned, unexpectedly, on civil society. We are told that society is formed for the good of all its members, and every individual is duty-bound to work towards the happiness of the rest. How does this duty arise? Pelli does not ask himself this question here, but it is consistent with his philosophy that the law of nature, which is ultimately divine law, has imposed this obligation, and that it carries over into civil society. He goes on: a society dominated by the interests of individuals or a few is a barbaric despotism. The interests of governors and governed may differ, but can be reconciled in the cause of the general happiness. Those who sabotage this project deserve to be excluded temporarily or permanently from society and its benefits. This has long been the practice in both civil society and the Church.

THE PROOFS

The First Proof (ch. 9) is that the death penalty is incompatible with the ends of punishment. These ends do not include either the satisfaction that is due to divine justice,[18] or vengeance, which is 'useless, inhumane and vile'. Pelli in effect conflates retribution with vengeance (or revenge), and in this way eliminates it as a just end of punishment. He will follow the same strategy later in discussing the *lex talionis* (in fragment 3). The legitimate ends of punishment are three (here Pelli is following Grotius and succeeding jurists): reform, security and example. In Pelli's analysis, these three ends flow into each other.[19] They all serve the aim of prevention of crime and deterrence of criminals, and point to the separation of the offender from society as the natural and ideal punishment. Seen against the background of the preceding chapters, one would expect this to involve exile. The other, more practicable, candidate as a secondary punishment, hard labour, is given brief support (but no prominence) further on in the treatise. Pelli had already shown that he favoured the latter punishment as an alternative to the death penalty well before he began writing on the subject. The entry in the *Efemeridi* for 15 September 1759 runs, 'I neglected to say yesterday that among some of my friends it was asserted that it would be better not to condemn to death any criminal for any crime at all, and to retain him for public labours. I am still of this opinion'.

He goes on to assert, in the same diary entry, 'the pointlessness of taking away the life of a man for a crime when he could in a thousand ways deliver partial compensation for the harm he has done to society'.[20] In the treatise as we have it, he is more or less completely absorbed in opposing the death penalty, and does not spend time and space debating the advantages of a substitute penalty. Beccaria, in contrast, stages an elaborate confrontation between death and forced labour. As for the end of punishment as reform, again Pelli is not interested in exploring this option in detail. How exactly offenders might be reformed is left unspecified: they will (somehow) learn to become virtuous 'through performing their duties'. This will benefit both them as individuals and society.

So much for the ends of punishment. What of their incompatibility with the death penalty? Pelli (in chapter 10) first summarises the standard view that the death penalty both prevents re-offending by the miscreant and 're-strains and corrects' others from following in his footsteps. Clearly the first of these ends is achieved by the execution of the offender (although Pelli doesn't say so).[21] He is right, of course that the 'terrible example' of death by execution has not put an end to crime.

More interesting is the assertion that follows.[22] Governments should seek to protect their subjects, and procure 'the greater good' by means of the lowest possible grade of evil, avoiding punishments which are excessive, pointless and unnecessary. Here Pelli anticipates the argument of Beccaria, that punishment is at best a necessary evil, and should be as limited and as moderate as possible. Any punishment beyond the bare minimum smacks of despotism (Beccaria) or vengeance (Pelli): the two reformers are at one in holding it to be useless and unnecessary.[23] Both invoke public utility as the prime desideratum, in their diverse ways. The main difference between them lies in the rationale for their claims. Beccaria supports the minimisation of punishments, with reference to the terms of the Social Contract, whereas Pelli invokes the dictate of 'Providence', which in his metaphysics means the Creator.[24]

The Second Proof is an argument from the right of self-preservation (chapter 10, first introduced in chapter 5). Humanity made the transition from the State of Nature to civil society through pacts or conventions, tacit or explicit. These were intended to be lasting, and were designed to give humans enhanced security and comfort. Pelli does not wish to go into the content of these conventions, but they would have included sanctions that enforced contracted obligations, and they must have authorised a public authority to make laws and punish their breach. But in addition, people brought with them into civil society a 'code of nature' comprising certain duties that were still essential for their existence and well-being. High up on the list of these duties or natural laws, coming second only to the acknowledgement of the 'First Being', was that individuals must seek self-preservation. The corollary is that they could not have consented to other duties which would have obliged them to give up their right to preserve their own lives, which in any case they lacked the authority to surrender.[25] No one, not even a criminal, can be required to ignore the command of divine and natural law to preserve himself. As is his usual practice, Pelli illustrates from classical literature and history, as others had before him.[26]

The Third Proof (in chapter 12) revolves around the non-utility of the death penalty. Through execution, individuals are removed whose survival might have been of benefit to society. Clearly society must be protected from further harm at their hands, as natural law dictates, but execution is extreme barbarity, and in any case only one of several options. It cannot repair damage and loss, it cannot dry the tears of bereaved widows and children. Pelli introduces the motif of reform alongside prevention, as he looks to punishments which carry 'advantages' for convicted criminals, by giving them the opportunity of making amends for their 'errors'.

Pelli views the death penalty as above all an instrument of revenge. In his account, the bloodthirsty 'spirit of vendetta' which inspires it faces off against pardon-seeking humanity and religion (and, a little later, equity and utility), and is found wanting. In the midst of the string of rhetorical questions and extravagant historical exempla that make up the rest of the chapter, Pelli asks rhetorically whether it wouldn't be 'a thousand times more profitable' to employ a condemned man in public works than to sacrifice him on the gallows. The profit he has in mind is partly economic, but partly also the comparative advantage of public labour as a deterrent. It is a matter of weighing 'the sight of their misery at labour . . . as an ever-present example to others' against 'the spectacle of a moment for anyone who derives pleasure from witnessing the depressing tragedy of his sufferings'.

This single, artfully constructed, rhetorical question in Pelli contains the essence of what is in Beccaria an elaborate, extended argument, in the course of which the latter strives to establish the greater deterrent value of hard labour as against execution, on the basis of their relative effect on the minds and sensibilities of spectators. It should be noted that both writers regarded it as essential that punishment be a public spectacle.

The Fourth Proof (chapter 13) is that the death penalty is excessive.[27] The argument is introduced as 'a new and comprehensive demonstration of my thesis'. It is based on the historical record, which demonstrates that the worst governments are those that most commonly enforce the death penalty. Such governments typically are despotisms, in which the sovereign reigns by force and fear over subjects who are tantamount to slaves. For exempla Pelli turns, as he regularly does, to ancient Rome: here, first, to Rome in the time of Triumvirs, who presided over a savage civil war in the transitional period between Republic and Principate, and second, Rome under the more tyrannical of the emperors. Despotism, he goes on to say, is patently contrary to nature, according to which the rights of rulers and the ruled are reciprocal. The penal system of a despotism is out of line with that of a monarchy or republic: in a despotism the death sentence is applied even for minor offences. There is a sting in the tail—for non-despotic regimes also execute offenders. Given that the death penalty is a natural fit with despotism, it cannot be an appropriate punishment in societies where moderation reigns. The death penalty in any regime is excessive ('un'esuberanza').

In setting out the Fifth Proof (chapter 14), Pelli says he is struck by the fact that so-called barbaric peoples imposed pecuniary rather than blood punishments,[28] whereas supposedly more civilised peoples execute offenders even for minor offences. Two principles should be applied in the selection of a penalty: first, it should be proportionate to the crime, and second, crimes should to be rated according to the damage done to society.[29] Pelli looks into the mind of the criminal and decides, reasonably enough, that were he to be faced with a choice between committing a more serious and a less serious crime he would opt for the former, should it be the practice to punish them with equal severity. In other words, such a penal system would incentivise rather than deter anyone contemplating serious breaches of the law. Pelli's next point explores further the mentality of the potential criminal: execution with all the extra, brutal embellishments that are available and commonly used would be no more terrifying to contemplate—and therefore no more of a deterrent—than a plain and simple execution. Execution is execution, whatever form it takes; the principle of proportionality simply ceases to be applicable.[30]

Pelli then lists crimes which do deserve to be punished severely, giving substance to his earlier assertion that harm to society should be the main criterion for assessing a crime and its appropriate punishment. By and large, these are offences that threaten the security of the ruler and his subjects and endanger the status quo.[31]

Moderate governments, those that actively pursue public happiness, can reduce the incidence of crime through the employment of mild punishments. Diligence in carrying out punishment, rather than severity of punishment, is the way to limit and control criminality, as Montesquieu wrote. Beccaria would stress that certainty and promptness in punishment were more effective deterrents than severity, as well as being more humane.[32]

The Sixth Proof is presented by Pelli (in chapter 15) as a means of deflecting an anticipated criticism of his thesis, to the effect that the death penalty has been applied everywhere and routinely,[33] and on these grounds may be considered legitimate, indispensable and unchallengeable. Pelli does not confront this objection directly, perhaps because at the time this would have seemed a losing strategy. Rather, he observes that there are flagrant inconsistencies in the way the death penalty is imposed between one polity and another. That cannot be right: justice should be invariable, everywhere.

This begs the question of how to decide what shape a just penal system might take, and how to decide between rival systems. Pelli feels that he has to give readers the assurance that to attack the current penal code, as he is doing, need not open the door to confusion and anarchy; does not, as he puts it, endanger public safety and the peace of the State or undermine justice and decorum. He claims that he knows the answer to the question of the proper structure of a system of punishment. He will provide an answer by surveying 'all the crimes', and in the process will address the issue of whether the death penalty is appropriate for any of them. He proposes to come up with 'a new and specific argument' for his thesis.

Pelli's final three chapters (16–18) provide rather less than such a survey, and less than is promised by the ambitious title (covering all three): 'Enumeration of crimes and examination of the penalty of death as it is customarily applied to them'. If we were looking to Pelli to come up with a list of alternative penalties graded according to their severity and paired off against a list of crimes, we would be disappointed. What he does come up with is puzzling. He goes through a list of natural laws, graded according to their importance. It runs as follows.

Gratitude to the Creator is the first of the natural laws, and the failure to obey this law, through blasphemy, heresy or idolatry, is punishable under a good government. Punishment lies with the offended, however, and civil governments should limit themselves to bringing offenders to their senses.[34] Pelli does not say how this end might be achieved, merely ruling that such offences should be punished, preaching the wisdom of toleration and the desirability of not keeping the company of unbelievers.

In the second rank of natural law are to be placed laws deriving from human relationships.[35] Of the many offences that come under this heading, governments are in a position to punish only suicide.[36] This is often not treated as a punishable offence, and in any case cannot be punished with death, and should not be so punished where it has been unsuccessful.

The third class of natural laws, finally, derives from the relationships issuing from the first two categories, and has to do with our responsibilities to one another. Offences in this regard range from lèse-majesté to breaches of contract. Civil governments do have to be active in this area, with codes of laws and a judiciary to implement them. Only lèse-majesté merits severe punishment, because it is most harmful to society and is a threat to the constitution. Pelli makes no recommendation as to a suitable penalty.

What is going on here? The work is unfinished. One can assume a fuller and more systematic treatment would have been forthcoming in a second draft. Meanwhile one can only speculate as to the direction of Pelli's thought. He emphasised, as we saw, that the civil law is governed by the natural law, and argued strongly for the thesis that natural law does not admit the death penalty; no more, therefore, should civil law do so. In the more substantial of the fragments, in which he launches an all-out attack on the *lex talionis*, Pelli strongly opposes the teaching of the Cocceji, father and son, to the effect that the *lex talionis* has a basis in natural law, thus legitimising the application of the death penalty in the positive law. These closing chapters 16–18 may perhaps therefore be seen as a bridging passage between the main text as it stands and an additional argument against the death penalty, perhaps based on fragment 3, on the *lex talionis*. This extra argument would be incorporated in the main text in a later, expanded version—which in the event was never composed.

Lex talionis

Pelli's definition of the ends of punishment (in his chapter 9) does not include retribution. He thinks of retribution as vengeance, a display of inhumanity which lowers men to the level of beasts.[37] The role of punishment, in his eyes, was to prevent the offender from re-offending, and through the example of his suffering, to dissuade others from turning to crime.[38] He would have been aware, however, that for many or most of his readers, retribution was the main aim and justification of punishment. More specifically, the *lex talionis*—an eye for an eye, retaliation in kind—was viewed as the logical and legitimate formula to be applied in punishing an offender. Talion was also widely believed to be sanctioned by the Bible, specifically the Old Testament. The door was therefore open for the application of the death penalty in certain cases. It was thus likely that Pelli would be drawn into discussing the *lex talionis*, and would make a contribution to the ongoing debate, initiated more than a century before by Grotius, and carried on by successive natural law philosophers such as the Cocceji, father and son, Heineccius and Pufendorf.

Fragment three (in four parts) contains a substantial argument against Talion and vengeance.[39] Pelli targets the Prussian jurists Cocceji, father and son, according to whom the Talion was prescribed by the law of nature, and must be part of the armoury of the sovereign who presided over the positive law. Pelli sided with Grotius, Pufendorf and Heineccius, who pointed to the impracticality of the law of Talion and its inefficacy in correcting the criminal and dissuading others from following his example. His discussion proceeds as follows.

The Cocceji, father and son, taught that Talion is required by the law of nature. Talion is impracticable, however. It is frequently difficult or impossible to measure or enforce an appropriate and just retaliation, for example where there is a status difference between offender and offended. In general, Talion implies an exact equality between injury and punishment, which is unrealistic and unattainable (fragment 3.1).[40]

The Cocceji were too tolerant of vengeance (fragment 3.2, entitled 'On vengeance'). Vengeance is a brutal and inhuman sentiment, as is conceded by Christian and gentile philosophers alike. It is inhumanity masquerading as justice (Seneca). Even Samuel von Cocceji admitted this, Pelli says, while claiming that it is consistent with the law of nature. And since it is inhuman, it is disproportionate, productive of no good result and excessive. It is to be noted that Pelli has here assigned these attributes to 'revenge *or Talion*', and from this point in the fragment the terms 'revenge/vengeance' and 'Talion' are used without discrimination. This is a strategic move: the latter term has taken over all the unfavourable connotations of the former.

Still with Samuel von Cocceji, Pelli finds fault with his application of the *lex talionis* to the causing of injury, because he has failed to explain how one can give satisfaction for an injury. He himself, in charting the response to injury, would follow a set of principles that he sets out in a series of axioms. First comes the New Testament instruction 'Do unto others . . .'. Next are that it is not worth doing things that are pointless; that the usefulness of a penalty or action must be calculated according to the consequences; and that if there is a choice, one should select the option that produces greater security and less harm.[41]

Heinricus von Cocceji says that there is no right to private vengeance. This according to Pelli is correct, but appears to cancel out a fully fledged *lex talionis*. In any case, public vengeance is another matter. Punishment is in the hands of the judicial authorities, and they have the right to assess the seriousness of an offence and apply an appropriate penalty; it lies within their power to substitute other penalties for death. It is not the case that magistrates are bound to implement the law of Talion on behalf of injured parties, who in accordance with that law uniquely have the right to retaliate in kind. Magistrates and governments in general are in place 'under the sole condition' that they promote the greater happiness, security and tranquillity of the citizenry. Pelli is here showing his colours as an advocate of a minimalist view of punishment. The fragment (3.2) ends with the comment that the *lex talionis* might seem to be the height of reason, but would in fact stir up never-ending war in the State of Nature and in whatever society it was the law.

In fragments 3.3 and 3.4, Pelli revives the argument of Grotius, that the law of Talion was sanctioned neither by the Old Testament nor by the New. He says that he is always wary of looking for 'universal rules' in the Scriptures and for the (hidden) rationale behind divine rulings. The Hebraic commandments are in any case a less safe guide than the Gospel message of gentleness and pity as opposed to revenge, even if humanity is more inclined to the latter than the former. The Deity reserved for himself the punishment of the likes of Cain, and threatened a much more severe punishment (seven times greater) than simple Talion for anyone who repaid Cain for his crime. This shows that in the Scriptures themselves Talion is not held to be an appropriate response, a just reparation, in accordance with the law of nature.

It is foolhardy to attribute the fate of certain historical individuals to divine intervention through Talion.[42] Stray passages in the New Testament,[43] supposedly supportive of Talion, merely confirm that some punishment is appropriate for crime—some proportionate punishment, for we are not obliged to follow the Hebrews, specifically in applying the death penalty for idolatry, murder and adultery.[44] Only the prejudiced or the over-imaginative could peddle the line that 'the Supreme Lawgiver' has prescribed the *lex talionis* for all crimes, and that the civil authorities should apply this law across the board. At this point, Pelli returns to his stated position on the end of punishment, with the firm assertion that the main aim of positive law is not to repay injury with injury, but 'to secure the safety, example and reform of men'. It only remains for him to remind the reader of the 'simple fact' that often the punishment of some offences through the *lex talionis* might constitute a 'new crime'.

To conclude: Pelli tapped into an ongoing debate on the *lex talionis*. He revisited the traditional arguments, but went beyond his predecessors in condemning the *lex talionis* root and branch. A key move on his part was to insist that this law was merely vengeance under another name, and vengeance was a passion unworthy of a human being. Vengeance has its roots in anger. It is the product of 'a boiling of the blood around the heart moved by a desire to transfer pain on to something else' (Eustratius on Aristotle's *Nicomachean Ethics*). Pelli was familiar with Seneca's *De ira* (*On Anger*), in which 'revenge' (*ultio*) is described as inhuman. A law that drew its inspiration from the uncontrolled passions of men had no place in any system of positive law, which must be constructed and enforced according to the principles of rationality and utility, prevention and deterrence. A state could not impose the *lex talionis* without committing in its turn inhuman acts, acts of cruelty.[45]

In the preface to his treatise, Pelli had railed against the 'germ within of capricious anger', 'the first impulse of boiling anger' as manifested in 'hating to death' a condemned man. In fragment 3, the *lex talionis* is presented as the very embodiment of 'the malice which is deeply rooted in us'. If Pelli had integrated this fragment into his text, his argument would have come full circle, and he would have produced a rousing finale to the first systematic and comprehensive attack on the death penalty of the Enlightenment.

CONCLUSION

Pelli looked back to the natural jurists and philosophers of the seventeenth and early eighteenth centuries rather than forward to the French and Scottish Enlightenment of his own period. The exception was Montesquieu, for whom he had great respect, as shown both in *Against the Death Penalty* and in the *Efemeridi*. Pelli was a keen reader and firm admirer of the historical works of Voltaire and d'Alembert, but had little sympathy with their moral and religious views and those of the *philosophes* of France (and Geneva) in general.[46]

Among the natural jurists, Grotius, who had the status of the founding father, is by far the most frequently cited by Pelli, for his seminal discussions of punishment, its definition and its ends, and for his teaching on the right to war, among other things. Heineccius, himself a keen student and sometimes (as was Pelli) critic of Grotius, receives attention, as does Pelli's older contemporary Vattel, also on the right to war, and the Cocceji, father and son, on the *lex talionis*. There is no explicit reference to Pufendorf, although he provided much of the raw material for Pelli's own arguments. In particular, it was Pufendorf's argument (contra Grotius) against the presence of punishment in the State of Nature that served as the springboard for Pelli's rejection of the presence of the death penalty in natural law. It may be that Pufendorf came to him second-hand via Heineccius,[47] or simply that Pelli leant heavily on Pufendorf and found little in him to disagree with. Among Pelli's closest associates and contemporaries, Lampredi was similarly immersed in the discussions and doctrines of the natural jurists. Pelli drew on Lampredi's *De licentia in hostem* and *De maiestate principis*, and shared his critical spirit.[48] He lacked his friend's self-confidence in committing himself to print.

Pelli inherited from the natural philosophers and jurists the grand theme of the transition of humanity from the State of Nature to civil society via the Social Contract. He also took over their method of presentation. In this tradition, erudition was very much on display. Pelli could play this game too, although at a rather lower level than Grotius or Pufendorf, and his citations from classical literature and history and elsewhere are frequently secondhand. His work fits into the genre of the juristic treatise, and was intended to do so. As such, it lacks the clarity and zest of Beccaria's work, which was more a manifesto than a learned treatise. Still, Pelli saw himself as a man with a mission. As he puts it in the *Efemeridi*, referring to *Against the Death Penalty*,

> I have charged myself with this work with the sole motive of bringing some benefit to my fellow men . . . May God lighten my path and give me sufficient strength to bring to a happy ending my undertaking, which has one object and one only, the well-being of others.[49]

He was well capable of writing with spirit and passion.

'May God lighten my path . . .': Pelli was a staunch Catholic. The Supreme Being hovers over his manuscript, and the doctrine of original sin is all-pervasive. Whereas sin, for Beccaria, is to be carefully distinguished from crime, whose origins are to be sought in social and economic conditions, in the poverty and backwardness of an underclass, for Pelli sin is the underlying cause of crime.[50] The task of the judiciary is to rid society of vice, the vice that is at the root of crime and also of the means by which it is opposed—for sin also permeates the judicial system which should be extirpating crime.

In assessing Pelli's achievement, one must bear in mind the intellectual setting and background and his intended audience, as well as the temperament of the author. Pelli came from a conservative background. He was a man of piety, who was nurtured, and remained, in the bosom of the Church. His world was one in which people, including men within the Church who held progressive views, were becoming increasingly sensitive to and intolerant of cruelty, the cruelty that was routine, and laid out for all to see, in the judicial system. Pelli in his more confident moments felt that if he could address this sensibility, he could start something. It bears repeating, and emphasising, that, as far as we know, *no one before him had undertaken a project such as his*. It is telling that Lampredi, who took up an independent position on many issues, such as the right to war, and who was completely familiar with the views of his friend, did not himself take up an abolitionist stance.

Pelli's educational and cultural background and his natural instincts led him to wage his war against the death penalty on a terrain laid out by others, for the most part the natural law jurists and philosophers, using weaponry forged by them and, where he judged it necessary, turning it against them. It was sometimes necessary. It was a commonly held view that the *lex talionis* was a, or the, just way of punishing criminals, and in general that retribution should be the essential ingredient in punishment. Pelli's arguments, on this terrain, and with this weaponry, were by and large convincing. Of course, from a modern perspective, his arguments (and also those of Beccaria) are dated: the State of Nature and the Social Contract have long ago vanished from debates about the death penalty.[51] The relevant question, however, is whether the contribution of Pelli was appropriate for his time, would have struck a chord with his intended audience, stirred up controversy and debate and stimulated a movement for reform of the law. My answer is: yes.

As for the inevitable comparison with Beccaria, in a sense this would never get off the ground, as we would be comparing two incomparables, one a manuscript that lay unfinished and unknown for centuries, the other a tour de force, launching a movement for penal reform that has lasted for two and a half centuries thus far. The two treatises are significantly different in their aims and content. Of the two works, Pelli's contains by far the more comprehensive and sustained attack on the death penalty; Beccaria's critique is more or less confined to one substantial chapter. It is of course regrettable that Pelli (in the draft as we have it) said little about alternative punishments and other aspects of the system of criminal law, including torture, and that his work tapers off before he had fulfilled his apparent promise to provide a detailed survey of the penal system.

We know enough about Pelli to be able to say that he was not equipped to be a 'young Turk' like Beccaria, who could distance himself from or bypass much of what had gone before (especially in the area of Roman, Dutch and German jurisprudence), and produce a pamphlet of extraordinary power and radicality that sent shock waves through Europe and beyond. It seems unlikely that a completed and polished version of Pelli would have had the vigour and bite of Beccaria, or, for that matter, the supple erudition and analytic power of Grotius. At the same time, it is fair to say that the publication of *Against the Death Penalty* in a finished form would have caused ructions in a country so firmly in the grip of conservative Catholicism as was eighteenth-century Italy.

Cesare Beccaria Bonesana
(1738–1794)

⋮

Texts

⋮

Beccaria against the Death Penalty and for Forced Labour

On Crimes and Punishments

Chapter 20 (excerpt): Violence

Some crimes involve attacks against the person, others against goods. The former ought without exception to be punished with corporal punishment: the grand and the rich should not be able to put a price on assaults on the weak and the poor; otherwise wealth, which is the reward for industry under the protection of the laws, becomes the seedbed of tyranny. There is no liberty when the laws in some circumstances allow a man to cease to be a *person* and to become a *thing*. Then you will witness the man who has power putting his efforts into securing out of the mass of civil relations those where the laws advance his interests. This discovery is the magic secret which transforms citizens into beasts of burden and becomes in the hands of the strong the chain with which the actions of the rash and the weak are shackled.

Chapter 22 (excerpt): Theft

Thefts which do not involve violence should be punished with fines. Anyone who seeks to enrich himself at the expense of another ought to suffer pecuniary loss himself. But as this is normally a crime issuing out of misery and desperation, a crime characteristic of those unfortunates whom the law of property (a law that is merciless and perhaps unnecessary) has deprived of all but bare existence (but as pecuniary penalties swell the number of criminals above the number of crimes and take bread from the mouths of the innocent while removing it from the guilty), the most appropriate punishment will be the only kind of slavery that can be called just, namely, the temporary slavery of the labour and person to society, in order that the offender may through a complete and personal dependency make amends for his unjust despotism against the Social Contract. But when violence is added to theft, the penalty should be a mixture of corporal and servile punishment.

Chapter 27 (excerpt): Moderation in Punishment

For a punishment to achieve its end, it is enough that the evil of the penalty be greater than the good that comes from the crime, and in any calculation of the evil there must be included the certainty of the punishment and the loss of the good that the crime might produce. Anything more than this is superfluous and therefore tyrannous. Men are guided by the repetition of evils that they are familiar with, rather than those of which they are ignorant. Take two nations, in one of which, in the scale of penalties set proportionately against the scale of crimes, the worst punishment is perpetual slavery, and in other, the wheel. In my view, the heaviest punishment in the former will produce as much fear as the corresponding punishment in the latter. Furthermore, if there were cause to adopt in the former the heaviest punishment of the latter, by the same token the consequence would be a stepping up of the punishment of the latter, so that there would be a gradual and hardly susceptible move from the wheel through slower and more cultivated torments to the ultimate refinements that tyrants know only too well.

Chapter 28: The Death Penalty

This pointless profusion of punishments, which have never made men any better, has driven me to examine whether the death penalty really is useful and just in a government that is well administered.

By what right do men consider that they are entitled to butcher their fellow men? It is certainly not the right from which sovereignty and laws derive: these are simply the sum of the tiny portions of the individual liberty that each man has; they represent the general will, which is the aggregate of those individual wills. Who at any time has voluntarily given others the authority to kill him? How could it ever be that the smallest sacrifice of liberty which every man makes includes the sacrifice of the greatest of all goods, namely, life itself? And if there were such a sacrifice, how is this to be reconciled with that other principle, that a man does not have the authority to kill himself? But he must be able to do so, if he can confer that right on another, or on to society in general.

The death penalty is not a right, as I have shown, but rather an act of war of a nation against a citizen, undertaken because it judges the destruction of his existence to be necessary or useful. If I can show, however, that such a death is neither useful nor necessary, I shall have won a victory for the cause of humanity.

The death of a citizen can only be regarded as necessary on two grounds: the first is where a citizen even though deprived of his liberty retains contacts and power such as to pose a threat to the security of the nation, where his very existence may bring about a revolution that would endanger the survival of the established form of government. The death of such citizens becomes necessary when the nation is regaining or losing its liberty, or at a time of anarchy when rioting takes the place of laws. But under the tranquil rule of law, when there is a government that has the consent of the whole nation, when it is safeguarded from without and from within by power and by public opinion, which is perhaps more efficacious than power, where authority lies with the true sovereign alone, where riches purchase pleasures rather than influence: under these conditions I do not see that there is any necessity to destroy a citizen, unless his death were to be the true and only restraint holding back others from committing crimes—and that is a second reason for holding the death penalty to be just and necessary.

When the experience of all ages, the ultimate punishment never having been a deterrence to men who are determined to outrage society, when the example of the Roman citizenry, when twenty years of the reign of the empress Elisabeth of Moscow, in the course of which she gave a shining example to the leaders of all peoples, worth at least as much as the many conquests bought with the blood of the sons of her homeland—when none of this has persuaded men for whom the language of reason is forever suspect, whereas they listen to the language of authority, it will be enough to consult the nature of man to perceive the truth of my assertion.

It is not the intensity of the punishment which makes the greater impact on the human soul, but its duration; for our sensibilities are more easily and forcibly moved by impressions that are very brief but repeated than by one

strong but passing disturbance. It is universally the case that habit governs
the life of every sentient being. Man speaks and walks and procures what he
needs with the aid of habit. In the same way, moral ideas are only imprinted
on the mind through lasting and repeated shocks. The most powerful check
on crimes is not the terrible but passing spectacle of the death of a criminal,
but the long-drawn-out example of a man deprived of liberty, who, trans-
formed into a beast of slavery, reimburses society by hard work for the offence he has caused. Much more potent than the idea of death, which always
seems dim and distant, is the refrain within ourselves, efficacious because it
often recurs: 'I too will be reduced to this never-ending and miserable condition if I commit like crimes.'

The impact of the death penalty, for all the impression that it makes, is
overshadowed by man's forgetfulness, something that comes naturally to
him even when matters of importance are at stake, and is quickened by the
passions. As a general rule, violent passions take men by surprise, but do not
last long. They are capable of producing the kind of revolution that turns
common people into ancient Persians or Lacedaemonians. But in a free and
peaceful regime, the impressions ought to be frequent rather than strong.

The death penalty is for most people a spectacle, and for some an object of
compassion blended with disdain. These are the two sentiments that take
hold of the minds of spectators, rather than the salutary terror that the law
claims to inspire. But with punishments that are more moderate and ongoing, the dominant sentiment is the latter, because it is the only one. The limit
that the lawgiver should set to the severity of punishments seems to be related to the point where the sentiment of compassion begins to prevail over
all others in the minds of those who are witnessing a punishment, which is
staged for them rather than for the criminal.

For a penalty to be just, it should have that grade of intensity which is sufficient to deter men from committing crimes. There is no one these days who
would, on reflection, be minded to opt for the total and perpetual loss of liberty, however advantageous a crime might appear to be. Thus the intensity of
the penalty of life-long slavery as a substitute for the death penalty is sufficient to deter anyone, however determined. I would say that it is more than
sufficient. A great many people view death with tranquillity and resolution,
one from fanaticism, another from vanity, which more or less invariably ac-
companies men beyond the tomb; yet another is finally and desperately resolved to put an end to his life or to escape from misery. But neither fanati-

cism nor vanity can stand fast in fetters and chains, under the rod or a yoke, or in a cage of iron. And the desperate man is not finished with his ills; for him they are just beginning. Our mind is less affected by violence and extreme but transitory suffering than by prolonged and unceasing toil. This is because it can, so to speak, compact itself for a moment in order to repel the former, whereas its elasticity, though great, is insufficient to resist the long-drawn-out and repeated imposition of the latter.

With the death penalty, every example that is given to the nation presupposes a single crime, whereas with the penalty of life-long slavery one individual crime provides plenty of examples which last. If it is important that men often witness the power of the laws, death penalties should not be far apart one from another. For that, crimes must be frequent. Thus for this penalty to be useful, it is necessary that it not make the full impression on men that it should make: that is, it has to be useful and useless at the same time.

To anyone who says that life-long slavery involves as much suffering as death and is thus equally cruel, my response is that if you add up all the miserable moments of slavery it will perhaps turn out to be even more cruel. These moments are extended over a lifetime, however, whereas the death penalty makes its full impact in one single moment. The advantage of the penalty of slavery is that it strikes terror in the spectator more than in the sufferer. That is because the thoughts of the former are directed toward the total sum of moments of misery, whereas the latter is conscious of the unhappiness of the present moment and is not distracted by the future. All the evils are amplified in the imagination, while the sufferer finds compensation and consolation unknown to and incredible to the spectators, in whom the hardened mind of the wretched offender is replaced by their own sensibilities.

This, more or less, is the reasoning that makes a thief or an assassin out of someone for whom there is no other countervailing factor than the gallows or the wheel to hold him back from violating the laws. I am aware that the development of the moral sensibilities of the individual mind is something instilled through education; but from the fact that a thief does not know how to express his principles properly it does not follow that he has none: 'What are these laws that I must respect which leave such a yawning gap between me and the rich man? He refuses me a coin that I beg of him, and evades me by telling me to go and find some work—of which he knows nothing. Who made these laws? The rich and the powerful who have never deigned to visit the squalid huts of the poor, who have never broken a mouldy loaf of bread in response to the innocent cries of famished children and a wife's tears. Let us break these bonds that are death to most people and of service only to some tyrants who are few in number and lazy; let us attack injustice at its source. I will return to my natural state of independence, I will live free and happy for some time on the fruits of my courage and industry. Perhaps the day of sorrow and penitence will arrive, but that time will be short, and one day I will suffer a single day of pain for many years of liberty and pleasure. King over a few, I will put right the mistakes of fortune and see these tyrants go pale and tremble in the presence of someone whom in their insulting pomp they regarded as beneath their horses and their dogs.'

Then religion enters the mind of the scoundrel who is abusive of everything, and by offering him an easy repentance and the near certainty of eternal felicity greatly diminishes the horror of that final tragedy.

But the man who sees ahead of him a great many years, or even his whole life-course, that would be spent in slavery and suffering, in the full sight of his fellow citizens among whom he is at present living a free and sociable life, a slave of the very laws by which he was protected, will set all this prudently against the uncertainty of the outcome of his crimes and the brevity of time in which he would enjoy their fruits. The ongoing example of those whom he sees as real-life victims of their own short-sightedness will make a much greater impression on him than the spectacle of an execution: that hardens rather than corrects him.

The death penalty is not useful, because of the example of atrocity that it gives to men. If the passions or the necessity of war have taught humanity to shed blood, the laws which moderate the conduct of men should not add to that cruel example, which is all the more disastrous in so far as a legal death is performed with studied formality. It seems an absurdity to me for the laws, which are the expression of the public will and detest and punish homicide, to commit a homicide themselves, and in order to deter citizens from committing murder prescribe a public murder. Which are the true and most useful laws? Those agreements and conditions that all would want to observe and propose while the voice of private interest, which is always heeded, is silent, or is in harmony with the public interest. What are everyone's feelings about the death penalty? We can read them in the indignation and displeasure which everyone directs at the executioner, who is simply an innocent agent of the public will, a good citizen who is making his contribution to the public good; who is as necessary an instrument for the security of the public within as valiant soldiers are without. What is the origin of these contradictions? And why is this sentiment fixed in men beyond all reason? It is because men, in the deepest recesses of their souls, those parts which more than any other still preserve the original form of their primitive nature, have always believed that their lives are in the power of none, outside that of necessity, which rules the universe with its iron rod.

What are men to think when they see wise magistrates and grave ministers of justice with calm indifference have a criminal dragged to his death with ponderous ceremony; or when a judge with icy insensitivity and perhaps even a secret satisfaction in his own authority passes by a miserable man writhing in his last agonies and awaiting the fatal blow, and goes on to revel in the conveniences and pleasures of life? 'Ah,' they would say, 'these laws are only the pretext for the use of force and for the considered and cruel formalities of justice; they are merely a language of convention to allow them to dispose of us with greater sureness, like victims destined in sacrifice to the insatiable idol of despotism. Murder, which has been preached to us as a terrible offence, we now see adopted without any sense of misgiving, without any repugnance. Let us exploit this example. Violent death has been presented to us as a terrible happening, but we can see it is a matter of a moment. How much less significant it will be for some who is not anticipating it, and is spared almost all the pain that is associated with it.' Such are the appalling sophisms, which, if not clearly, at any rate confusedly, make men disposed to crimes, in whom, as we have seen, abuse of religion can be more influential than true religion.

If someone were to object that in virtually all ages and in virtually all nations the death penalty has been prescribed for some crimes, my reply is that his argument dissolves before the truth, against which there is no denial; that the history of mankind appears as a massive sea of errors, in which some truths, few and far between, are floating in confusion. Human sacrifice was common to virtually all nations, but who would be brazen enough to justify it on these grounds? That some few societies, and only for a short time, have abstained from prescribing death is an argument for rather than against me. For this is the fate of the great truths: they last for as long as a single shaft of light in contrast with the long dark night that engulfs humanity. That fortunate age has yet to come in which the truth belongs to the majority, as error has belonged thus far. And up till now the only exceptions to this universal law have been those truths that the infinite Wisdom has chosen to reveal as distinct from the others.

The voice of a philosopher is too weak to counter the tumult and the shouting of the many who are driven by blind habit. But the handful of wise men who are sprinkled over the face of the earth will find an echo of my thoughts in the depths of their hearts. If truth, struggling against the infinite obstacles that keep it away from a monarch against his wishes, were able to penetrate as far as his throne, then he should know that it comes with the secret prayers of all humanity; that truth in his presence will silence the bloody fame of conquerors; and that posterity, with justice, will award him trophies of peace ahead of those of the Tituses, the Antonines and the Trajans.

Blessed would humanity be if such laws were promulgated for the first time, now that we see seated on the thrones of Europe benevolent monarchs who are breathing life into the virtues of peace, the sciences and the arts, who are fathers of their peoples, crowned citizens. Their increased authority is bestowing happiness on their subjects in so far as they are dispelling that obstructive despotism, the crueller because less stable, which had suffocated the always sincere wishes of the people, desires always fortunate when they can reach the throne! If they let the ancient laws survive, I say, this is because of the enormous difficulty of removing the venerated rust of the errors that has built up over many centuries. This is a reason for enlightened citizens to wish with ever greater ardour that their authority will continue to increase.

Chapter 33 (excerpt): Smuggling

But must a crime go unpunished when committed by someone who has nothing to lose? No. There is smuggling which is so closely related to the nature of taxation, which is such an essential and so problematic a part of a good system of legislation, that such a crime deserves a considerable penalty, as serious as imprisonment itself and servitude, but imprisonment and servitude of a kind that fits the nature of the offence itself. For example, the conditions of imprisonment of a tobacco smuggler should not be comparable with those of a cutthroat or a thief, and, for it to be the most fitting to the nature of the penalty, the labour imposed on the former should be limited to work and service in the very department that he set out to defraud.

LAW OF GRAND DUKE LEOPOLD OF TUSCANY, AGAINST THE DEATH PENALTY (1786; EXCERPTS)[1]

Prolegomenon

Since our accession to the throne of Tuscany we considered it one of our main responsibilities to examine and reform the criminal legislation, which we had seen early on to be too severe. It evolved out of principles introduced in the less fortunate times of the Roman empire and in the turbulent periods of anarchy in the Middle Ages that followed, and was signally unsuited to the mild and gentle character of the nation. We sought as a first step to moderate its rigour with instructions and orders to our tribunals. Specifically, we issued edicts abolishing the penalty of death and torture, and punishments that are excessive and disproportionate to the crimes and to contraventions of the fiscal laws, until we were in a position to reform the entire criminal law, having subjected it to a serious and thorough examination, and having seen how these new dispensations worked in practice.

With the greatest satisfaction to our paternal inclination, we have finally come to the recognition that the moderation of penalties, when combined with the most vigilant attention to the prevention of criminal acts, the expeditious conducting of trials and the swift and sure application of the penalty to those who are truly criminals, far from increasing the number of crimes has considerably reduced those that are most commonly committed, and virtually eliminated the most serious of them. Therefore we have come to the decision not to hold back any longer the reform of the criminal law. Having as a fundamental principle totally abolished the death penalty, which we consider unnecessary for achieving the end set by society of punishing criminals; having eliminated completely the use of torture, [and] the confiscation of the goods of convicted criminals—a measure which tends for the most part to cause harm to their innocent families who played no part in their criminal acts; having removed from the law the multiple crimes which have gone under the name of lèse-majesté that were invented with the refinement of cruelty in perverse times; and in fixing penalties that are proportionate to the crimes but executed without fail in the respective cases, we hereby enact, in the fullness of our supreme authority, the following regulations. [...]

Chapter 33

We confirm with our sovereign authority and with particular emphasis the abolition of torture which already for some time with our approval has been suspended in the tribunals of the Grand Duchy. We permit no exception of any kind; we except no case, nor any of the modality of execution for which it had been practised in criminal trials in the past.

Chapter 51

We have witnessed with horror the facility with which in earlier legislation the death penalty was prescribed for crimes of no gravity, and having judged that the end of punishment should be, first, to give satisfaction for injury to a private individual or to the public; second, to correct the delinquent—who is still a son of the society and the State and of whose reformation we can never despair; third, security, in the case of the more grave and atrocious crimes, that the criminals concerned not remain in liberty to commit others; fourth and finally, the example given to the public that the government, in the punishment of the crimes and in employing such punishment in the service of the ends towards which it is uniquely directed, is always expected to make use of the methods that are most efficacious and cause the least possible suffering to the criminal. We find moreover such a combination of efficacy and moderation achieved less by the death penalty than by the penalty of public labour. This latter serves as an example continuous over time, rather than providing a moment of terror, which often degenerates into compassion. Moreover it removes the possibility that the delinquent will commit new crimes, while preserving the possible hope of witnessing the return to society of a useful and reformed citizen. Having judged in addition that a quite different system of laws might be more in tune with the greater gentleness and docility of the manners of the present age, in particular those of the people of Tuscany, we have come to the decision to abolish, and in fact we have abolished with the present law forever, the imposition of the death penalty on any criminal whatsoever, whether he is under arrest, or has absented himself, or has confessed to and has been convicted of any crime declared capital by the laws promulgated up till now. We declare all such laws null and void and abolished.

Chapter 53

And since those condemned of capital and grave crimes should continue to live in order to pay for their evil deeds through useful ones, we prescribe as the ultimate punishment, to substitute for the death penalty now abolished, the punishment of public labours for life in the case of men, and imprisonment equally for life in the case of women. We abolish absolutely the custom of allowing those condemned to the stated penalty of public labours for life the possibility of petitioning for their freedom, as if it were owed to them, after they have served their sentence for the space of thirty years.

Chapter 54

We have already abolished in our edict the penalty of branding imposed by the laws of 6 February 1750, and by a special order directed at our judges and tribunals the punishment of the rope or the cord, so familiar from the ancient laws of the Grand Duchy, equally remain abolished. In confirmation of these our dispositions, we forbid our judges and tribunals the use of such punishments, either in matters of ordinary justice or in police matters, and to this end and therefore in addition to the demolition of the gallows wherever they are to be found, we command that the ropes and the pulleys are not to be put on public view anywhere but are to be removed from all the tribunals. And since in many statutes of the cities of the Grand Duchy there still survive prescriptions for the barbarous and inhuman punishment of the mutilation of limbs for certain crimes, although this has been in disuse for many years, we repeal and annul from our side and as a necessity these statutes and any other law which imposes such penalties.

Opinion ('Voto') of Beccaria, Gallarati Scotti and Risi against the Death Penalty (1792)[2]

The Criminal Law Committee, in drafting the prolegomena to the new penal code which is to be submitted for the approval of the sovereign, and is modelled on the basic principles laid down in section 3 of the Royal Imperial Dispatch of 13 August 1790, had to enumerate and rank the various penalties that will be prescribed in this code, that they might be then assigned to the various crimes, with due attention to proportionality, and have followed the praiseworthy example of the Austrian and Tuscan codes, which are proposed as authoritative models in the aforementioned Dispatch.

The Committee was from the start confronted with the highly important and much debated question of whether the death penalty should be numbered among these penalties. The members of the Committee have been divided on this matter, so that at first it seemed unlikely that any progress could be made in drawing up the penal code before presenting the variant opinions in all humility to the sovereign oracle of His Majesty to await your decision, unless as many different codes were to be produced as there were opinions among the respective members of the Committee. That, however, would be an utter waste of time and labour. But on reflecting that we were all agreed on this, that the death penalty should be limited to a very few crimes, and that the pure and simple execution of the death penalty was to be regarded as the ultimate punishment, completely ruling out as useless and cruel those additional exacerbations which in the ancient codes habitually accompany the death penalty in the case of the more serious crimes, it was immediately apparent that the Committee could proceed with its work of allocating the ultimate punishment to the most serious crimes, while providing an explanation, in the margins, of those votes in favour of the death penalty and those in favour of a substitute penalty. The latter penalty would in our view be public labour of greater or lesser duress in proportion to the gravity of the crimes in question.

In fact, we the three signatories were of the same opinion, that the death penalty should not be imposed except where there was a positive necessity for it. Moreover, we have been unable to envisage any such positive necessity, in a society in a peaceful state and with a regular administration of justice, apart from the case of a criminal involved in plotting to subvert of the State, who although imprisoned and closely guarded, might, through his external or internal contacts, be in a position to disturb society and put it in peril anew. Some Committee members have been of the opinion that one should add to that case that of an accused who had committed a crime in itself capital but aggravated by murder. An example would be a highway robber who in seizing goods with violence takes the life of the person he is assailing. Finally, other members have believed it necessary to extend the death penalty to a number of other crimes, albeit all of a most serious nature. We are all however agreed on the opinion that, in the case of open sedition, rioting and gatherings of men in arms, these may be crushed then and there, even with the death of those perpetrators of the sedition who resist, for this is to be judged not as the execution of a penalty of death as prescribed in the law, but rather as a response to a genuine declaration of war.

We owe it to ourselves, and to our zeal for our sovereign and our responsibility to the public that inspire us, to present candidly and succinctly the reasons that have led us to arrive at this view and to uphold it under the guidance of the combined examples of the Austrian and Tuscan codes which have been presented to us as authoritative models to follow. The first of these, at article 20 of chapter 2, part 1, lays down clearly that there should be no place for the death penalty beyond the cases of so-called statarial, that is, most summary, procedure. It is clear from the context and supported by reason that such statarial procedure is only admitted and admissible where there is imminent danger to the State, as in cases of sedition and rioting. The second of the codes, at chapter 51, abolishes the aforementioned punishment for any capital crime whatsoever, adducing the most sound and plausible reasons. It is to be noted also that both codes also exclude the death penalty for those crimes which have to do with offences of any kind whatsoever which are directed against the person of the prince.

Leaving aside for a moment the authority that the two aforementioned codes must have over our own subaltern intuitions—for they must be the ultimate authority for us—and following in the luminous footsteps of the aforementioned article 51 of the Tuscan code and the trails blazed by those most worthy men who have held the same opinion, we believe that the death penalty is not applied appropriately except in the cases set out by us above. That is, first, not simply because it is unnecessary, but second, because it is less efficacious than a perpetual punishment accompanied by adequate and repeated public exposure, and third, because it is irreversible.

To show that it is unnecessary it is sufficient to reflect that, for a penalty to be just it should carry only those grades of intensity that suffice to deter men from engaging in criminal activity. There is no one today who on considering the matter would opt for the total and perpetual loss of their freedom, however advantageous a crime might be. Thus the intensity of the penalty of perpetual slavery as a substitute for the death penalty is sufficient to deter any mind, however resolute. We add that it is more in harmony with human nature to put death above perpetual and miserable slavery.

Those who deem the death penalty to be necessary for the purpose of providing an example for the repression of the most serious crimes would need to demonstrate this from the facts. It would have to be shown that where the death penalty has been applied most frequently, such crimes were far less numerous than in those places where the same death penalty was less common or not common at all. As it is, if we care to look with the impartial and calm eye of the legislator, at times past, and at countries near and far where the death penalty has been limited to the more serious offences, we would find that precisely the opposite is true: where penalties have been milder while at the same time imposed on criminals inexorably, there being less reason for letting them go unpunished, crimes have been seen to be less frequent, because the nature of men has little by little been moulded in line with the moderation of the laws.

In order to demonstrate that the death penalty is less efficacious than perpetual and public punishment it is sufficient to reflect that it is not so much the gravity of a punishment as its inevitability that is the most effective means of repressing crimes, provided that punishments are proportionate to crimes; just as the more effective restraint on crimes is not the terrible but passing spectacle of the death of a delinquent, but the long-drawn-out and repeated example of a man deprived of freedom, who by his labours gives recompense to the society that he has offended. This is efficacious because, when we are repeatedly reminded, with reference to ourselves, that we too would be reduced to an equally long-lasting and miserable condition if we commit like offences, this has a much more powerful effect on us than the sight of a death. People invariably view death as something vague and distant, on the assumption that they themselves will avoid it, and with a feeling of compassion for those who actually suffer it. In addition, with the death penalty, every example that is provided to the nation presupposes a crime. In the case of the penalty of perpetual slavery, one individual crime provides a great many examples over an extended period of time; and if it is important that men should frequently be exposed to the reality of the power of the laws, then applications of the death penalty should not be very far apart, which presupposes a frequency of crimes. But this means that for this penalty to be efficacious, it does not have the impact on men that it should; in other words, that it is efficacious and inefficacious simultaneously.

The death penalty is less efficacious because, since we are all agreed on its limits, namely that it should be reserved for the most serious and terrible crimes, it is not possible, its imposition being immediate, that it be easily applied in proportion to the number and atrocity of such crimes. This is because it is clear that, however barbarous a murderer might be, there might be another criminal who commits crimes even more barbarous and more numerous. Hence in order to avoid the inexpedient policy of punishing with the same penalty the more serious and numerous crimes, the death penalty would have to be supplemented, in reality and not just in appearance, with more horrible and recondite punishments, thus adding a legal exemplar of cruelty to what is already an illogical punishment of one homicide with another.

Finally we infer that the death penalty is inappropriate because it is irreversible; we bear in mind the inevitable imperfection of human judgements. Even if the death were a just penalty, even if it were the most efficacious of all punishments, in order for it to be justly applied to a particular criminal it would be necessary that he be proven to be guilty in such a way that the possibility of the contrary is excluded. This follows clearly from the irreversibility of the death penalty. As it is, if such proofs are required for the sentencing of a criminal, there would never be a case where such a penalty could be applied. Nor could one say that it would be expedient to leave it prescribed in the code solely for the purpose of intimidation, because with the reality of the execution of the penalty removed, gone too is the greater degree of efficacy of the example, which consists in the inevitability of the punishment; reduced also is the power of the rest of the penal laws. Yet reality shows, and an examination of all legislation confirms, that the proofs sufficient for sentencing a criminal to death have never been such as to exclude the possibility of a contrary verdict. Therefore neither the testimony provided by witnesses, even if there were more than two, nor the multifarious and independent pieces of evidence, confirmed though they may be by the confession of the accused, are such as to reach the limits of moral certainty, for that on close scrutiny offers a high level of probability but nothing more.

Not unheard of are examples from virtually all nations in which alleged criminals were sentenced to death on the basis of supposedly watertight proofs. It does not follow that we should invariably accuse judges of inexperience or negligence or bad motives: the fault lies rather with the necessary imperfection of the laws. Whenever these virtually inevitable errors of magistrates have failed to escape the attention of the public, and whenever the innocence of the supposedly guilty has been promptly revealed, such an occurrence has always been treated as a public calamity, and the magistrates have been the target of public condemnation through no fault of their own. If, therefore, we are in the situation of having to follow in sentencing an accused the light of moral certainty—which is sometimes not entirely clear—there is no comparison between a penalty that is in some way reversible while the accused is still alive, and the death penalty, which cannot be reversed once the accused has been deprived of life, even on the assumption that the punishment was intrinsically just, and more efficacious in reality than a penalty that lasts for life. And this is an assumption that we are far from subscribing to.

One might say that even in the single case where we allow for the issuing of a death sentence, an accused man is subjected to the same disadvantage, namely, that the possibility exists of the contrary verdict. But one should bear in mind that in our unique case we are caught between two conflicting necessities: one necessity is saving the State from the imminent danger of subversion, the other is facing the extremely remote danger of killing an innocent man. Between these two dangers it is evident that we must confront the latter out of plain necessity in order to avoid the former, which would at most provide an exemplary, a juridical necessity. Thus it is not a misdirected compassion for the wicked which persuades us to do away with the death penalty, much less a desire to contest the right of the sovereign legislator to prescribe the death penalty if in the light of his superior judgement he should consider it necessary to repress crime. If we were to judge it to be necessary, we would regard it as our absolute duty to propose it, and to plead with him to deviate from the sublime example given by our present August Sovereign who has abolished it in all cases in Tuscany. As it is, we have dared to do so in the single case of the criminal who, despite being held in prison, might be capable of playing a role in the subversion of the State. This matter also should however be left for the decision of the Sovereign alone, after consulting with the Supreme Magistrate.

Before concluding our considered opinion, we must take it upon ourselves to lay down an addendum, namely that the penalty that we would substitute for the death penalty implies a sufficient and repeated punishment that is public; and therefore that a prison hidden away in a corner of the province does not appear the most suitable means of providing the repeated and efficacious example to the public that we have had in mind. We would maintain, therefore, that it would be preferable to set up prisons in the various cities, so that the punishment would be open to the public gaze.

Distinguishing between, and classifying, different kinds of imprisonment would also be of use in order readily to identify those public works which are appropriate to serve as punishment and which would cope with the problem of the disorder that would result if criminals who have offended in different ways, and those who have been condemned to different grades of punishment, should be thrown together in a single place.

This not the place to develop these ideas. It is enough to have made a note of them here. The Committee for its part will give them more careful consideration. Suffice it that we have touched on here what is for further demonstration: first, that the penalty of public labour can be the most efficacious and useful for meeting the objective of all good criminal legislation, which is first and foremost the correction of the condemned when this is possible and in all circumstances, while giving an example to innocents to distance them from criminal activity; and second, that the death penalty, even if it is swiftest way of getting rid of criminals, is not the most suitable punishment for the repression of crime.

Gallarati Scotti
Beccaria Bonesana
Risi

Context

⁝

Lombardy

Lombardy, unlike Tuscany, was under the direct rule of the Austrian Habsburgs, from the early eighteenth century. In contrast with previous rulers, the Italian Sforzas and then the Spanish Habsburgs, the rule of the Austrian Habsburgs was reformist: over the course of a little less than half a century they introduced far-reaching changes into the society, economy and administration of Lombardy, in a concerted attack on the institutions and culture of the Old Order. Lombardy served as an experimental terrain for Habsburg reformism.

The first stage of reform was already underway in the late 1750s, under the direction of two high imperial officials of impressive stature who served Maria Theresa (empress 1740–80) and her eldest son Joseph II (co-ruler with Maria Theresa from 1765, sole ruler 1780–90). The officials in question were Wenzel Anton, Count (later Prince) von Kaunitz (1711–94), chancellor in Vienna for around four decades, who ran the newly formed (in 1757) Italian Department within the Austrian State Chancellery, and Count Karl Joseph Firmian (1708–82), governor of Lombardy from 29 July 1759 until his death. Together they formed a powerful axis with an agenda of reform for Milan and Lombardy.[1] They enrolled as active agents in their programme a wide variety of men, some outsiders, some Italians from elsewhere, such as the Tuscan Pompeo Neri, but increasingly they also drew recruits from the aristocracy of Milan and Lombardy. The local nobility was at first hesitant or even hostile, and some of them remained so, but there were also individuals and groups who themselves nurtured ambitious plans for reform, and saw the attractions of service in the imperial administration.[2] The 'Lombardian Enlightenment' was the product of the working together of these two forces.

The 1760s and 1770s was the period of maximum cooperation between the imperial power and the progressive aristocracy of Milan and Lombardy, although collaboration was never straightforward.[3] From the early 1780s, under Joseph II, however, the momentum of reform picked up speed: he introduced wholesale changes in the administration and economy in Lombardy and in the monarchy at large, and imposed a wide range of ecclesiastical and monastic reforms, practising 'a more extreme absolutism than almost any other monarch in history'.[4] His aggressive interventionism alarmed his younger brother Leopold, who as grand duke of Tuscany made moves (soon quashed by Joseph) to create a constitution for Tuscany to protect the Grand Duchy from arbitrary rule. In Lombardy, Joseph infuriated the deeply entrenched patriciate, accelerating the corrosion of their privileges and monopoly of office and the process of opening up their ranks to new men. The senate of Milan, the proud stronghold of the nobility, was abolished. Even some of the reformist nobles who in principle were in favour of a more meritocratic and egalitarian society, and looked to enlightened monarchs to engineer this change, reacted adversely to the dictatorial methods of an emperor whose accession they had greeted with enthusiasm.[5]

The most prominent of the progressive nobles were the small group which for around three years from 1762 met in the house of Count Pietro Verri: the self-styled Accademia dei Pugni ('Academy of Fisticuffs'). Beccaria was twenty-four when he joined the group.[6] From the first they threw in their lot with the Habsburg empire, perceiving that they had a common cause in the reform of the economy and society of the city and the province. At the same time, they cherished the hope of high office in the imperial service, which would give them fame as individuals and as a group, and the means of putting their ideas into practice. They were, in political terms, reformists rather than revolutionaries. Their leader and spokesman Pietro Verri was outspoken in his support for enlightened despotism. As he wrote in 1781, in welcoming the accession of Joseph II,[7]

In my opinion, subjects ought never to fear the power of the sovereign when he himself exercises it and doesn't surrender any essential part of it into other hands ... I think and feel that the best of all political systems will always be despotism, provided that the sovereign is active and in overall control and doesn't give up any portion of his sovereignty.

Verri's friends followed his lead: Beccaria in his attack on the death penalty placed his hopes in progressive princes. Verri, returning (in early 1761)
from service in the Austrian army in the Seven Years' War, disillusioned and
ready to devote his energies to the advancement of his *patria*, immediately
made overtures to governor Firmian, looking to impress him and his superior
in Vienna, von Kaunitz, with his ideas and counsel on political economy, issued in the form of pamphlets; he harnessed his newly founded group to follow his example.[8] Their main mouthpiece was the lively journal *Il Caffè*
(modelled on *The Spectator* of Addison and Steele launched in the 1710s),
which was published every ten days between June 1764 and May 1766. Verri
led the way with his first production, *Elements of Commerce*; Beccaria followed (in 1762) with a pamphlet on the monetary system of Milan. Although
the (informal) academy soon imploded, through literary and sexual rivalry,
most of its individual members went on to pursue successful careers as administrators and advisers in the service of the empire, in some cases in bitter
competition with each other.

Politically quiescent, the Academy of Fisticuffs similarly steered clear of
religious controversy. This was not easily done, given their full exposure to
the radical Enlightenment in France and elsewhere, and the secular flavour of
their mission to place sociability, public utility and the rights of the individual at the centre of their programme for social and cultural change. To attack
ecclesiastical and monastic privilege was one thing—that after all was a central plank of the imperial reform programme, pursued energetically by von
Kaunitz and Firmian and at a frantic pace by Joseph II in the 1780s. But anti-
clericalism was difficult to distinguish from anti-Catholicism, and attacks on
Catholicism, or on religion as a whole, would have been a step too far for
their allies in the imperial administration, not to mention the Austrian censors and the rulers themselves. Despite the fact that Beccaria in *On Crimes
and Punishments* avoided direct confrontation with the Church and the
Christian religion, the work was, entirely predictably, seen as anti-religious,
and encountered strong opposition from within the ecclesiastical hierarchy
and the monasteries, and from ideological supporters of traditional thought
and values in general.

If religion was a dangerous terrain, economics, or political economy, was a
relatively safe one, and the fact that it was the main interest of the Verri and
his colleagues does much to explain their successful careers as officials and
consultant administrators within the Austrian empire. Beccaria's subject

matter was the criminal justice system, however, and this *was* a contested area. The Inquisition had not yet released its grip on parts of northern Italy (for example, Lombardian Mantua), and the regime of torture and cruel punishments, though somewhat in decline by the second half of the eighteenth century, was still current in the secular courts of the day, on both sides of the Alps, as displayed notoriously in the brutal torture and breaking on the wheel of Jean Calas in Toulouse (1762) and the equally barbarous treatment of Giovanni Battista Torriggia in Milan (1767).[9] That Beccaria was fully aware of the controversial nature of his subject and the opposition that his treatise was likely to arouse is shown by the procedure that he followed in bringing his work into the light of day.

ON CRIMES AND PUNISHMENTS

On 16 July 1764 a press in Livorno printed out an anonymous work entitled *On Crimes and Punishments (Dei delitti e delle pene)*. Livorno was in Tuscany, rather than Lombardy, and thus lay outside that part of Italy which was under the direct rule of the Austrian Habsburgs. The author, as was later revealed, was Marchese Cesare Beccaria of Milan. When the book appeared, he was twenty-six years old (b. 1638).

The work is of modest length. Ferdinando Facchinei, a Vallombrosan monk who published a ferocious critique of it, also anonymously, six months later (6 January 1765), mocked it for its brevity: 'Our author's short book contains a mere one hundred and four pages, in a small octavo, printed in a rather large typeface.' The philosopher and Encyclopedist André Morellet answered him well: 'It is of primary importance that a work composed to be written and thought about should be short, for all the world to read.'[10] This remark appears in Morellet's letter of congratulation to Beccaria, dispatched in February 1766 together with an unsolicited translation of Beccaria's work and proposed alterations to the layout of the text.

On Crimes and Punishments was quickly and repeatedly reprinted, in Italian and in French translation. By the end of 1766, there had been at least six Italian and seven French editions (the latter with a print-run of a thousand copies each), and many more were to follow. The first English translation was published in 1767. Some of the most prominent philosophers of the time were impressed. Voltaire, in 1766, wrote a *Commentaire* on the book, hailing

it as 'a little book that is in the moral sphere the equivalent of the few remedies in medicine that are capable of relieving us of our ills'.[11] In Britain, the
book was a major influence on leading jurists and legal philosophers, including William Blackstone, William Eden, Jeremy Bentham and Samuel Romilly.
The Founding Fathers of the American republic read it avidly and put into
practice its key ideas. Some European emperors and monarchs came under
Beccaria's spell and moved towards significant reform of their criminal justice
systems. There was a hostile reaction from within the Catholic church, with
the monk Facchinei, as noted above, in the vanguard. The work was added to
the Church's list of prohibited books on 3 February 1766.

The book came out of the blue. Nothing of the sort was expected, and particularly not from Italy. Morellet condescendingly recorded in a letter to Beccaria that until he read his work he had been unaware that 'la bonne philosophie' had crossed the Alps.[12] True, other progressive thinkers had prepared
the ground to some extent—in particular Montesquieu in *De l'esprit des lois*
(1748), as Beccaria acknowledged. In Italy, the historian Lodovico Antonio
Muratori, in his *De' difetti della giurisprudenza* (1742), had pointed to some
of the faults of the existing legal system in Italy, without, however, touching
on the criminal law.

The book made a deep impression because of its content and presentation.
Beccaria summarises the content, under the heading 'General Thesis', thus:

> Lest punishment be an act of violence committed by one man or many
> men against a private citizen, it is essential that it be public, immediate,
> necessary, the minimum possible in the given circumstances, propor-
> tionate to the crime, and dictated by the laws.[13]

This brief résumé gives few details of the argument and passes over its infrastructure. In particular, Beccaria ruled out the use of the death penalty for all
offences except in specific historical circumstances when the liberty of the
nation is at stake and anarchy has undermined the rule of law, and in its place
prescribed hard labour, lifelong or short-term. Torture should be abolished.

Beccaria's proposals for reform of the administration and execution of the
system of criminal law would have involved the dramatic reform or abandonment of current laws and procedures in Italy and elsewhere in Europe. He
leaves us in no doubt, without going into details, about the iniquities and
brutalities of the existing system, as practised by the Inquisition and the secu-

lar courts under its influence. And he mentions right at the start three prominent jurists of the past, whose opinions, he says, constituted the current
laws which are 'the dregs of the most barbarous ages': Benedikt Carpzov
(1595–1666), professor of law in Leipzig, and two Italians, Giulio Claro
(1525–75), a Piedmontese statesman and lawyer who, like Carpzov, wrote
extensively on criminal law, and Prospero Farinacci (1544–1618), Roman
judge and lawyer, who served two popes and whose speciality was torture.

There is much more to the book than penology. The argument for penal
reform is set within a broad programme for the formation of a society based
on sociability, justice, individual rights and utility. This reflected the reformist interests and ambitions of the group of intellectuals from which it emerged,
the 'Academy of Fisticuffs'.

CAREER

We know comparatively little about Beccaria—if he composed an equivalent
of Pelli's diary it has not survived—and most of what we have comes from
hostile sources.[14] After the Academy of the Fisticuffs broke up in acrimony,
some of Beccaria's former friends and associates, specifically its founder and
leader Pietro Verri and his brother Alessandro, indulged in a prolonged campaign of character assassination against him.

In a letter to Morellet of 1766, Beccaria complains bitterly about his Jesuit
schooling in Parma which gave him 'eight years of fanatical and servile education'. There he met his future mentor (and nemesis) Pietro Verri for the first
time, although the two are unlikely to have seen much of each other in this
period, Verri being his senior by ten years.[15] He took a degree in jurisprudence from Pavia, graduating in September 1758, and soon after joined the
Accademia dei Trasformati, a literary society in Milan of which Verri was a
member. Verri took him under his wing. He managed the (contested) admission of Beccaria into the patriciate of Milan (24 December 1759),[16] and or-
chestrated the reconciliation of Beccaria with his parents two years after they
had expelled him from their house, hostile to his marriage on 22 February 1761 to Teresa Blasco (aged sixteen). It is probable that Verri supported
him financially: his situation, already somewhat precarious, had significantly
worsened following his alienation from his family. In the same year (1762)
Verri enrolled him as a founder member of the Academy of Fisticuffs and

commissioned him to compose and publish a work on the monetary system of Milan. This was part of a strategy, which at this stage did not reap dividends, of seeking employment, for himself and his colleagues and friends, with the Austrian administration.[17]

Beccaria first made his mark as a mathematician, receiving from his classmates the nickname Newtoncino, and he soon developed a special interest in the economy. He never abandoned these concerns: after holding the post of professor of cameral science (that is, political economy) at the Scuole Palatine in Milan from 1769 to 1772,[18] he spent the rest of his working life, that is, the best part of a quarter of a century, as an administrator and consultant on the economy of Habsburg Milan and Lombardy. His regular employment as a civil servant began on 29 April 1771, with his appointment by royal decree as a member of the Council for the Economy.[19] How these highly significant career moves were engineered will be discussed shortly. By the end of 1766, however, the 'Fisticuffs' had come to blows with one another, their informal organisation and collaboration had collapsed, their journal *Il Caffè* had been wound up and the individual members had gone their several ways. They mostly headed in the same direction, namely, into the service of the Habsburg empire, competing with each other for influential posts.

Before these extraordinary happenings, and while the Academy of Fisticuffs was in full swing, Beccaria had turned his attention to law. It is likely that Pietro Verri (whose own specialty was political economy) made the initial suggestion that he produce a critical analysis of the criminal justice system, aware of his younger colleague's training in jurisprudence and impressed by his intellectual gifts.

The results surprised everybody, including, and perhaps most of all, Beccaria. Ironically, the very success of the book led to a total breakdown in his relationship with the Verri brothers. The proximate cause was an aborted visit to Paris in October 1766. Beccaria, accompanied by Alessandro Verri, was expected to receive the plaudits of *les philosophes* and to bring reflected glory to his *équipe*, in particular, to its founder and leader. But Beccaria cut the visit short, returning early to Milan, missing his family and particularly his wife, according to his companion Alessandro, to the latter's embarrassment and humiliation and that of his sponsor Pietro, who had organised and partially financed the event.[20] To rub salt into the wound, Beccaria had given the impression to his Parisian hosts that it was he who had written the riposte to Facchinei's broadside, rather than the actual authors, the Verri brothers.

The Verri had made what turned out to be the strategic error of writing it anonymously in the first person, as if the author was replying on his own behalf.[21] In December 1766, the brothers broke with Beccaria. Their letters to each other at the time and for years to come are full of splenetic abuse of their former colleague.[22]

After this disaster, Beccaria retreated from the area of law and criminality. For the best part of two decades, he composed for his Austrian employers numerous reports on a wide range of subjects to do with the administration and economy of Milan and Lombardy.[23] It was only in the late 1780s that he was called upon by Habsburg emperors, first Joseph II (in October 1787), then Leopold II (the ex-Grand Duke Leopold of Tuscany), to work, with others, on the preparation of a general code of crimes and punishments for Austrian Lombardy.[24] We have his considered opinion on the death penalty, dated to 1792, composed with two others, as a member of a committee charged with revising the criminal law. This appears to be essentially his work, as it repeats much of the argumentation against the death penalty of his classic treatise of 1764.[25] There is, however, no substantial work on criminal law among his writings after *On Crimes and Punishments*.

It was in any case not as a jurist, but as a philosopher, that he composed *On Crimes and Punishments*. Around five years before its publication in 1764, he was 'converted to philosophy', as he tells his correspondent Morellet. There is no systematic discussion in this work of the institutions of criminal justice (such as a jurist might have provided), nor for that matter any build-up of factual information or careful documentation (as one might have expected from a legal historian). Instead, we encounter sustained, meaty, theoretical argument, advanced with striking clarity, and in a spirit of deep humanity. Morellet refers several times to 'the warmth' of the work, and Voltaire calls its author 'this lover of humanity'.

Milieu, Authorship, Character

Where did the treatise *On Crimes and Punishments* come from? The deeper intellectual influences behind Beccaria's work will be explored in the commentary on his argument, below. Here we discuss the milieu in which he operated, and the vexed question of authorship: how far Beccaria was responsible for the text that goes under his name.

The Academy of Fisticuffs was the incubator of the work. The group (as we have seen) debated a wide range of political, social, legal, economic, literary and philosophical subjects, and produced sundry monographs and papers, and a highly influential periodical (*Il Caffè*). All of their work came under the critical scrutiny of their colleagues. *On Crimes and Punishments* simply flew far higher and further than all their other productions.

Group discussion and debate will have contributed to the infrastructure of Beccaria's central argument. The 'Fisticuffs' shared a vision of a society arising out of a Social Contract, in which the social cohesion of its members would be promoted on the basis of equality and individual rights, with a view to securing the greatest happiness of the greatest number. Beccaria would have drawn on this common store of beliefs and aspirations in the process of setting out, and justifying, his dramatic programme of penal reform. At the same time, it is clear that the foundations of his work were laid down by research that he conducted with great intensity over a short period of time, from his conversion to philosophy in 1761; the research entered a second phase around September 1762, with his discovery of Rousseau's *Social Contract* and the works of Francis Bacon.[26] For all the contributions of other members of the group, from Pietro Verri down, it seems unlikely that a collective could have produced *On Crimes and Punishments*. Its brilliance, power and durability derive from the genius of an individual—Cesare Beccaria.

One should, however, consider the claims made by Pietro Verri, who wrote in one of several letters 'to his brothers and friends in Milan' as follows:

Regarding the book *On Crimes and Punishments*. The book is by the Marchese Beccaria. I gave him the argument, and the greater part of its thoughts result from the daily conversations between Beccaria, Alessandro [Verri], Lambertenghi and myself. Our society passed the evenings with everyone working in the same room. Alessandro had the History of Italy in his hands, I my economic political works, others read, Beccaria bored himself and the others. Out of desperation he asked me for a topic, and I suggested this [i.e., crime and punishments], knowing it to be appropriate for an eloquent man with an extremely lively imagination. But he knew nothing of our criminal methods. Alessandro, who was Protector of Criminals, promised him assistance. Beccaria began to write some ideas on various pieces of paper. We supported him with enthusiasm. We encouraged him so much that he produced a great multitude of ideas. After lunch we went walking, we spoke of the horrors of criminal jurisprudence, we discussed, we queried and in the evening he wrote. But it is so difficult for him to write and it costs him so much that after an hour he falls over and cannot continue. Having amassed his materials, I wrote it and gave it an order and a book took shape.[27]

This letter was written after the collapse of the group.[28] It is coloured by an unwillingness to acknowledge the achievement of a younger colleague who had outshone his mentor and patron. Verri does recognise, in an offhand way, Beccaria's brilliance as a writer and creative thinker, and it should be noted that in happier times, Verri spoke glowingly about his intellectual qualities.[29]

Beccaria's acquaintance with the day-to-day workings of the judicial system may well have been limited, as Verri asserts, and Alessandro Verri would have been able to give him graphic information about the condition of prisoners.[30] Pietro Verri was on hand as a copy-editor, and will have contributed to the preparation of the final text for publication. Finally, one of his comments rings true, and is confirmed much later by his brother, as we shall see shortly: Beccaria worked in short bursts; he lacked stamina and staying power. He was a creative thinker who found composition enervating.[31]

There are indications that the long-standing animosity of the brothers eventually ran its course, and that they adopted a somewhat more emollient tone when speaking of their former companion. When Alessandro composed the letter that follows, in 1803, he was the only survivor of the three (Beccaria died in 1794, Pietro in 1797).

How the treatise *On Crimes and Punishments* turned up among the writings of my late brother Pietro of vivid memory, transcribed in his own hand, I do not know for sure. However, I do seem to have some recollection that Marchese Beccaria used to compose the work little by little, writing it out in his own hand, and as the script was full of second thoughts and crossings outs, my brother out of friendship would transcribe a fair copy. If my memory serves me well, my brother's hand was neat and clean. Coming back now to the story of the work, I welcome the opportunity to repeat the truth that appears not yet to prevail; for some reason it does not tally with the rumours that circulate among so many of our citizens. In vain did my brother while still alive insist to the point of exhaustion that the work was not his, in vain have I consistently delivered the same testimony as witnessed by me in person and worthy of trust. Now I am ready to declare and confirm, as if in a testament, my first-hand knowledge of the truth of this. . . . I was at the time employed as Protector of Prisoners, an experience given to young men with a leaning toward forensic studies. Thus it came about that I frequently gave thought to the subject of criminality and found myself at odds with the barbarity that I encountered in the literature and likewise in the methods employed in reaching judgements and in the judicial process. Count Pietro thought the subject worthy of the pen of his friend Beccaria and proposed to him that he treat it. Marchese Beccaria took up the project. Like many other eminent geniuses, he was well up to the task, but at the same time baulked at the hard work involved in composing it. Thus to make things easier for himself he used to spend every evening in the rooms then occupied by my brother. I was there too, studying . . . Count Pietro would go out on business, and I used to spend the evening with Marchese Beccaria, studying in that end room of the apartment on the ground floor right below the first-floor lounge decorated with the animal paintings. Marchese Beccaria was there, I saw him, at Count Pietro's table, writing away, composing the work *On Crimes and Punishments*. I remember that he spent a lot of time in thought before writing. He couldn't keep at his work for more than two hours, and when they had passed he put down his pen. At the end of the evening Count Pietro would return to the house. The Marchese read him what he had written and sometimes made changes and corrections in accordance with his advice. But as the Marchese wouldn't go to the trouble of producing clean copy out of a draft, which was always full of crossings-out, I remember that my brother made a point of making a clean copy with his own hand. He was always encouraging Beccaria to press ahead with it, and predicted that Europe would sing its praises. I myself was thus persuaded, from that time on, that I had to concede to him that his was the original script that I had seen taking shape under his own hand in the space of round about two months, evening after evening.[32]

Alessandro's insistence that the work was Beccaria's own is striking: his is not merely a 'testimonium', it is (he says) tantamount to a 'testamentum': it has almost the status of an oath, as taken in court. Alessandro came back to the group with harrowing stories of the brutal treatment of prisoners. His brother sensed there was a prospect of a book and proposed to Beccaria that he write it. Beccaria took up the challenge. Alessandro, it should be noted, rates him as a genius. The failings which he goes on to retail are apparently to be expected in men of exceptional brainpower. Beccaria produced substantive copy, even if it was untidy. He was so drained by the creative process of writing (Alessandro has him working with intensity for two hours at most, while Pietro allotted him a single hour) that he couldn't even bring himself to make clean copy out of his drafts. This was a 'service' that Verri was prepared to perform.

So much for Alessandro's testimonium or testamentum. We can sum up the situation in this way. It was Beccaria who composed the text, which Verri took upon himself to (literally) tidy up. His motivation is not hard to divine. The cause was one he believed in, and he hoped or expected it would bring fame and fortune to the author and his associates, in particular no doubt to himself as leader of the group and instigator of the project. He comes across as the motivator, the practical man, the director of research (as it were). Beccaria, in contrast, is someone caught up in, entranced by, and exhausted by, the process of intensive research, creative thought and composition.

What we do not have to believe is that Verri modified the text on a regular basis during the process of composition. Confirmation that the central text was Beccaria's is provided by a manuscript of the first version, in the hand of Beccaria and signed by him, now in the Ambrosian Library of Milan. Verri did introduce changes in the text before handing it over to the printer, and these are visible if we compare the Ambrosian text with that delivered by Verri, but these were introduced at the end of the process, not in the course of composition.[33]

What all this says about Beccaria's relationship with Verri and its effect on his personality is worth a moment of speculation. The fact is that he had no choice but to accept Verri's assistance and interventions, and one wonders if this might have accentuated his natural tendency to lethargy and passivity. He was deeply in Verri's debt, and owed him deference. The experience of being dominated, prodded into action, having his drafts subjected to constant criticism and in general being dependent on another might well have been psychologically burdensome and at times traumatic for Beccaria. He already had a tendency to depression—no doubt aggravated by his personal situation—and he admitted to hypochondria.

The phenomenal success of the book brought about a dramatic change in the chemistry of the relation between patron and client. Both sides found this hard to handle. Beccaria was unable to deal with the publicity and fame (and notoriety) that his book brought him, from supporters and opponents both. At the same time, he showed insensitivity to the feelings and interests of the Verri brothers. He was surprised and shattered by the breakdown of his relationship with them. As he confesses in a letter to Morellet of late 1771 (five years after the collapse of the Academy), he was stunned into silence:

> A cruel misanthropy invaded my soul. It was not produced by friends in France . . . but by those in Italy. As a result I began to neglect my correspondence, and a form of aversion to writing induced me to keep this ungrateful silence.[34]

At the same time, he was seemingly unable or unwilling to associate his Italian 'friends' in his success. For his part, Pietro Verri could not swallow the reversal of their roles, his former client's monopolisation of the applause gained by a book which he, Verri, regarded as at least a joint enterprise and his client's failure to show him the gratitude that he deserved.

Beccaria beat a retreat, as soon as he could, into the Viennese imperial administration. He became a docile, obedient and efficient civil servant. The assessments of two colleagues, both dated to 1791, are explicit and revealing:

> Beccaria has spirit and is very well-informed, but he is not a man of action and he lacks energy. He knows nothing about practical matters, and he follows the opinion of others even when he expresses his own.
>
> Despite his great talent and impressive knowledge, his corpulence affects his morale. He is naturally vague, and energy is not his strong point. He never has the courage to disagree with anyone who is in a position to do him good or evil.[35]

What neither observer mentions or perceives is the effect that long-term service for an imperial power which was increasingly (under Joseph II) interfering and critical with regard to its employees would have had on a man who was already over-sensitive and insecure.[36] He had exchanged one relatively pliant master for a rather more exacting one.

PATRONAGE AND PUBLICATION

Pelli did not publish, Beccaria did. Both anticipated an unfriendly reception. How was Beccaria able to publish and get away with it? If a comment made in the first of his letters to André Morellet is to be believed, his heart was in his mouth as he wrote *On Crimes and Punishments*:

> In writing my work, I had in front of my eyes Galileo, Machiavello and Gianone [*sic*]. I have heard the chains of superstition stir and the howls of fanaticism suffocate the whimpers of truth. This determined me and forced me to be obscure and to wrap the lights of truth in a sacred fog. I have wanted to be the defender of mankind without being its martyr.[37]

But Beccaria's critics had no difficulty penetrating the 'sacred fog'. He needed more than obfuscatory language to escape their wrath. One part of the answer to my leading question is Pietro Verri; the other part is Firmian and von Kaunitz.

Among the many benefits that the patronage of Pietro Verri bestowed on Beccaria (some have been highlighted in the above discussion) was protection from attacks from outside that might have endangered his person and his prospects. Verri was a man of status and influence in Milan, a blue-blood patrician whose family (and contemporaneously his eminent father) had held high office in the city for centuries. That Beccaria was his protegé counted for a great deal—once, that is, it became known that he was the author of *On Crimes and Punishments*. The work was initially thought to have been written by the same hand as an earlier work, *On Happiness*, also published from Livorno, and also anonymously; the authorship of the latter was pinned (correctly) on Pietro Verri. Despite the unpopularity of both works in conservative circles, religious and secular, Verri succeeded (after a long and vigorous campaign) in being co-opted by the Austrians on to the Supreme Economic Council set up in 1765. Verri's relationship with the governor and effective ruler of Lombardy, Firmian, and his superior, the chancellor von Kaunitz, was not an easy one. Early on, Verri was brought to order by von Kaunitz himself for revealing more than was considered prudent about the Milanese balance of trade in a work that he composed on the subject.[38] Verri did not repeat the mistake, and in general steered away from politically sensitive subjects. He remained, however, a source of tension and turbulence within the administration, critical of official decisions, and feuding with some of his colleagues, in particular of course with his former client Beccaria. In one letter of 1770 to Vienna, Firmian's irritation with Verri (who is not named) bubbles over:

> For some time now I have been concealing the impertinence of certain persons with connections here; in order to exalt their own mainly chimerical ideas, they put every effort into discrediting the ideas of others, publishing biting criticisms of measures taken by the government, condemning and ridiculing them.[39]

As to the second factor in Beccaria's good fortune—von Kaunitz and Count Firmian—it was crucial that the chancellor and the plenipotentiary governor of Lombardy were themselves committed to a crusade against the surviving structures of the Old Order and for the modernisation of Lombardy, and were on the lookout for men of intelligence, motivation and knowledge to serve them in this project. Beccaria's treatise on money of 1762 did not impress Firmian, and his early overtures were rebuffed. But the Austrian censors did not wield the censor's axe over *On Crimes and Punishments*. On the contrary, when the intelligence reached them (in 1767) that Catherine the Great was interested in engaging Beccaria to redraw the law code of Russia, they moved fast and created a chair in the cameral sciences for him in Milan. Von Kaunitz, writing to Firmian in 1767, voiced his concern lest the government lose

> a man who is not only well furnished with knowledge, but who would appear, *at least on the basis of his book,* to be well used to thinking; and this is particularly worrying, given the dearth of thinking men and philosophers in the provinces.[40]

Beccaria repaid them handsomely. The pioneer of penal reform, famous the world over for a work of originality, imagination, passion and humanity, was a productive, loyal—and docile—servant of the Austrian empire for more than two decades.

Argument against the Death Penalty[1]

.
.
.

Chapter 28, on the death penalty, is the longest chapter in *On Crimes and Punishments*. It is the only one devoted specifically to this subject, and it comes about two-thirds of the way through. There are forty-seven chapters in all, together with a 'Note to the Reader' and an introduction. What are the implications of this arrangement?

Beccaria's treatise was a broadside against the whole system of criminal justice, the penal code and the way it was administered by judges and magistrates. The death penalty was not his sole target, but it was at the acme of the structure of punishments. As such it represented all that was wrong with the existing criminal law. Beccaria was very much aware that a critique of the death penalty (as distinct from, for example, the advocacy of proportionality between crimes and punishments) would be novel, highly provocative and difficult to clinch. He needed to prepare the ground with care. We find him in the preceding chapters laying down the foundations of an argument that would culminate in the displacement of the death penalty from the top rung of the ladder of punishments. Chapter 28, in other words, cannot be read in isolation from the earlier chapters, which provide the building blocks for his argument therein.[2]

The argument against the death penalty which Beccaria regarded as decisive is derived from his version of Social Contract theory.[3] The theory enters first in the 'Note to the Reader', and is never far from his discussion. The abuses of the existing system of criminal justice, which are roundly attacked from the very beginning,[4] are the creation of human convention, that is to say, legislation supplemented by jurisprudential opinion, which have strayed from the 'enactments' of the Social Contract. The quarrel is not with divine law or natural law, but with positive law, which is distinct from the other two categories and must be treated separately.[5]

There follows, in the 'Introduction', a statement of the fundamental principle which the laws representing the contracts made among men should seek to uphold, namely, 'the greatest happiness shared among the greater number'. What Beccaria meant by this is not crystal clear. Elsewhere he talks in terms of the happiness *of individuals*, and this is likely to be what he had in mind here.[6] In this, he lines up with his patron and mentor Pietro Verri, whose *Meditazioni sulla felicità* (*Meditations on Happiness*) was published anonymously in 1763, that is, in the year before Beccaria's own work saw the light of day. Verri wrote,

> The end of the social pact is the well-being of each of the individuals who join together to form society, who do so in order that this well-being becomes absorbed into the public happiness or rather the greatest possible happiness distributed with the greatest equality possible.[7]

Both Verri and Beccaria were influenced by Helvétius, who, with his *On Spirit* (1758), was instrumental in elevating an early version of utilitarianism to the status of an established philosophical doctrine. It has been convincingly argued that Helvétius is the unnamed philosopher to whom Beccaria, in the next sentence but one following his statement of the 'greatest happiness' principle, extends praise and the gratitude of humanity. His admiration for and debt to Helvétius are further emphasised in his letter of January 1766 to the French philosopher André Morellet.[8]

The compatibility of contractualism and utilitarianism has been questioned, but it should be emphasised that the latter doctrine was at a formative stage when Beccaria was writing. Bentham had not yet spelled out his principle of the greatest happiness of the greatest number and declared both contractualism and natural law theory redundant.[9] If there was for Beccaria a decisive principle governing the penal system, it was the avoidance of public harm and the promotion of private good. In any case Beccaria was not alone in his period in combining a (fully fledged) Social Contract theory with a (proto-)utilitarian position emphasising the happiness of the individual. Evidently the two in combination did not pose problems for him, and they appear side by side (as well as singly) throughout his treatise.[10]

The first three chapters, on punishment, are basic to the argument. Above all they provide a preliminary statement of Beccaria's minimalist view of punishment that will figure in chapter 28. In summary form, it is this: 'a criminal justice system is justified if and only if it results in the least possible evil'.[11]

Punishment has its origin in the Social Contract. Beccaria, unlike Grotius, does not locate punishment in the State of Nature,[12] although, against Hobbes, he does not rule out the existence of 'duties and obligations' in that state. This is one of the very few explicit references to predecessors or contemporaries.[13] Otherwise, his position bears some resemblance to that of Hobbes: in the State of Nature men were free and independent, but their freedom was of dubious value to them because of the constant state of war.[14] In Beccaria's account men gave up a portion of that freedom (the smallest portion that they could) out of necessity, in the pursuit of security and tranquillity. The sum of these mini-portions is the right to punish. The Social Contract places an obligation on both parties, individual and society, that is, its representatives, sovereign or legislature: the latter is bound to protect citizens against the despotism and private usurpations of individuals.[15] Anything that goes beyond that end is not a matter of right, or justice, but an abuse. In another formulation (echoing Montesquieu), Beccaria labels punishment which is not necessary as tyrannous. Extreme punishment is useless.

The term 'useless' (also 'extreme punishment') remains for the moment unexplained. For enlightenment, we can turn to chapters 11–12, on public peace and on the purpose of punishment, respectively. In chapter 11, 'useful' is linked with 'necessary' and 'just'. The three terms are not of course identical in sense,[16] but are very closely associated in Beccaria's argument, and all derive their meaning from the Social Contract. In this same chapter, and for the first time, the death penalty enters the discussion, rather unexpectedly, in the context of brawls, revels and fanatical demagogy. The question should be asked, Beccaria says, whether death is really a useful and necessary punishment for the security and good order of society. Chapter 12 points the way to his answer in a short, sharp statement, in which he dismisses the motive of retribution (the punishment of an offender simply because he has offended, independent of any notion of utility),[17] and states categorically that the end of punishment is prevention (of additional crimes committed by an offender) and deterrence (of others from committing crimes). In chapter 28, Beccaria will face down the traditional, accepted answer to this question in relation to the death penalty (namely that it does successfully deter), and reply in the negative: the death penalty is not efficacious as a deterrent. Hence it is neither 'necessary' nor 'useful'.

Chapter 6, on proportionality as between crimes and punishments, provides another crucial stepping-stone on the way to chapter 28. This doctrine has clear implications for the plenitude of minor offences that in Beccaria's day were punished by death. The purpose of punishment as a deterrent is worked into the argument: if an equal punishment is laid down for two crimes which damage society unequally, men will not have a stronger deterrent against committing the greater crime. The way forward is to make a scale of offences with punishments to match, bearing in mind the Social Contract, which represents men's need to come together, and the criterion for ranking the gravity of crimes, namely the degree of damage done to society.

Another thread leading into chapter 28 is the criticism of judges, magistrates and jurisconsults, which occurs with some regularity. The judiciary is put firmly in its place as early as chapters 3 and 4: magistrates are there to impose the law, not interpret it; their task is simply to confirm or deny the facts of the case. Weak and corrupt judges have established 'petty tyrannies', which have brought suffering to the innocent. Right-minded citizens are urged to challenge those who misuse their authority. In the case of the jurisconsults, Beccaria goes for the jugular: 'It would be a happy nation in which law was not a profession.'[18] After all this groundwork, the reader will be better prepared for the visceral attack on the judiciary in the rhetorical outbursts of chapter 28, some of which, but not all, are put in the mouths of fictional spectators and lower-class citizens who are weighing up the options between criminality and going straight.

Finally, chapter 27 on leniency in punishment serves as a curtain-raiser for chapter 28. The first substantive sentence of chapter 27 goes to the heart of the matter: 'One of the most effective brakes on crime is not the harshness of its punishment, but the certainty of it.' Deterrence is the end of punishment, but this is not achieved by severity, unless we mean by this the severity of a judge in enforcing the law, but that, to be useful to the cause of virtue, must be accompanied by a lenient code of laws:[19]

> For a punishment to achieve its end, it is enough that the evil of the penalty be greater than the good that comes from the crime, and in any calculation of the evil there must be included the certainty of the punishment and the loss of the good that the crime might produce. Anything more than this is superfluous and therefore tyrannous.

Ferocious penalties merely provoke and justify inhuman crimes. 'The same brutal spirit that guided the hand of the lawgiver also moved the parricide's and the assassin's.' This incendiary language softens up the reader for Beccaria's dramatic characterisation of the execution of a citizen, in chapter 28, first as 'war', and later as 'public murder'. The two chapters taken together constitute a powerful attack on severe punishments, their supposed necessity, utility and justice.

And so to chapter 28.

Chapter 28 in Outline

This pointless profusion ['inutile prodigalità'] of punishments, which have never made men any better, has driven me to examine whether the death penalty really is useful and just in a government that is well administered.

This dense opening sentence of chapter 28 needs unpacking. 'Useful' and 'just', along with 'necessary' (as we have seen) are general, desirable properties of punishment.[20] 'Questa prodigalità', here labelled 'useless', carries the charge that punishments, in the here and now, are excessive in both quantity and kind, and have no rationality behind them. The present penal system is 'useless' in as much as it does not achieve the proper end of punishment, to make men better. This is the main thrust of the argument in chapter 28: that harsh punishment, specifically the death penalty, does not make people more virtuous, in the sense that it does not turn them away from crime.[21] That is the true end of punishment—(simply) to deter and prevent. Beccaria is advocating a radical conception of punishment, which sees its purpose as strictly limited. In the words of Philippe Audegean, he 'defines punishment as a legal form of violence which, as such, can only be justified in negative terms: legitimate only if it reduces the overall rate of violence in society at large.'[22] Beccaria sidesteps the other putative ends of punishment that were put forward by a succession of natural jurists from Grotius on (having put paid to retribution earlier, in chapter 12).

The clause 'which have never made men better' has a second programmatic function in that it anticipates an argument from history. There are two historical interventions in the chapter. In one, Beccaria maintains that over the centuries men have not been turned away from crime by the presence of the death penalty (nor, for that matter has its absence, which is rare, made a difference); in the other, he claims that the apparent near universality of the death penalty in the course of history is not a good argument for its retention, serving merely to underline the errors into which humanity has fallen. Beccaria does not set much store by such arguments, and he gives them only a minor role. He may be expecting his critics to employ them, and for this reason moves to neutralise their impact.

Finally, Beccaria asks whether the death penalty can be useful and just 'in a government that is well administered': this is an important qualification, and anticipates the discussion that will follow shortly about exceptional cases where the death of a citizen might be considered justified.

After the opening salvo, Beccaria moves on rapidly to pose the question, 'By what right do men think they are entitled to butcher their fellow men?' His answer is that no person or institution has the right to inflict the death penalty. No such right could have been included in the Social Contract. In the passage from the State of Nature to society individuals gave up a small part of their liberties to a sovereign-legislator, but the abandonment of their right to self-preservation by the law of nature was not part of the package. This proposition, besides, cannot be reconciled with the denial of a right to kill oneself.[23]

A succession of thinkers in the contractualist tradition (Grotius, Hobbes, Locke, Vattel, Helvétius and Rousseau, among others) had insisted on the right of self-preservation.[24] As Hobbes put it in *Leviathan*,[25]

> A Covenant not to defend my selfe from force, by force, is always voyd. For (as I have shewed before[26]) no man can transferre, or lay down his Right to save himselfe from Death, Wounds, and Imprisonment (the avoiding whereof is the onely End of laying down any Right).

Specifically, the right to resist could not be abandoned in the Covenant:

> and therefore the promise of not resisting force, in no Covenant transferreth any right; nor is it obliging ... This is granted to be true by all men, in that they lead Criminals to Execution, and Prison, with armed men, notwithstanding that such Criminals have consented to the Law, by which they are condemned.

It is characteristic of Beccaria that he does not discuss the various accounts of the Social Contract by preceding authorities, let alone adjudicate between them; nor for that matter does he himself set out a comprehensive account of the Contract.[27] What he presents is a message stripped down to its dramatic essentials: an outright rejection of the idea that a right to kill was carried over from the State of Nature into the society or commonwealth, and a reinterpretation of the Social Contract in terms of necessity and utility. It was necessity, the urgent need for greater security, that forced humans to come together in society. In doing so, they bargained away the smallest possible portion of their liberty, and that bare minimum fell far short of conceding their most valuable possession, the right to life.

The upshot is that the execution of a citizen is an act of 'war'. Here Beccaria was in open conflict with Rousseau (though he does not say so); and the recently published *Social Contract* would certainly have been on his desk. Rousseau had written that a criminal was at war with the State, not vice versa:

> Besides, every evil-doer who attacks social right becomes a rebel and a traitor to the fatherland for his crimes, by violating its laws he ceases to be a member of it, and even enters into war with it. Then the preservation of the State is incompatible with his own, one of the two has to perish, and when the guilty man is put to death, it is less as a citizen than as an enemy. The proceedings, the judgement are the proofs and declaration that he has broken the social treaty, and consequently is no longer a member of the State. Now, since he recognised himself as one, at the very least by residence, he must be cut off from it either by exile as a violator of the treaty, or by death as a public enemy; for such an enemy is not a moral person but a man, and in that case killing the vanquished is by right of war.[28]

Beccaria now considers some exceptional circumstances where a case might perhaps be made for applying the death penalty, namely, if society was in upheaval and the government and the rule of law were in danger of collapse into anarchy and chaos.[29] For Beccaria, those would be highly abnormal circumstances, and the description of normalcy that he provides is intended to embrace established governments of his time, more particularly the Austrian regime in Lombardy which he was hoping would co-opt him into active service. It is important that Beccaria is not here admitting, or pondering whether to admit, *a particular class of offences*, namely crimes of high treason, as meriting the death penalty. Rather he has in mind *particular historical situations* in which there might be a case for capital punishment.[30] A second situation where a possible use of the death penalty might be thought 'just and necessary' involves an offender whose execution might be thought the only means of deterring others from crime. This is a false trail, a phantom hypothesis, for Beccaria will spend the rest of the chapter refuting the idea that the death penalty can legitimately be considered the only way of preventing crimes.

The way forward, the way to prove his point about the inefficacy of the death penalty, is 'to consult human nature'. What, in the realm of punishment, makes an impression on the sensibilities of human beings? What feelings occupy the minds of the spectators of punishment-in-practice?—and Beccaria is insistent that punishment be public if it is to deter. Are the passions invoked by the sight of the suffering of condemned men—primarily that of 'fear'[31]—appropriate, given that the prime aim of punishment is, and must be, deterrence?

That Beccaria's argument takes this particular twist should come as no surprise, given that passions and emotions and their contest with reason are a central concern of moral philosophy from the seventeenth century onwards.[32] But it is above all his focus on deterrence as the end of punishment that leads him to stake so much on the argument from human nature. He also clearly has a taste for rhetoric, which he indulges fully in the sections that follow. His hated Jesuit schooling, which put such a heavy emphasis on rhetoric, had left its mark on him.

The execution of a condemned man may be intense, but it also momentary, and as such is much less dissuasive and off-putting than the long-drawn-out hard labour of a man reduced to the status of a beast of burden. The passions of bystanders at an execution are as fleeting as the penalty itself, and the passions involved are the 'wrong' ones, those of spectators at a day out, or equally inappropriately, 'compassion blended with disdain'. When compassion threatens to take over as the dominant emotion, then we will know that the appropriate level of harshness in the punishment has been reached.

Beccaria's second suggestion as to how to arrive at the correct level of intensity in a punishment is that it must be sufficiently intense (and no more) to act as a deterrent. He then restates his conviction (for it is essentially a subjective judgement)[33] that perpetual servitude is more efficacious than death; this time he focuses not on the attitude of the spectator, but rather on

that of the condemned man facing death, or alternatively, the endless drudg-
ery and fatigue of hard labour.

At this stage, an argument that was never tight becomes increasingly frag-
mentary. We are first presented with a sophism. If the death penalty is effective as a deterrent, then it should be applied frequently, which however implies the frequent occurrence of capital crimes. So capital punishment cannot
achieve its purpose. It must be both useful and useless at the same time.[34]
This is neat, but would be unlikely to persuade those not already on Beccaria's
side. He then assesses the criticism that perpetual servitude is actually as
painful and therefore as cruel as the death penalty. This objection would
seem to have some point: there is good evidence that 'death by hard labour'
was a common enough phenomenon.[35] The first part of his riposte, to the effect that the pain of perpetual servitude is spread over a lifetime and is less
acute at any given moment, only scratches the surface. Beccaria may well
have felt that the second part is more persuasive, and it certainly fits better
with his central arguments: the point of the punishment is to scare potential
criminals, rather than the condemned himself. Thus this issue is settled, as are
others, including the riddle of the Social Contract itself, by reference to the
purpose of punishment as a deterrent.

After this, there is a descent into a series of episodes of lively, passionate
and incendiary rhetoric, with prosopopeia, used twice, a conspicuous feature. First, the stage is given to a poor man debating whether to turn to crime.
He inveighs against a justice system that is run by corrupt judges in the interests of men of power and wealth. He calculates that some years of profitable if
illegal activity, even if they end in one day of excruciating pain, is to be preferred to a lifetime of poverty and hunger. Such a man, Beccaria adds, might
even look to religion for 'easy' salvation in the end. In short, the prospect of
punishment by death will not dissuade him from a life of crime. In contrast,
the would-be criminal who is faced with the prospect of a life sentence of
hard labour will calculate (correctly) that it is better to go straight. Beccaria
does not afford this man the opportunity to speak for himself.

Beccaria proceeds to expand on his earlier accusation that the death penalty
is murder: it is public, legal murder, the very crime that the laws legislate against,
a prime example of atrocity. This is strong language. He is now speaking in his
own person, though claiming to be representing the sentiments of everyone.

'Everyman' is then given the opportunity to launch into a virulent attack
(in direct speech) on the judicial system, echoing the words of the pauper

whom Beccaria has 'consulted' a little before. This, Beccaria says, is 'appalling sophistry', but he still ascribes to Everyman the conviction—recalling the opening argument which is the kernel of his whole case—that

> men, in the deepest recesses of their souls, those parts which more than any other still preserve the original form of their primitive nature, have always believed that their lives are in the power of none, outside that of necessity, which rules the universe with its iron rod

The treatise ends (after a second, rather inconsequential, dip into history) with an admission of his lack of influence as a philosopher, and an appeal to the benevolent monarchies of Europe to reform the laws. This peroration is worth more than a passing glance. Is it in effect an exhortation to the enlightened king to seek counsel in philosophy, and more especially to listen to a particular philosopher, even though his voice, which is the voice of truth, might not be as loud as the raucous shouts of the crowd? Was Beccaria making a covert bid for a position as court philosopher?

Commentary

Readers of the anonymous work *On Crimes and Penalties* were in for a shock if they were expecting a learned jurisprudential treatise in the style of any previous writer who had treated the subject of criminal law and punishment.[36] This was a manifesto. The author was launching a crusade; his was a root-and-branch critique of the criminal law and procedure of the time.

The work was, besides, a pamphlet rather than a large tome after the example of Grotius, Hobbes or Pufendorf. The argument is cut down to the bone. Thus deterrence or prevention is the only end of punishment that Beccaria considers in any detail, and it dominates his discourse, in chapter 28 as elsewhere.[37] This means, for example, that he will show no interest in an economic argument for the penalty of hard labour which is his preferred substitute for the death penalty: namely, that the execution of criminals was wasteful of human manpower, which might be usefully employed on public works.

Beccaria does not engage in debate with his predecessors. Various eminent thinkers had philosophised about the Social Contract, but Beccaria gives exclusive coverage to his own theory, without, however, setting it out in any detail. There is one small exception: Hobbes is mildly chided by name in the preface for his alleged denial of the existence of 'duties and obligations' in the State of Nature. In general, Beccaria very rarely mentions, let alone cites, authorities. Again there is one exception (apart from Hobbes): Montesquieu. Beccaria pays him a compliment early on, while observing that he has not followed the path of the 'immortal president' at every turn. He leaves it to the reader 'to distinguish my steps from his'. Montesquieu, as it happens, had defended the death penalty, with a logic that foreshadowed that of Rousseau, but Beccaria leaves it to his readers to do the detective work here.[38]

The tone of the work is forthright, not to say aggressive. Heads are sent rolling left and right, those of judges and magistrates, legislators and jurisprudents. The language can be violent and abusive. Beccaria knows and exploits all the resources of rhetoric, with the end in view of making as great an impact on the emotions of his readers as he can. The justification of his approach is that he is fighting the cause of humanity. In effect, he is lodging a passionate appeal, above the heads of the ranks of the official judiciary, to, on the one hand, benevolent monarchy (and its high functionaries), and on the other, Everyman. Overall, Beccaria comes across as pessimistic about human moral attitudes and behaviour, but he nonetheless appeals to man's elemental convictions and emotions: he believes, or would like to believe, that ordinary people have a basic, innate respect for the sanctity of human life. Fierce resistance to his message was predictable from the bulk of the establishment, both religious and political, who had a vested interest in the status quo and were apparently unmoved by the atrocities and brutality of the criminal justice system. But it was to be hoped that the 'few wise men who are scattered across the face of the earth' of chapter 28 would act as a counterweight against 'the so-called wise men' who on a day-to-day basis operated the 'barbaric and useless tortures' evoked at the end of chapter 27.

Beccaria's sharp focus on his own theory had the consequence, as we have seen, that he was very selective in his argumentation. One striking omission is the argument from the irreversibility of the death sentence, which is perhaps the most potent weapon in the armoury of the abolitionist. It would certainly appear to be a better argument than the particular combination of contractualism and utility that Beccaria pushes hard. The Contract was not a historical reality, but a theoretical construct, and one can legitimately entertain doubts about any particular version that a philosopher or jurisprudent might come up with. This is not the case with the argument from irreversibility. Death is final, and there is little or no scope for the assertion that the guilt of the dead man is always certain. It is not as if Beccaria was ill-equipped to make this argument. He shows awareness, at several points in his work, particularly in chapter 16 on torture, that the innocent might suffer, and do suffer, under the existing system.[39]

Beccaria made amends (so to speak) a generation later (in 1792), when he composed, along with two colleagues, Gallarati Scotti and Paolo Risi, an *Opinion on the Reform of the Criminal Justice System in Austrian Lombardy with Regard to the Death Penalty*. For a cool, rational discussion of the case against the death penalty from the pen of Beccaria (and associates) it is to this text rather than to *On Crimes and Punishments* that we should turn. Gone is the rhetoric, the polemic and the passion. There is not a whiff of Social Contract theory, although the theory of punishment that emerges is still minimalist and utilitarian. The longest, most carefully composed, and most persuasive section is devoted to the irreversibility, or irreparability, of the death penalty.[40]

The context explains the difference. This is work to order, the result of a commission from the Austrian imperial regime. It is not the uninhibited outburst of a young man urged on by a group of highly caffeinated intellectuals anxious to establish their credentials as radical reformers. It is a minority report from within a larger committee, among whose members there was considerable resistance to abolitionism. And almost thirty years of lively debate and controversy had passed since the Beccarian bomb had detonated. Finally, Beccaria himself was a changed man as a result of his long-term service in the imperial administration. His inner convictions remained basically the same— the argument in many respects follows closely that of the original treatise—but the presentation is very different.

As already observed, Beccaria does not make a practice of referring to authorities. He does not get into a genuine argument with anyone. Similarly, he does not acknowledge his intellectual debts. So where did he 'come from'?

Beccaria was by no means making a clean break with the past, in particular, with the long tradition of scholarship associated with natural law theory and indeed Roman law. The Social Contract, which he revisits and reinterprets, is central to his discussion. He was undoubtedly steeped in the work of Grotius and his successors. Grotius was a pioneer in the field of Social Contract theory.[41] Moreover, the longest chapter in his great work of 1625 *De iure belli ac pacis* (*The Rights of War and Peace*) is devoted to punishment. He provides, in addition, an extended treatment of slavery, and his typology of slavery includes the category of slavery as a punishment for crime. This is a notion that Beccaria will utilise in conceptualising his own 'surrogate' punishment of hard labour. He consistently characterises this punishment as slavery. The concept had its roots in classical Roman law, which invented the category of *servus poenae*, penal slave.[42] There is a long sequence of learned commentaries on this term (and on variants such as *servitus poenae*) from the sixteenth century to the eighteenth, into which Beccaria will have tapped. We know that one of the books that he took with him when he left his family home under a cloud was a work of Heineccius.[43] When he later sold his library, he kept back Heineccius. Heineccius, a professional jurist, unlike Beccaria, provided an analysis of *servus poenae*. He followed Grotius in classifying slavery as the consequence of a judicial sentence, and he specified that serious felony was involved. Heineccius also had something to say about the utility of punishment and natural law theory—this too would have attracted Beccaria's attention, even if in both areas he took an independent line.[44]

Beccaria's work begins with a scathing condemnation of the laws of the Romans and the Romanist jurisprudential tradition 'that passes for law across a large portion of Europe'. But he himself was unable to shake off the shackles of the past. That said, whatever his intellectual background, his spiritual allegiance lay elsewhere, across the Alps. In the well-known letter to Morellet of 26 January 1766,[45] he traces his 'conversion' to philosophy to Montesquieu (specifically to the *Persian Letters*), and speaks with awe of the 'revolution' that Helvétius brought to his thinking. His roll of honour is a list of French philosophers of the Enlightenment: Morellet himself, Diderot, d'Alembert, Helvétius, de Buffon, de Condillac and, from Scotland, David Hume. To a different correspondent he might have admitted the impact on his thought of Hutcheson and Bacon, not to mention Voltaire and Rousseau. His exposure to the liberating, secularist philosophies from across the Alps is conspicuous in his argumentation. Under their influence, 'criminal law emerged desacralized from his hands.'[46]

Postscript: From Forced Labour to Penal Servitude

⋮

Preliminaries

Beccaria's work had an immediate impact on philosophers, jurists, politicians and church leaders in Italy and abroad.[1] The debates and controversies that it provoked concerned far more than the death penalty, for he had surveyed the whole system of criminal justice with a fiercely critical eye. To track the reception of his ideas on the death penalty in particular, and the mixed fortunes of the movement for abolition which he launched, would require another volume.[2] I focus here on Beccaria's surrogate penalty of hard labour, which has received rather less attention than his views on the death penalty and other aspects of criminal justice. As we have seen, the two penalties are closely intertwined in his discussion. Beccaria set up a direct confrontation between the death penalty and forced labour, from which the latter came out as the clear winner, as in his view the more effective deterrent. I am particularly interested in the fact that he conceptualised his substitute penalty as perpetual slavery, and in how this formulation was received and utilised by some of his successors—with special reference to Jeremy Bentham in Britain and Thomas Jefferson in America. I explore in addition the process by which the favoured surrogate penalty of the two Italian reformers (for Pelli as well as Beccaria advocated forced labour) evolved into the punishment that is routinely characterised as 'penal servitude' by contemporary legal historians and criminologists. I will naturally be focusing on the role of Beccaria in this development, for his work entered the public domain whereas Pelli's remained invisible. But, in addition, Beccaria, as I have said, conceptualised his surrogate penalty as slavery or servitude, whereas Pelli did not. Without slavery, no 'penal servitude'. Beccaria would seem to be a strong candidate for the (unenviable) title of 'Father of Penal Servitude'.[3]

There are two preliminary observations to make. First, the last remark should be qualified straightaway. The search for the paternity of a particular concept such as the one in question is likely to be unprofitable. Beccaria was a link in a long chain of jurists, philosophers and theologians who knew that slavery might follow a court sentence. He tapped into this tradition, and fed into it his own thoughts. What is worth investigating is his place in this tradition, and whether, and in what manner, his contribution influenced thinkers and politicians who followed.

As to predecessors of Beccaria, a major component of his penology, namely, slavery as a punishment for a capital crime, was already in place in Roman law, thanks to the creativity of classical Roman jurists of the second and third centuries AD, from Salvius Julianus in the Antonine period to Ulpian under the Severan dynasty. They invented the category of *servus poenae*, 'slave of the penalty'.[4] We shall see below ('Beccaria on Forced Labour', in particular at the second, fourth and sixth points) that Beccaria, whether consciously or not, had absorbed the fundamental characteristics of the Roman law of slavery. Further, in the post-classical period, that is, by the time of Justinian in the sixth century, the standard form taken by slavery-as-punishment involved hard labour: one might say that this was in embryo Beccaria's preferred punishment for the more serious offences.[5] Looking ahead to the late medieval and early modern period, we encounter (as we have already seen) a long line of juristic commentators who composed treatises on penal law in the Roman tradition, and discussed, sometimes centrally, *servus poenae* (and its equivalents, such as the abstraction *servitus poenae*).[6] Beccaria would have been familiar with Grotius's typology of slavery, which included a category of slavery as a punishment following a judicial sentence. He would also have taken in, among other things, Heineccus's definition of *servus poenae* and its characterisation as the condition of an offender condemned for a serious felony.

One predecessor of Beccaria who has attracted very little attention is the anonymous author of a letter dated to 1754, composed therefore a decade before the publication of *On Crimes and Penalties*, and addressed to the British prime minister Henry Pelham.[7] This document, purporting to be a response to the call of King George II for advice on how to deal with a perceived increase in crime in English society, set out the advantages of forced labour as against the death penalty, asserted its superior efficacy as a deterrent, calling it without apology 'slavery',[8] and advocated the imposition of slavery throughout the country as an appropriate penalty for a wide variety of crimes. The author cites Grotius precisely for his recognition that a criminal might be sentenced to slavery. The document, as far as we know, made no impact whatsoever on the government at the time or on policy makers, jurists and philosophers in Britain or elsewhere in the decades that followed. It was as if it had never seen the light of day. I can suggest one reason why the document might have been ignored or even buried (see below).

My second preliminary observation is that both Pelli and Beccaria made reference to their preferred alternative punishment as forced labour, not as imprisonment at hard labour.[9] Beccaria makes an exception for the most serious cases of smuggling, for which he prescribes 'imprisonment and servitude'.[10] They knew of course that forced labour entailed the confinement or imprisonment of the condemned. Looking ahead, we find that Beccaria, together with two colleagues, in presenting their minority opinion to the Commission for Legal Reform in Lombardy in 1792, made it clear that their preferred alternative to the death penalty was 'public labour' (also referred to in the document as 'perpetual slavery' and 'perpetual and public labour'), but recognised, in passing, the need for prisons to house the convicts.[11] The three signatories in addition declared that, in recommending the abolition of the death penalty, they were following the example set by Leopold II when he had been grand duke of Tuscany, in his law of 1786. And in fact Leopold, while he had replaced the death penalty with perpetual forced labour in the case of male felons, prescribed imprisonment for life for female felons, presumably because the physical demands of hard labour were considered too severe for them.

Beccaria (and Leopold, and Pelli) do not appear, therefore, to have thought of imprisonment as a central aspect of their favoured, most serious, penalty. How is this to be explained? Traditionally (and this was a tradition that can be traced back to ancient Rome[12]) imprisonment was not officially a penalty, but a temporary measure for the holding of a defendant prior to their trial or repayment of a debt, or of a condemned person prior to the execution of their punishment. In practice, imprisonment even for these purposes might be of long duration, especially but not only in the case of debt. It is now recognised, however, that in the early modern period, in continental Europe and in Britain, imprisonment gradually established itself as a judicial punishment alongside its employment for short-term detention. Beccaria and Pelli would have been fully aware of this development when they composed their treatises. The wider use of imprisonment as a penalty, and the expansion of the prison as an institution, were developments of the later eighteenth and the early nineteenth centuries.[13]

There is however another very relevant consideration. Beccaria (in particular) was concerned to argue that his preferred surrogate penalty had greater deterrent value than the death penalty *as a public spectacle*. He might for this reason have passed over the confinement element in the punishment. It is significant that in the one instance where he does explicitly prescribe imprisonment, it is for a crime, namely, smuggling, which he doesn't rate highly because (he says) it does not provoke public outrage, and by implication would not attract, let alone deter, a crowd of spectators. And to return to the *Opinion* of 1792 of Beccaria and colleagues, they were insistent that the prisons that housed convicted felons should be located in cities rather than hidden away in some 'corner of the province', in order that the punishment be visible and serve as an effective deterrent.[14]

Our pioneer abolitionists therefore make it clear that their preferred alternative to the death penalty was hard labour: in the wording of the document of 1792, 'public labour' (or 'perpetual and public labour' or 'perpetual servitude'). The impression given by the secondary literature, however, is that 'penal servitude' became at an early stage the normal term for imprisonment at hard labour. For example, it is employed in the standard English translations of Beccaria's treatise.

The history of 'penal servitude' is not straightforward. First, there is no exact Italian equivalent of the term 'penal servitude' in Beccaria. What he did produce is a conceptualisation of forced labour as slavery or servitude. The relevant expressions in Beccaria's text are not accurately translated as 'penal servitude'.[15]

Secondly, in the British context, the term 'penal servitude' did not enter official parlance until the middle of the nineteenth century. It did not appear in a statute as a recognised punishment, or in parliamentary debates, before 1853. On 20 August 1853, the British Parliament passed an Act carrying the title, 'An Act to substitute in certain cases other punishments in lieu of Transportation'.[16] Clause II of the Act reads,

Any person who, if this Act had not been passed might have been sentenced to Transportation for a Term of less than 14 years, shall be liable, at the discretion of the Court, to be kept in Penal Servitude for such Term as hereinafter mentioned.

On 11 July, the bill received its second reading in the House of Lords. The chancellor, Lord Cranworth, who was directing its progress through Parliament, is reported in *The Times* of the following day as being 'anxious . . . to leave, as far as possible, the class of those who would have been transported for 7 years, but who were now kept *in what he would call penal servitude* for a term of 4 years, in the same condition'.[17] Cranworth seems to have thought he was introducing a new term. If so, he was mistaken. The term crops up in a colonial context in a few documents from Colonial Office files, from the 1820s on, in connection with the ongoing discussion and controversy over the efficacy and propriety of convict transportation.[18] But the point to stress is that it did not enter official discourse until the statute of 1853. Once employed in that statute, the term stuck. It reappears in a whole series of statutes, which made various adjustments to the content of the penalty up until 1948, when it was abolished.[19] Interesting for my purpose is the fact that, even before the term made sporadic appearance in the colonial context, the jurist and philosopher Jeremy Bentham had toyed with using it, while it was avoided (I use the word deliberately) by establishment jurists such as William Blackstone. Both Bentham and Blackstone were avid readers of Beccaria.[20]

Thirdly, 'penal servitude' first appears in American law only in the second half of the nineteenth century. It appears to have been a direct descendant of the term 'servitude in consequence of a judicial sentence' (or equivalents). This category of servitude goes back to the time of Jefferson and the Northwest Ordinance 1787 which he promoted. Jefferson was also a keen reader of Beccaria. The year 1865 brought an intriguing twist to the story. In the Thirteenth Amendment of that year, it was laid down that 'neither slavery *nor involuntary servitude except as a punishment for crime whereof the party shall have been duly convicted* shall exist in the United States'.[21]

The point to note, therefore, is not so much that the term 'penal servitude' came into play, as the fact that it took a long time to arrive and become established.

BECCARIA ON FORCED LABOUR

Six points emerge from Beccaria's discussion. First, although he says little about the treatment that he envisaged for those sentenced to his surrogate punishment, it certainly involved corporal punishment and hard labour. The frontispiece of the third edition of *On Crimes and Punishments* (of March 1765) and subsequent editions, based on a sketch provided by Beccaria himself, shows Justice Personified rejecting an executioner's offer of three severed heads, and turning in favour towards a heap of tools and shackles that lie, together with the scales of justice, at her feet.[22]

Second, this penalty is characterised as slavery. Beccaria is completely upfront about this. For the most serious offences the punishment is perpetual slavery (*schiavitù perpetua*). He also envisages slavery for a shorter period (*schiavitù per un tempo*).[23] Slavery in perpetuity stands at the top of a sliding scale.[24]

Third, as already indicated, Beccaria does not use an exact equivalent of 'penal servitude'. There is no *schiavitù penale, servitù penale, servitù di pena* or *schiavo penale*. His favoured word for the punishment is *schiavitù*.[25] Exceptionally, he writes *servitù*.[26] No obvious distinction emerges between these two terms. In addition, he talks of the punishment as a blend of corporal and servile.[27] He twice uses *servigio*, which is presented as labour typically performed by animals, that is, beasts of burden.[28] The closest he gets to 'penal slavery' is 'slave of the laws' (*schiavo ... [delle] leggi*: see the end of this section).

Fourth, Beccaria knows exactly what slavery involves in legal terms. When someone is enslaved, he is no longer a person, but a thing (*una cosa*).[29] This faithfully reflects classical Roman law, which held that the slave was a thing (*res*). Again, the loss of liberty that is involved in his alternative punishment is a repeating theme in Beccaria. This too mirrors the Roman law doctrine, that one is either free or a slave.

Fifth, the penalty in question is a *just* form of slavery—what's more, the *only* just form. It is just, because the criminal has violated the social pact. In chapter 22, on theft, Beccaria talks of 'unjust despotism' exercised against that pact.

Sixth, to the question of to whom or what is the criminal a slave, Beccaria's answer is that he is not the slave of any individual master, but rather a slave to society, ('alla comune società'), having breached the social pact (again, see chapter 22, on theft). In chapter 28, on the death penalty, another idea is introduced: the condemned man is 'slave of the very laws by which he was protected'.[30]

Beccaria and Bentham[31]

It happens that a situation arose in Britain in the 1770s which prima facie was tailor-made for the introduction of the Beccarian recommendations on an alternative punishment to the death penalty, together with the author's terminology. In Britain, transportation had long been the preferred secondary punishment to the death penalty.[32] It is true that imprisonment appears as a punishment alongside its primary employment for detention, notably from the sixteenth century on, with the invention of bridewells or houses of correction for the 'undeserving poor' (such as prostitutes, vagrants and beggars);[33] and, at the other end of the social spectrum, 'state prisoners' (such as the conspirators against William III in 1696) might be punished with imprisonment, and for long periods of time. In the 1770s and 1780s, however, there was a rapid rise in the number of prisoners to be dealt with in ways other than by the gallows. America was closed to convict transportation from 1775, and Australia did not open up for this purpose until 1788. In addition, French prisoners of war began to arrive in numbers from 1778.[34] It is no coincidence that a bill was passed in 1779 establishing a comprehensive system of penitentiaries for the custody of convicted felons. The reform was stillborn. The scheme was considered too expensive, landowners were unwilling to sell, and governments were still hoping to find a destination abroad for convicts. Moreover, Blackstone's death in the following year removed a key advocate who had been able to keep the three commissioners appointed to execute the project from fighting among themselves—which they proceeded to do.[35] Eventually, Australia came to the rescue: the First Fleet sailed into Botany Bay on 26 January 1788 to establish a penal colony.[36] Thus the British authorities had the convict transportation system back again as the secondary penalty, and could shelve any thoughts of a national penitentiary system for the moment. The building and rebuilding of prisons continued, but at a slower space and on a much less ambitious scale than envisaged in the bill of 1779.[37]

The jurist who played a large part in drafting the 1779 bill, William Blackstone, refers to it in his correspondence variously as the Convict Bill, the Hard Labour Bill, the Felons Bill, but never as the Penal Servitude Bill.[38] Blackstone and his parliamentary allies—in the first place William Eden, a former pupil, author of the reformist volume *Principles of Penal Law* (1771) and now a minister of state—had it within their grasp to introduce a new vocabulary. We know from Blackstone's celebrated *Commentaries on the Laws of*

England (1765–68) that he leant particularly on two sources: Justinian's *Corpus of Civil Law*, and Beccaria's *On Crimes and Punishments*. Blackstone's citations of Beccaria reach double figures in Book 4 of his work *On Punishments*. Yet he avoids the language of slavery when describing the punishment of felons.[39]

Why did Blackstone and Eden bypass the vocabulary of slavery in 1779; why did they not take a leaf out of Beccaria's book? I suggest as at least part of the answer a sensitivity of the British, the British establishment, on the subject of slavery. As early as 1701, the lord chief justice of England, Sir John Holt, had pronounced in a celebrated ruling (Smith v. Brown and Cooper), 'As soon as a negro comes to England, he is free; one may be a villein in England but not a slave.' The ruling is evoked by Blackstone in the first chapter of the first book of his *Commentaries*. Blackstone frequently returned to the theme that love of liberty was distinctively English, and that only in England did liberty remain the keystone of the constitution. In the 1770s, British jurists and legislators were unwilling, in my view, to establish a penalty with a name that implied the creation of a whole class of slaves at home, as distinct from the colonies. That would have been controversial at any period; as it happens, the anti-slavery movement was already rearing its head at about this time.[40]

There was one English jurist who did not share the sensitivity of the legal and political establishment: Jeremy Bentham.[41] In 1778, he obtained a draft copy of the Hard Labour Bill, and rushed out a pamphlet entitled *A View of the Hard Labour Bill*, which he sent to Blackstone and the bill's other promoters. The surviving manuscript shows that at one point he used the term 'penal servitude', but then excised it, substituting the neutral term 'punishment'. However, 'penal servitude' does occur twice, in Bentham's own hand, and is allowed to stand, in manuscripts associated with *The Rationale of Punishment* (see below).[42] In addition, he uses the term 'servitude' fairly freely in *A View*.[43] He also touted a motto to be inscribed over the entrance to his ideal prison, reading 'Violence and knavery are the roads to slavery'.

In the preface to *A View*, Bentham says that he is putting the finishing touches to a work on punishment (from which he evidently drew in composing *A View*). This must be the *The Rationale of Punishment* (though Bentham's own working title appears to have been *Theory of Punishment*). This treatise has a curious history. Essentially composed in the mid-1770s, it was never published or even completed by Bentham. Apparently, it was never conceived by the author as a distinct work, but rather as a part of a longer introduction to the penal code that he was hoping to draft. Étienne Dumont of Geneva produced a version in French on the basis of the manuscripts (and complained mildly in his introduction of the author's lack of cooperation), as part of his *Théorie des peines et des récompenses* (1811). There was no English version until Richard Smith, a civil servant who worked in the Stamp and Taxes Office, produced one in 1830, two years before the death of Bentham at the age of eighty-four. In Smith's version, 'penal servitude' occurs twice and 'public servitude' once: it was therefore Smith rather than Dumont who accurately reproduced the vocabulary employed originally by Bentham.[44] No one, however, had access to this work of Bentham (thus edited by Smith) for almost half a century after it was written, that is, until the 1830s. Even so, there are indications that the 'approved' text remained that of Dumont, in which French equivalents of 'penal servitude' and 'servitude' do not occur.[45]

In general Bentham had no inhibitions about comparing condemned criminals to slaves, and describing the hard labour that they did as servitude. In doing so, he was fully aware that he was being controversial. In *The Rationale of Punishment*, we read the following:[46]

> Liberty: Under this heading there is little to be said. All punishment is an infringement on liberty: no one submits to it but from compulsion. Enthusiasts, however, are not wanting, who without regarding this circumstance, condemn certain modes of punishment, as for example all imprisonment accompanied with penal labour, as a violation of the rights of man. In a free country like this, they say, it ought not to be tolerated that even malefactors should be reduced to a state of slavery. The precedent is dangerous and pernicious. None but men groaning under a despotic government can endure the sight of galley-slaves. When the establishment of the penitentiary system was proposed, this objection was echoed and insisted on, in a variety of publications that appeared on that occasion. Examine this senseless clamour, it will resolve into a declaration that liberty ought to be left to those who abuse it, and that the liberty of malefactors is an essential part of the liberty of honest men.[47]

In sum, in Britain, Bentham stands out as a direct heir of Beccaria, to the extent that he was prepared to describe the hard labour alternative to the death penalty as slavery.[48] He even used on occasion the term 'penal servitude'. Bentham was a maverick and a loner. The grand plan for a model penitentiary which he pressed on successive British governments (and later tried to sell to the Americans) cut no ice with them. Nor did they pick up his vocabulary. As transportation dried up with the progressive closure of Australia as a destination for convicts, 'penal servitude' had a second chance of entry into official parlance, via the colonial route, and this time it made it.

BECCARIA AND JEFFERSON

In the new American republic, Pennsylvania led the way in instituting a penal system involving the abandonment of the death penalty in the case of most capital crimes and its replacement by imprisonment combined with hard, public labour. This gave way by the 1820s to the 'house of repentance', again pioneered in Pennsylvania. By the end of that decade, penitentiaries were falling into disrepute and the systematic contractual labour of imprisoned convicts was introduced, in the first instance at Auburn prison in New York. This system became dominant, especially in the northern states, and prevailed until the 1890s, when it too collapsed, under pressure from organised free labour.[49]

When in Pennsylvania the death penalty was dropped for 'robbery, burglary and the crime against nature', on 15 September 1786, it was replaced by 'servitude at hard labour'.[50] The records show that this was a sentence commonly imposed in courts of law in Pennsylvania in the 1780s and 1790s.[51] Servitude seems to have been regarded as synonymous with imprisonment and the confinement that accompanied it. We occasionally come across 'imprisonment at hard labour'. Later records suggest that this variant became the norm in many states.[52] The significance of the change is not transparent. It is clear, however, that in the early history of the republic, the judicial authorities of Pennsylvania at least had no inhibitions about using the language of slavery in this context. They treated it as synonymous with imprisonment and the confinement that went with it.[53]

This same period witnessed the conceptualisation of the condition of the condemned criminal as a form of servitude. The context was the promulgation of the Northwest Ordinance, a process that began in 1784 and was approved by Congress in 1787.[54] The Ordinance laid down regulations for the governance of the extensive newly-acquired territories north of the Ohio River.

The area was taken over from France by Britain in 1763 after the Seven Years' War, seized for Virginia by George Rogers Clark in 1779 and finally ceded to the national government in 1784. The Ordinance, among other things, prohibited slavery and involuntary servitude in the designated region, thus:[55]

> Art. 6. There shall be neither slavery nor involuntary servitude in the said territory, *otherwise than in the punishment of crimes whereof the party shall have been duly convicted.* Provided, always, That any person escaping into the same, from whom labor or service is lawfully claimed in any one of the original States, such fugitive may be lawfully reclaimed and conveyed to the person claiming his or her labor or service as aforesaid.

It is somewhat surprising that Article 6, which on paper excluded slavery, passed through Congress with the support even of the southern states and of its many slave-owner members. The article was added at the last minute, it was at odds with other articles and there was no debate. In any case, without an enforcement clause it was a blunt weapon. Once the significance of Article 6 was recognised, a prolonged campaign was waged against it from the regions where most of the slaves were held, the (later) states of Indiana and Illinois. The clause survived because Congress stood by it and applied it whenever a state sought incorporation in the Union. It gradually gained the status of a 'sacred text', which explains how it found its way into the Thirteenth Amendment of 1865, which abolished slavery:[56]

> Neither slavery nor involuntary servitude, except as a punishment for crime whereof the party shall have been duly convicted, shall exist within the United States or any place subject to their jurisdiction.

In the course of the debate over the amendment, Senator Charles Sumner of Massachusetts had suggested that this formula was out of date and should be replaced by one that used language taken from the French Declaration of Rights of 1791:

> All persons are equal before the law, so that no person can hold another as a slave; and the Congress may make all laws necessary and proper to carry this article into effect everywhere within the United States and the jurisdiction thereof.

This was turned down following an interjection from Senator Jacob Howard of Michigan:

> Now, sir, I wish as much as the Senator from Massachusetts in making this amendment to use significant language, language that cannot be mistaken or misunderstood; but I prefer to dismiss all reference to French constitutions or French codes, and go back to the good old Anglo-Saxon language employed by our fathers in the ordinance of 1787, an expression which has been adjudicated upon repeatedly, which is perfectly well understood both by the public and by judicial tribunals, a phrase, I may say further, which is peculiarly near and dear to the people of the Northwestern Territory, from whose soil slavery was excluded by it.[57]

There is irony in the fact that the very measure which abolished 'slavery' gave constitutional status for the first time to another kind of involuntary servitude: that which issued from a court sentence, or 'penal servitude', as it came to be called in the following decades (see below). For white southerners determined to subvert the new bi-racial social order imposed on them as the price of their defeat in the Civil War, the clause in question provided the legal foundations for the 'neo-slave' system which took over in the south from the 1870s to the 1940s: black convicts were forced to work in mining, industrial and agricultural enterprises, as part of the punishment for ostensible or trivial offences (labelled as crimes in laws specifically promulgated to intimidate blacks), under conditions that rivalled or exceeded the brutality and coercion of the pre–Civil War slave system.[58]

Thomas Jefferson was chair of the small committee, set up on his initiative immediately after the cession of the northwestern territories by Virginia, which worked on drafts of the Northwest Ordinance. We know that the legal sections were his responsibility.[59] The first draft of what was to become Article 6 was defeated in Congress (by one vote, on 19 April 1784).[60] Soon after (on May 7), Jefferson was appointed to the post of American ambassador to Paris and vacated his seat in Congress, and the passage of the Ordinance was left to others, initially Rufus King of Massachusetts, and finally Nathan Dane, also from Massachusetts. There is no doubt that Jefferson was the instigator and inspiration behind the clause.[61] What is interesting for present purposes is the resemblance between Jefferson's concept of 'involuntary servitude' as a punishment for a crime, and Beccaria's singling out of the slavery which followed a judicial sentence as a just, the only just, form of slavery. Jefferson was taking a leaf out of Beccaria's book. It is recorded that he copied large sections of Beccaria into his notebooks, and in addition harboured an ambition to redraw the penal code of his state, Virginia, along Beccarian lines.[62]

As for 'penal servitude', the earliest occurrences of the term as a judicial sentence in America are dated to 1870 (a case from Hawaii), 1871 (Virginia), 1874 (Missouri) and 1875 (California).[63] Thereafter it became the standard term for a sentence that imposed imprisonment and hard labour. It looks as if the Americans took it over from the British, who had themselves begun to use it systematically only two decades earlier. It is true that the antebellum period throws up one or two possible outliers. In a case of 1884 (New Jersey), there is a reference back to a case of 1856, which alludes to a sentence of 'penal servitude'. It is unclear, however, whether these were the *ipsissima verba* of the original judgement.[64] Six years earlier, in 1850, Daniel Webster, in the course of his famous speech in the Senate in which he pressed for compromise between the two sides in the dispute over slavery, made a passing reference to peonage as 'penal servitude'. So he knew of the term, even if he applied it inaccurately.[65]

Some of the detail of Webster's speech, which lasted three and a half hours, is worthy of attention for our purposes. In the first place, he held up the Northwest Ordinance of 1787 as a model to follow. Secondly, he delivered what might be called a 'brief history of slavery', in the course of which he credited Roman jurists with a typology of 'servitude—slavery, personal and hereditary', which included 'being placed in a state of servitude, or slavery, for crime'. Webster was a lawyer, but it is still striking that he was familiar with the Roman jurists' invention of the notion of penal servitude. Indeed, if we are to focus on penal servitude and see it as the progeny of a centuries-long development of penal law, then there is a case for identifying not only a 'Beccaria moment' in the mid-eighteenth century, but also a 'Julian moment', after the Roman jurist of the second century AD Salvius Julianus, the likely father of the concept of 'slave of the penalty'.[66]

NOTES

INTRODUCTION

1. This title is not the same as Pelli's, which translates as *Outline of a Disquisition on the Death Penalty*. In calling the work *Against the Death Penalty*, I am following the example of the editor, Philippe Audegean. His argument may be summarised as follows: Pelli's is not a genuine title; it is a general description designed to facilitate the classification of the manuscript among his personal papers. We cannot know what title Pelli would have chosen had he published the work. The advantage of the present title is that it reflects very well the content of the work and its character as a polemical pamphlet.

2. See Pasta 1990, and further n. 8 below; Audegean 2012; Audegean, ed. 2014 (= Pelli, *Contro la pena di morte*, Padua 2014); Audegean, ed. and transl. 2016 (= Pelli, *Contre la peine di mort, précédé de Correspondance avec Beccaria*, Paris 2016). All students of Pelli are immensely in debt to these two scholars.

3. It is possible, and even likely, that he had composed some preliminary drafts or made systematic notes before the date that he signals as his starting date.

4. Winstanley, *New Law of Righteousness*, 515ff. However, he advocates a harsh penal code, including the death penalty, in the later work, dedicated to Oliver Cromwell, *The Law of Freedom* (1652); see Corns et al., eds 2009, vol. 2, pp. 331ff.; also Bellers, *Essays about the Poor*, 102–4. See Rogers 1996; Reungoat 2012.

5. Cantarella 2007: 45–48.

6. *Solon Secundus: or Some defects in the English laws: with their proper remedies, by a hearty lover of his country*, London 1695; A Student in Politics, *Proposals to the Legislature, For preventing the frequent executions and exportations of Convicts, in a Letter to the Right Honourable Henry Pelham, Esq.*, London 1754. Solon Secundus, whose name recalls the great Athenian legislator and statesman of the early sixth century BC, has some trenchant criticisms of public executions on the grounds that they are inefficacious as a deterrent, here anticipating the arguments of both Pelli and Beccaria. I thank Wilfrid Prest for bringing this text to my

attention. For the preference of the Student in Politics for forced labour, which he calls (as does Beccaria) 'slavery', as a punishment, see pp. 12–13 of his tract

7. Natale, *Riflessioni politiche*. See Berti 2018.

8. Thanks especially to Renato Pasta, the greater part of the *Efemeridi* can now be accessed on the internet. On the *Efemeridi*, see Pasta 1997; Pasta 2002; Capecchi 2006.

9. Another line of enquiry, which I cannot develop in the context of this book, is the contrast between the views of Pelli on punishment and those of the 'Neapolitan School', of whom the most prominent members were Antonio Genovesi (1713–69) and his pupils Francesco Mario Pagano, and Gaetano Filangieri, all of whom produced major work on penal law in the second half of the eighteenth century and were firm believers in punishment as retribution, and the *lex talionis*. One can safely predict a spirited response to Pelli, had he published. The bibliography is extensive. See, e.g., Ippolito 2012, 105–27; Ippolito 2008, 157–222; Berti 2003, 473–502; Berti 2014.

10. See, e.g., Reinert 2018, 8–9: 'The short pamphlet remains one of the most famous and influential publications of its age, and certainly the most lionized work to emerge from the Italian Enlightenment, constituting nothing less than "the most widely read text on penal reform in the western world"'.

11. It is striking that what is arguably the 'best' argument against the death penalty, namely its irreversibility, is not employed by either Pelli in 1760 or Beccaria in 1764. It does appear, however, in the 'Voto' of Beccaria and colleagues of 1792. See here pp. 115–21.

12. See Audegean and Delia 2018. As the editors argue in their introduction (here I paraphrase), the origin of modern penal law lies not so much in the short work that appeared in 1764 as in the intense debate and discussion that it provoked in the decades that followed and thereafter. One might add that in relation to our present interest, the death penalty, Beccaria did not so much advance clinching arguments against it, as make its presence in law codes, and its application in courts of law, deeply problematic.

TEXTS

1. In the translation I have followed the text of the treatise (and the fragments) as presented in Audegean, ed. 2014. There is also the 2016 French translation and edition by Philippe Audegean, likewise noted at Introduction, n. 2 above. I refer to the treatise elsewhere in this volume, passim, as *Against the Death Penalty*.

2. Pelli has in his mind Jean-Jacques Rousseau, *Discours sur les sciences et les arts* (1750) and *Discours sur l'origine et les fondements de l'inégalité parmi les hommes* (1755). There is a parallel passage in *Efemeridi* (hereafter *Efem.*) 1.8, p. 119, 22 November 1762. Earlier in the same year Pelli had expressed his distaste for *Emile* (which he had not read): *Efem.* 1.7, p. 150, 4 July 1762. For Pelli's attitude to Rousseau over time, see here pp. 57; 86; 168n17; 174n4; 177n46.

3. Benedetto Menzini (1646–1704) was a Florentine poet.

4. Pelli here refers, first, to the arrival in Rome of texts from ancient Greece after the capture of Constantinople by the Turks in 1453, and second, to a plot against Pope Leo X by a doctor and five cardinals in 1517.

5. Pelli had been reading G. Buondelmonti, *Ragionamento sul diritto della guerra giusta*, at p. 535, and Montesquieu, *De l'esprit des lois* 10.3; 24.3.

6. Elisabeth (1709–62) ruled Russia from 1741, and abolished the death penalty by decree in 1753 and 1754.

7. For this distinction, see Heineccius, *Elementa iuris naturae et gentium* II, viii, § 158. 'Civil punishment' is understood as that imposed by positive law, 'conventional' as that to which one submits of one's own volition.

8. Heineccius, *Praelectiones academicae* II, xx, 1; cf. Pufendorf, *De iure naturae et gentium*, VIII iii, § 4, in *Gesammelte Werke*, ed. Schmidt-Biggemann, vol. 4.2, p. 762.

9. Pelli's source is Voltaire, *Histoire de Charles XII* iii, 303.

10. D'Alembert, *Mémoires et réflexions sur Christine, reine de Suède*, 274–75.

11. Cf. Heineccius, *Elementa iuris* II, viii, § 158, note.

12. 'illo trahite damnatos, quo non sequuntur . . . nulla poena est nisi invito', Pseudo-Quintilian, *Declamationes XIX maiores* XI, 6 (p. 227); cf. Pufendorf, *De iure naturae* VIII, iii, § 4 (see n. 8 above); Heineccius, *Elementa iuris* II, viii, § 161.

13. Properly Atilius, but the text has Attilius. See Livy, *Summaries (Periochae)* 18.

14. Vattel, *Le droit des gens* III, 3, xli.

15. Heineccius, *Elementa iuris* II, viii, § 160.

16. Grotius, *De iure belli ac pacis* II, xx, § vi, 2. There is some confusion concerning the second end of punishment, as between 'retribution' (in Grotius), 'security', as here in Pelli, and 'satisfaction', as in Barbeyrac's translation of Grotius, in Heineccius, and here, later, in Pelli.

17. Ravaillac assassinated Henri IV of France and was executed in 1610; Robert François Damiens's attempt on the life of Louis XV of France was punished with death in 1757; ten people were executed after the attempted murder of Joseph I of Portugal in 1758.

18. Plutarch, *Solon* 17.2–3.

19. Herodotus 2.177.2.

20. Stobaeus, *Florilegium* (= *Sermones*) 17; Plutarch, *Lycurgus* 11.

21. Ulpian on natural law: *Digest* 1.1.1.3; on force and armed force: *Digest* 43.16.3.9.

22. I, vii, § 182, note, p. 142 (cited in both Greek and Latin).

23. Cicero, *De orat.* 1.54.232.

24. Sigonio, *M. Tullii Ciceronis consolatio*, p. 848.

25. 'Multo plures extincti sint homines ipsa hominum saevitia et acerbitate quam omni reliquo genere calamitatis.'

26. Diog. Laert., *Solon* 1.2.

27. Herodotus 5.25.

28. The governor of the Low Countries, the duke of Alba, under orders from Philip II, had the counts of Egmont and Horn executed for rebellion in 1568.

29. Jan Hus of Bohemia was burned at the stake for heresy in 1415.

30. Montesquieu, *Esprit des lois* 6.16.

31. Montesquieu, *Esprit des lois* 6.12.

32. Montesquieu, *Esprit des lois* 6.9.

33. Livy 1.28, cited in Montesquieu, *Esprit des lois* 6.15.

34. Gellius reports that theft was lawful and encouraged among young Spartiates in order to 'make their minds keen and strong for clever ambuscades and for endurance in watching and for the swiftness of surprise'.

35. See *Efem.* 1.3, p. 90, 12 September 1760: Catherine Howard, fifth wife of Henry VIII, was executed for adultery.

36. What Pelli appears to have in mind, as Philippe Audegean has suggested to me, are other crimes in the religious sphere which are punishable not, as in the case of the first three crimes mentioned, by the ecclesiastical authority, but by the civil authority. Such crimes might include those grouped by the penal law of the Ancien Régime as sacrilege, such as simony, usurpation of benefices, profanation of churches, etc.

37. *Sic.* Cf. fragment 1, referring to Matt. 10:14.

38. Leibniz, *Theodicy* 3, 241, citing the same passage from Grotius that Pelli cites via Heineccius.

39. Pelli distinguishes *legge*, the laws, or legislation, of a civil society, from *gius naturae*, the norms that operate in the State of Nature.

40. Matt.10:14.

41. John 8:3–11.

42. Xenophon, *Constitution of the Lacedaemonians* 2; Plutarch, *Lycurgus* 17.5–6 and 18.1; etc.

43. See translation ch. 14, citation from Montesquieu.

44. By the principle of Talion, the punishment corresponds to the crime.

45. For the history of this saying, see Audegean, ed. 2014, p. 126 n. 6.

46. Heinrich von Cocceji on Grotius, *De iure belli* II, xvii, prop. iii, vol. 3, p. 186.

47. Cited by Grotius, *De iure belli* II, xx, § v, 1. Cf. on anger Aristotle, *De anima* 1.403a–b; Seneca, *De ira* 12.19.3. See the discussion on anger in Audegean's commentary in Audegean, ed. 2014, 39–48.

48. Ch. 9 of main treatise.

49. It is in fact Samuel (not Heinrich) von Cocceji, in Grotius, *De iure belli* II, xx, ad § xiii, vol. 3, p. 355.

50. 'Est jus quo quisque tantumdem patitur, ac fecit.'

51. Pelli is saying that it would be impossible to reproduce those circumstances on which the original injury was inflicted.

52. See fragment 1, here pp. 37–38.

53. The passage in Seneca, *De ira* 2.32.1 is already cited by Samuel von Cocceji on Grotius, *De iure belli* II, xx, ad § v, vol. 3, p. 338.

54. Seneca wrote, 'igitur fatebatur verbum ultionis pro iusto quidem receptum sed inhumanum esse'.

55. The reference is to Plutarch, *Dio* 47.8, cited in Latin and Greek in Grotius, *De iure belli*, II, xx, 2.

56. Lucretius, *De rerum natura* 5.1147–51.

57. In modern editions, this is Dissertation XII: Max. Tyr. *Oratio* 12.6. The text is cited in Greek and Latin in Grotius, *De iure belli* II, xx, § viii, 4, note.

58. Another text borrowed from Grotius, *De iure belli* II, xx, prop. iii, addition, vol. 3, pp. 321–22.

59. The full reference is to Samuel von Cocceji on Grotius, *De iure belli*, II, xx, add. to 44.

60. Cf. Montesquieu, *Esprit des lois* 6.19.

61. The correct references for Pausanias are: Pausanias, *Messenia* 17.4; *Corinth.* 9.4–5.

62. *Adv. Jud.* 3.10.

63. With 'his opinion' Pelli would seem to be referring back to Heinrich Cocceji, who thought that adultery should be punished by death. See fragment 3.2.

64. Boccaccio, *Decameron* 6.7.

65. See Beccaria, *Carteggio I*, nos 85, 89, 98, 188.

CONTEXT

1. For the historical background, see Venturi 1969; Woolf 1979; Beales 1987–2009.

2. In the struggle with the Church over its privileges, Richecourt had an ally in Giulio Rucellai, descended from an old patriciate family of Florence, although they did not always see eye to eye.

3. Cf. the brothers Richard, younger contemporaries of Pelli, who rose faster and went higher than he did in career terms. See *Efem.* 1.4, p. 66, 16 February 1761: Pelli comments that they were in a position to control the affairs of Tuscany at their pleasure.

4. See Venturi, ed. 1965, 258–300. See pp. 83–85.

5. *Efem.* 1.27, pp. 106–7, 2 April 1771. Siena was omitted at first but was then included in the following year. See *Efem.* 1.29, pp. 128–29, 17 July 1772.

6. Woolf 1979, 49, citing Caracciolo 1968, 85.

7. *Efem.* 1.1, p. 99, 29 August 1759.

8. See Rosa 1999.

9. See, briefly and succinctly, Beales 1987–2009, vol. 1, 60–63.

10. Pelli rejected at least one marriage proposal, and elsewhere comes down against marriage, e.g., *Efem.* 1.8, pp. 34–35, 11 September 1762. His attitude to women was conservative and traditional, though he was not immune to their charms. *Efem.* 1.8, p. 86, 26 October 1762; 1.8, p. 115–16, 16 November 1762; etc. See *Efem.* 1.3, pp. 6–7, 20 June 1760 for an intimate conversation with a woman.

11. E.g., *Efem.* 1.1, p. 70, 29 August 1759.

12. *Efem.* 1.1, pp. 11–12, 29 August 1759.

13. There was no salary attached to his job as assistant to the secretary of state. Finally, after much lobbying, he was awarded one hundred scudi per annum by favour of the emperor. He had expected more.

14. See, e.g., *Efem.* 1.2, pp. 52, 146, 168, respectively 4 February, 22 May and 31 May 1760. For his 'poverty', see, e.g., *Efem.* 1.2, p. 92, 16 April 1760.

15. The work spans eighty volumes and twenty thousand pages. See Introduction, n. 2 for bibliography; and n. 16 below. From early 1763, Pelli was keeping a record of his activities, reading and other intellectual pursuits, in parallel to his *Efemeridi*, in volumes, which he called *Filze giornaliere*. By 1802, he had amassed seventeen volumes of these materials. I have been unable to locate a copy of this production. The National Library of Florence has the index to the *Filze*, in his own hand, but not the text itself. See *Efem.* 1.9, p. 60, 21 February 1763.

16. Ancient introspection and modern autobiography are radically different, and there is a strong case for saying that the latter was born precisely in the era of Pelli. See Capecchi 2002 and 2006; Betri and Maldini Chiarito 2002; Pasta 2009, ix–xxxiii.

17. *Efem.* 1.1, p. 104, 4 September 1759 (Pelli purchased Montaigne's *Essays*, which he says he had not yet read); see also 1.1, p. 170, 28 November 1759; 1.1, p. 155, 26 October 1759; 1.2, p. 1, 29 November 1759 ; 1.3, pp. 159–60, 11 November 1760. For comparison with Rousseau, see, e.g., *Efem.* 2.10, p. 1,832^v, 11 July 1782: 'How much more I like my Montaigne! How much more naturally he

speaks of himself!' Cf. 2.10, p. 1,829^v, 7 July 1782: 'This latter became my favourite writer, my best teacher, my almost constant companion.'

18. *Efem.* 1.3, p. 88, 10 September 1760: 'Do I buy too many books? It's my passion'; cf. 1.9, p. 127, 1 April 1763: 'I buy books every day'.

19. *Efem.* 1.4. p. 15, 23 December 1760; cf. 1.3, p. 153, 1 November 1760, on weather forecasts.

20. *Efem.* 1.8, p. 30, 5 September 1762.

21. *Efem.* 1.8, pp. 64–65, 10 October 1762. He makes this statement just before beginning the composition of the dissertation *Against the Death Penalty*.

22. Mazza and Tomasello 2005.

23. For the date of the official announcement of the appointment, see *Efem.* 1.7, p. 8, 11 February 1762. He announced his abandonment of the work on the death penalty on 6 January 1761, *Efem.* 1.4. p. 29.

24. A comment at the end of the draft of his dissertation *Against the Death Penalty* is consistent with this statement: 'I have suspended this work because when I was displaced from the State Secretariat and moved to the secretaryship of the Pratica Segreta of Pistoia and Pontremoli, a post which gave me influence in criminal trials, it seemed to me to be imprudent to treat such matters.' See Audegean, ed. 2014, 63.

25. It is true that the reasons he gives in his diary entry of 6 January 1761 (*Efem.* 1.4, p. 29) for giving up the project are 'internal': he was not satisfied with his argument; and he feared criticism. An 'external' obstacle to the completion of the work, his appointment as a criminal law judge, is introduced five years later. I will argue below that 'external' factors intervened rather earlier than his appointment as a judge.

26. It is also reasonable to suppose that he would not only have completed the content of the treatise, but also polished it up in preparation for publication. He believed in achieving 'un certo grado di perfezione' in the finished project. See *Efem.* 1.3, p. 156, 8 November 1760.

27. *Efem.* 1.3, p. 175, 25 November 1760.

28. Recent additions to a succession of volumes are Audegean and Delia, eds 2018; and on Beccaria and Britain, *Diciottesimo Secolo* 2019. See Victor Hugo's reference to a monument for Beccaria (Jean, ed. 1979, 198: 4 March 1865): 'je serai fier de voir mon nom parmi les noms éminents des membres de la commission du monument à Beccaria . . . Elever la statue de Beccaria, c'est abolir l'échafaud.' One can only speculate on what the reaction *of Beccaria* might have been to Pelli's work had it been published before his own. Pelli's response to Beccaria's work was generous. For the relations between Pelli and Beccaria, see Timpanaro Morelli, ed. 1976, App. 2, 693–714.

29. We can add that Beccaria wrote a single chapter on the death penalty, albeit a powerful one and the longest chapter of his forty-seven.

30. For that matter, nor does Beccaria.

31. See, e.g., on the Jesuits, *Efem.* 1.7, p. 142, 25 June 1762; cf. 1.8, pp. 39–40, 16 September 1762, on the Inquisition.

32. Beccaria did work on a book on the 'Ripulimento delle nazioni' until 1768 and abandoned it definitively at the end of 1771. This coincides with the cessation of his lectures on the economy and his assumption of a career as a civil servant with the Habsburg administration.

33. It is unclear for whom the diaries were composed, if for anyone apart from the diarist. Clearly they were not for general public consumption. Pelli never (to my knowledge) refers to an intended audience, apart from himself—for he did read and reread them. Occasionally he drops a hint that someone else might have access to them. So at *Efem.* 1.3, p. 51, 12 August 1760, he expresses himself unwilling to talk about proceedings in the State Secretariat, on the grounds that he had taken an oath of secrecy.

34. *Efem.* 1.1, p. 114, 15 September 1759.

35. *Efem.* 1.3, p. 174, 24 November 1760.

36. *Efem.* 1.4, p. 29, 6 January 1761.

37. It is of course no easy matter, then as now, to come up with an argument against the death penalty that might be judged 'decisive'. Meanwhile it is worth pointing out that Pelli does not bring into play what is arguably the most powerful argument against the death penalty, namely that it is irreversible. See here pp. 119–20; 147–48.

38. *Efem.* 1.7, pp. 56–57, 1 April 1762 (italics mine).

39. Leopold of Habsburg-Lorraine became grand duke of Tuscany in 1765, and developed into just such a reforming ruler, delivering, in 1786, a comprehensive reform of the criminal code, which among other things abolished torture and the death penalty. Whether Pelli had anything to do with this development is unclear.

40. *Efem.* 1.7, p. 116, 1 June 1762.

41. *Efem.* 1.11, p. 107, 13 January 1764.

42. *Efem.* 1.11, p. 183, 31 March 1764.

43. *Efem.* 1.12, pp. 115–16, 23 July 1764.

44. And see his statement at the end of the draft of his *Against the Death Penalty* (n. 24 above).

45. The intellectual origins of the ideas that form the content of the dissertation are discussed in the next chapter.

46. It is true that Pelli and his friends discussed not infrequently human nature and issues of social morality. On the former, see, e.g., *Efem.* 1.3, p. 126, 17 Octo-

ber 1760: 'the nature of man-as-animal, his contradictions, vices, ignorance, etc. etc.' Pelli's thinking on these topics is a basic building block of his dissertation.

47. For criticism of the death penalty before Pelli, see Introduction; also Audegean's Italian edition of Pelli (Audegean, ed. 2014), 20–21, with bibliography.

48. For Montesquieu's views on punishment, see Ippolito, 2016; also the translation of this work by Philippe Audegean (2019).

49. This was not a true academy, but rather a group of friends who jokingly called themselves an academy. For fuller discussion of the group and Beccaria's place in it, see pp. 123–34. See now the important study of Reinert 2018.

50. E.g., *Efem.* 1.1, p. 135, 2 October 1759.

51. E.g., *Efem.* 1.1 pp. 9–10, 29 August 1759: 'my best friend'.

52. *Efem.* 1.3, p. 112, 4 October 1760.

53. Lastri also disappears from the diaries in this period. Pelli does not walk with him again (it seems) until 7 May 1761: *Efem.* 1.4, p. 189.

54. As Pelli reveals, *Efem.* 2.20, p. 4,529, 31 May 1792.

55. In a letter to his friend Perini of 7 March 1758, Lampredi wrote, 'In my present state I have everything I could desire. Three hundred scudi per annum could not put me in a better situation, but this of course depends on the good will of another. If you knew how much this vexes me. I hate the grandeur that is sustained by someone else.' See Timpanaro Morelli 1978, 153–98, App. 6.

56. Pelli's obituary notice in his diary is strikingly caustic. See *Efem.* 2.21, pp. 4,786–87, 20 March 1793.

57. *Efem.* 1.1, p. 135, 2 October 1759; also *Efem.* 1.4, p. 31, 7 January 1761: Adami survived the 'cut' in the number of senators from forty-eight to twelve, despite his low birth ('nascita piccola').

58. *Efem.* 1.1, p. 157, 27 October 1759.

59. *Efem.* 1.3, p. 4, 18 June 1760.

60. Timpanaro Morelli, ed. 1976, 621–22.

61. This woman may be a mere figment of Lampredi's imagination. But see *Efem.* 1.2, pp. 53–54, 7 February 1760 for Pelli's unrequited love for a singer.

62. It seems that Pelli was happy to join in the merriment. See *Efem.* 1.4, pp. 3–4, 13 December 1760; pp. 9–10, 18 December 1760.

63. Lampredi/Hilarion in another letter to Pelli/Verecundo does (pretend to?) find fault with historical biography, with specific reference to Pelli's work in progress about the life of Dante, although that 'criticism' would have been equally applicable to a biography of Machiavelli on which Lampredi was employed.

64. The works in question were *De licentia in hostem* and *De maiestate principis*. Pelli himself treated the subject of *ius in bello*—whether there should be limits to the exercise of violence against an enemy in war—in his dissertation. Both men were joining in the debate inspired by Buondelmonti, who opened up the sub-

ject to an Italian audience in his publication of *Ragionamento sul diritto della guerra giusta* (read before the Accademia della Crusca on 30 August 1755, published in the same year and then again in 1757).

65. Comanducci 1981, 257.

66. *Efem.* 1.1, p. 24, 29 August 1759; 1.1, pp. 63–64, 29 August 1759.

67. *Efem.* 1.1, p. 70, 29 August 1759.

68. *Efem.* 1.1, p. 25, 29 August 1759.

69. *Efem.* 1.1, pp. 18–19, 29 August 1759.

70. See *Efem.* 1.1, p. 5, 29 August 1759, for his role in Giuseppe's baptismal ceremonies.

71. *Efem.* 1.1, p. 20, 29 August 1759.

72. There follow nine names, including Pelli's own, cf. *Efem.* 1.1, p. 21, 29 August 1759.

73. *Efem.* 1.9, p. 2, 7 January 1763.

74. See Fratoianni and Verga, eds 1992, in particular, Rosa 1992: 87–102.

75. See esp. *Efem.* 1.17, p. 37, 15 August 1766; *Efem.* 1.18, p. 184, 4 June 1767 (a report on *mani morte* with documentation is handed to senator Adami); *Efem.* 1.19, p. 117, 7 September 1767 (the report is finally published through the agency of Adami).

76. Pelli has by no means completed the preliminaries to the diary proper, that is, the day-by-day account of his doings. In fact there is roughly three times as much introductory material to come, on his health, personality, habits, interests, and way of life: *Efem.* 1.1, pp. 24–100, 29 August 1759.

77. *Efem.* 1.3, p. 46, 1 August 1760; cf. 1.3, p. 50, 8 August. On this occasion, Marchese Lorenzo Casimiro degli Albizzi took the initiative. This institution had responsibility for the grain supply. The position in question cannot have been trivial, if it was held previously by a senator (Venturi) although Pelli dismisses it as 'a simple benefice', and underpaid: 'bringing in around 60 scudi'.

78. *Efem.* 1.3, p. 68, 28 August 1760. The ceremony of admission took place on 3 September (1.3, pp. 74–75; his colleagues are named here) and his tenure ended on 28 February 1761 (1.4, p. 81).

79. *Efem.* 1.3, pp. 98–99, 22 September 1760.

80. *Efem.* 1.4, p. 55, 6 February 1761.

81. See *Efem.* 1.4, p. 31, 7 January 1761; and see n83.

82. *Efem.*1.4, p. 55, 6 February 1761.

83. For the first reference to the secretaryship of the Pratica Segreta, see *Efem.* 1.4, p. 31, 7 January 1761, where the same Piccolomini comes up in a list of newly appointed senators, and is described as the holder of the two secretarial positions in question. Coincidentally, the previous diary entry records Pelli's abandonment of his dissertation on the death penalty.

84. Reautan had not long before been given a position in the State Secretariat comparable with Pelli's own; he was replacing cavalier Mozzi, who had been appointed at the same time as Pelli, more than two years previously. This fact may well have encouraged Pelli to seek high office.

85. *Efem.* 1.6, p. 88, 20 November 1761.

86. *Efem.* 1.7, p. 38, 7 March 1762.

87. *Efem.* 1.7, p. 8, 11 February 1762. His immediate reaction is that the salary was low, he was hard done by (and will therefore be enabled to ask for more in due course) and he should have been allowed to hold on to his position in the State Secretariat. However, he admits to feeling some guilt because of this. See *Efem.* 1.7, p. 10, 12 February 1762. The decision to deprive him of the latter post was in fact reversed, for a time.

88. As we saw (*Efem.* 1.7, pp. 56–57, 1 April 1762), Pelli dropped a hint when he was a little more than a month into the job that he had not completely given up the idea of resuming and completing his work on the death penalty. He was apparently yet to face any court case that might have embarrassed him. This suggestion of Pelli cannot be taken as an indication of firm intent to take up the project again, but nor of course is it a firm statement of an intention not to do so.

89. *Efem.* 1.27, pp. 107–8, 3 April 1761. Siena was omitted at first, but included in the following year. See *Efem.* 1.29, pp. 128–29, 17 July 1772.

90. Note that it was Pelli who was asked to provide an honorary inscription for the grand duke to celebrate the reform of the criminal law. See *Efem.* 2.14, p. 2,746ᵛ, 25 December 1786.

91. *Efem.* 1.1, pp. 65–68, 71–74, 29 August 1759. These entries contain a penetrating analysis of his character. Closely allied to timidity were melancholy and the hypochrondria of which he was also a victim. See also *Efem.* 1.2, p. 103, 26 April 1760; 1.3, p. 43, 30 July 1760; 1.5, p. 154, 16 August 1761; 1.13, p. 152, 9 February 1765, etc.

ARGUMENT OF *AGAINST THE DEATH PENALTY*

1. Hence my decision to discuss the content of his thought more or less as it appeared from his pen, rather than risk giving the impression that the argument is more orderly and logical than it is. The argument of the treatise receives learned, thorough and incisive analysis from Philippe Audegean in his editions of the work.

2. See *Efem.* 1.8, p. 10, 16 August 1762. He says he was going to revise it completely ('da capo'), correcting, improving and expanding it, with the aid of his priest friend Marco Lastri. When Lastri withdrew (see *Efem.* 1.8, p. 63, 8 October 1762), he resolved to do the job himself, in stages.

3. *Efem.* 1.7, pp. 116–17, 1 June 1762, with pp. 47–48.

4. Pelli in his diary is quite complimentary about *The New Eloise*, but comes down hard on *Emile*, as did the authorities in France, Geneva and elsewhere: *Efem.* 1.7, p. 150, 4 July 1762: 'They say that this book teaches pure materialism. Truly this is the age of unbelief . . .'; cf. *Efem.* 1.8, pp. 119–21, 22 November 1762: 'This book appears to have written with the sole purpose of reducing everything to natural religion. We have the book here but I have not wanted to read it, because I disapprove of the bad principles of this doctrine.' He goes on to say that if it fell to him to punish the author, he would have him locked up in a lunatic asylum. The entry ends with the admission that he very much respects Rousseau for his 'capacity, his method of reasoning and especially his eloquence', but not for the 'strangeness' of his ideas, and the 'barefaced arrogance' which leads him to advance 'the most impious and false opinions in the world'. Much later in his life, Pelli was prepared to grant him high stature, at least for his autobiographical writings (the *Confessions* was published posthumously in 1782), alongside Augustine and Montaigne. See *Efem.* 2.15, p. 2,784, 4 March 1787; 2.17, p. 3,267ᵛ; 27 January 1789, etc.

5. In the diary entry of 22 November 1762, he reports that he is at present reading the work. See *Efem.* 1.8, p. 122. He stopped writing *Against the Death Penalty* in January 1761.

6. See *Efem.* 1.8, pp. 131–34, 29 November 1762: 'an ingenious work, well-conceived, full of solid truth, if one excepts Book 4 chapter 8 in which he speaks of civil religion, and perhaps some other passages'; p. 147, 8 December 1762.

7. See e.g. *Efem.* 1.1, p. 156, 26 October 1759, on Montesquieu: 'I consider him the finest fruit of intelligence that has appeared for several centuries. He is, so to speak, my delight.'

8. See Audegean, ed. 2014, Introduction for a convincing advocacy of the influence of Pufendorf on Pelli. Although Pufendorf is not mentioned in Pelli's treatise, an entry in the diary proves, if proof were needed, that Pelli had been reading him. See *Efem.* 1.9, p. 6, 8 January 1763: 'Before this day, I had never purchased the work of Grotius *De iure belli ac pacis* and that of Pufendorf, *Del diritto della natura e delle genti*, although I had made use of these two authors at appropriate times. In the end, seeing that I cannot do without them and that I need to consult them on a day-to-day basis, I acquired them, in the translations made by the celebrated Barbeyrac.' In addition, *Efem.* 1.8, p. 96, 31 October 1762, appears to indicate that Pelli had been reading Pufendorf's *De officio hominis et civis*, in the translation of Barbeyrac.

9. Compare, still in the preface, the following passage: 'Man, as he is, is subject to all the storms of passions great and small, driven by a blind *amour propre*, by self-interest and by pleasure, vulnerable to the temptations of sin, infinitely change-

able in his thoughts and resolutions, scant in self-knowledge, the victim of injuries inflicted by perverse fortune or the malice of others, seduced by the appearance of the good and oblivious of the consequences of the bad.'

10. There is an unexpressed Christian assumption in this argument, that a man will be judged by the same standard as he uses to judge others.

11. *Efem.* 1.4, p. 29, 6 January 1761.

12. The civil/conventional distinction is taken over from Heineccius, who defines 'conventional' sanctions as those to which one submits of one's own volition, as opposed to those prescribed by positive law. See here p. 165n7.

13. In the judgement of Audegean, ed. 2014, Introduction, the section interrupts the flow of the argument and is misplaced.

14. Pelli is here contributing to a debate launched by Grotius in his *De iure belli ac pacis* (1625) and pursued by the Cocceji, Pufendorf, Heineccius and Vattel (among others). It is important for Pelli's argument that he refutes the argument of Grotius that punishment existed independently of all positive jurisdiction and before the establishment of civil law, and that just warfare came within the category of punishment.

15. This argument would be especially weighty with Catholic readers.

16. Pseudo-Quintilian, *Declamationes* XI; Hobbes, *Leviathan*, quoted here at p. 142.

17. Later Pelli will admit that exile, the physical removal of an offender from society, was not a realistic possibility as a punishment. See his ch. 12.

18. Here Pelli is following Heineccius.

19. Pelli substitutes 'satisfaction' for 'security'. He is evidently uncomfortable with this, as he immediately admits that 'satisfaction' may seem like revenge. But he will interpret the word solely as putting a check on evil, not enjoying someone's suffering. Grotius read it as prevention, and so will he. Beccaria, for his part, selects out prevention/deterrence, and is not interested in debating the ends of punishment with his predecessors.

20. *Efem.* 1.1, p. 114, 15 September 1759. There are echoes of this language in his ch. 12: e.g., 'a thousand times more profitable'.

21. Pelli says first that the dead man is not corrected, but his spokesman for the death penalty does not make this claim.

22. He first rules out 'public vengeance' as a justification for the death penalty. Vengeance is an obscene notion for Pelli. Here he concedes that some states permit private vengeance, for example through duels, but this is a provocation that can lead into a kind of continuous warfare.

23. *Efem.* 1.3, p. 174, 24 November 1760: 'This morning's conversation with a friend has led me to resolve to turn my hand to a dissertation "On the Penalty of Death", with the aim of demonstrating that it is excessive, unnecessary and perhaps unjust when applied to any crime whatever.'

24. See here *passim*.
25. Cf. ch. 5 of the treatise: we are trustees, not owners, of our lives.
26. Here, inter alia, he refers to Heineccius's citation of Oedipus justifying his patricide. Beccaria's citations, in contrast, are minimal.
27. The argument takes its inspiration from Montesquieu, who stops short, however, of ruling out the death penalty.
28. Pelli here cites Montesquieu, *Esprit des lois* 28.36.
29. Both principles are also enunciated by Beccaria. Pelli calls the first of them, proportionality, indisputable, but he is likely to have been just as firmly convinced by the second. The principle of proportionality was advanced by Montesquieu, though he is not explicitly credited with this here.
30. This point seems less plausible. One might argue in this way: there are two fears, (a) of death, and (b) of suffering. Both are natural to us. It is true that as far as (a) is concerned, decapitation and (say) the wheel are equal, but they are not equal as regards (b). So there is reason to think that a criminal would fear being broken on the wheel more than simple decapitation. Pelli does not make the (legitimate) point that, even if natural law gave us a justification to execute, it does not give us a justification to impose pain and suffering.
31. In Beccaria, such offences involve revolutionary or anarchical activity. Also highlighted by Pelli are crimes 'that bring shame to humanity'. Presumably he had in mind offences against religion and morality. There is brief treatment of these subjects in the closing chapters.
32. At the end of his ch. 14, Pelli revisits the argument of the previous chapter (and proof), to the effect that the penal system of a despotism is harsher than that of a republic, with special reference again to ancient Rome.
33. Beccaria's response to this point is simply that this demonstrates the ubiquity and continuity of human error in the principles and practice of penal law.
34. In the interests of public peace and in order to discourage slanderous accusations, and prevent martyrdoms for false causes.
35. Pelli has in mind here precisely laws deriving from relations men have *with themselves*; that is, essentially, the duty to preserve oneself. There are clearly many ways by which individuals might harm themselves, suicide being the most extreme, and, for Pelli, the only offence in this category that governments might consider punishing. I owe this insight to Philippe Audegean.
36. Strictly speaking, there can be no punishment of suicide, only of attempts at suicide—as the rest of the paragraph in question goes on to make clear.
37. As did Beccaria.
38. In a brief summary of his position on the ends of punishment in fragment 2, Pelli says the ends boil down to two, security and example.

39. Already in fragment 2, Pelli had condemned the *lex talionis* as 'excessive, inconclusive and so on'. He adds that reparation is not achieved by imposing on an offender the evil that he has done to another.

40. At the end of fragment 3.2, Pelli returns to this theme with the comment that the much-vaunted equality implicit in the *lex talionis* was utterly fanciful.

41. The same axioms appear in a different order in fragment 2.

42. The examples are taken from Greek and Roman antiquity.

43. Matt. 7:1; 26:52; Apocal. 13:10.

44. Pelli favours the clemency advocated by the New Law above the vengeance prescribed by the Old Law. The fragment ends with a citation from Tertullian *Adv. Jud.* 3 to this effect, with reference to idolatry. He returns several times in his treatise to the punishment of adultery, which he points out is punished in radically different ways in different societies, and in any case does not merit the death penalty. His final comment on the subject comes in fragment 4, over the cause célèbre of Donna Filippa Pugliesi, as recorded in Boccaccio, *Decameron* 6.7.

45. Cf. Beccaria's charge that the state would itself be committing a murder if it executed a citizen.

46. On Rousseau, see n. 4 above. There is a relatively measured judgement (for Pelli) of the 'powerful, modern spirits Rousseau, Helvétius, Voltaire, the Encyclopedists, etc.' at *Efem.* 1.19, pp. 86–87, 13 August 1767. In this passage he distances himself not only from these philosophers, but also from the theologians of the Sorbonne who have been persecuting them.

47. As Audegean suggests: 2016, xvii.

48. Audegean 2016, xiii–xviii, shows that Pelli had a close personal and intellectual relationship with Lampredi and drew on the latter's publications in specific areas, such as punishment and the right to war. Lampredi, like Pelli, tapped into the natural law tradition as represented principally by Dutch and German jurists.

49. *Efem.* 1.3, p. 174, 24 November 1760.

50. On this point, see Audegean 2016, p. xxx.

51. Philippe Audegean, however, writes pertinently (pers. comm., transl. mine): 'Probably the vocabulary would not be the same today, but the method which consists of defining the conditions of legitimacy of a society while starting from the hypothesis that such a society does not exist has not disappeared. Social contract theorists did show *definitively* that no society was natural, that any society results from a choice and, given that that is the case, that there is always a possibility of changing it. The consequence is that the question of the conditions for legitimacy of any particular society is always an open one.'

TEXTS

1. I translate from the text as presented in Venturi, ed. 1965, 258–300.
2. I translate from the text as presented in Romagnoli, ed. 1958, 735–41, n. 59.

CONTEXT

1. At the time, the city of Milan was the largest and wealthiest city in Lombardy, with more than 120,000 inhabitants; the population of the Stato di Milano numbered more than one million. See Reinert 2018, 48.
2. There were around three hundred patrician families in Milan: Reinert 2018, 74.
3. The early efforts of Pietro Verri and Beccaria to impress the Austrians were not well received. See Capra 2016, 87–110.
4. Beales 2009, 358; also 496, for a succinct summary of his measures in the religious sphere.
5. See n. 7 below.
6. On the (informal) Academy, see now the excellent and comprehensive study of Reinert 2018. Members of the group included, in addition to Pietro Verri and Cesare Beccaria, Alessandro Verri, Gian Rinaldo Carli, Gian Battista Biffi, Paolo Frisi, Luigi Lambertenghi, Alfonso Longo and Giuseppe Visconti di Salicento. They took names from Roman antiquity: Beccaria was Atticus, the faithful friend of Cicero, and Pietro Verri was Sulla the dictator.
7. Beales 2009, 357. Verri's enthusiasm cooled when he failed to obtain preferment from the new emperor. He was hoping and expecting appointment as the president of the economic section of the administration.
8. Verri had already encountered von Kaunitz in Vienna in 1759.
9. Voltaire famously intervened post mortem in the case of Jean Calas. See his *Traité sur la tolérance à l'occasion de la mort de Jean Calas* (Toulouse 1763). On Torriggia, see Reinert 2018, 26–32. On the death penalty in Italy, see Mereu 1982; Cantarella 2007.
10. Beccaria, *Carteggio I*, 192: André Morellet to Beccaria, Paris, 3 January 1766: 'un ouvrage fait pour faire écrire et penser doit être d'abord fort court, parce que tout le monde le lit'.
11. Voltaire, *Oeuvres complètes*, vol. 61A, 81: 'petit livre ... qui est en morale ce que sont en médécine le peu de remèdes dont nous maux pourraient être soulagés'.
12. Beccaria, *Carteggio I*, 348: André Morellet to Beccaria, Paris, 17–30 July 1766: 'Si quelque chose est capable de soutenir notre courage, c'est de voir qu'à deux

cent lieues de nous, dans un pays où nous ne soupçonnions pas que la bonne philosophie eût encore pénétré, il y a d'excellents esprits, des amis chauds de l'humanité et de la raison.'

13. From ch. 47.

14. His correspondence is quite voluminous and is a vital source of information. See Beccaria, *Carteggio I*.

15. Beccaria, *Carteggio I*, 219–28: Beccaria to Morellet, 26 January 1766; Capra 2016, 87. Verri was in Austria from May 1759 to January 1761, and probably had little to do with Beccaria before the latter's marriage in February 1761.

16. Capra 2016, 88, writes of the Beccaria family, 'for the whole of the seventeenth century they had held modest posts of treasury officials and procurators in the service of the civil and ecclesiastical authorities, and finally secured their objective of gaining admission to the patriciate only through the efforts and genealogical fraudulence of the uncle of Cesare, the collegiate jurisconsult Nicola.' Verri, in contrast, came from a family that was enrolled in the patriciate virtually from its foundation in the sixteenth century, and was the son of Gabriele Verri, a leading senator and official. There was also a very significant difference between the financial resources of the two men.

17. Verri failed to impress Firmian with this work. The breakthrough, in the first instance by Pietro Verri, came in 1765, when the latter was appointed as a member of the Supreme Economic Council then established. Another 'pugilist', more senior and of higher standing than Beccaria, Gian Rinaldo Carli, was also successful in 1765. Beccaria tried twice to follow his colleagues on to the Council, in 1765 and 1766, but without success. He was co-opted on to the Council only in 1771. See below, and for bibliography, next note.

18. For the cameral sciences, see, succinctly, Reinert 2018, 312–14; in detail, Tribe 2006, 525–46.

19. For his career in the Habsburg administration, see Capra 2017, 177–93.

20. See, briefly, Reinert 2018, 299–301.

21. See Beccaria, *Dei delitti e delle pene*, 219, n. 1 for the angry letters that passed between the brothers Verri reporting on the Paris visit and Beccaria's outrageous claim to authorship of the *Apologia*.

22. For a catalogue of the expletives employed by the Verri brothers, see Francioni, ed. 1984, 220; also Capra 2016, 104.

23. His main areas of responsibility included the grain supply, money, mines, weights and measures; to these were added commerce, roads and frontiers, factories and manufacture. See Capra 2017, 178.

24. At the end of 1789, following Joseph's reconstruction of the administration, he was put in charge of a department with responsibility for, among other things, the police, penal institutions and the codification of the criminal law.

25. See here pp. 115–21.

26. See a letter of Pietro Verri to Giambattista Biffi, a member of the Accademia dei Pugni, of 20 September 1762; also Francioni, ed. 1984, 224ff. According to Pietro Verri, 'the work' (he presumably means the composition of a definitive text) began in March 1763 and was completed by January 1764. The text was ready for the printer in mid-April 1764. Verri received the first copy on 16 July 1764. See Francioni, ed. 1984, 222.

27. Cited Venturi, ed. 1965, 122–23; Francioni, ed. 1984, 222–23 (Italian); Reinert 2018, 125 (English).

28. The letter was allegedly written on 1 November 1765, but the date is a false one. See the discussion of Francioni, ed. 1984, 222ff. It is pertinent to note, in connection with the issue of authorship, that subsequent to the break-up of the group, Pietro Verri, in correspondence with his brother, had critical things to say about the content of the book (including that Beccaria had plagiarised Montesquieu, Helvétius and Voltaire), and proposed writing his criticisms up for publication. Fortunately, he stayed his hand. See Francioni, ed. 1984, 220 n. 1.

29. See, e.g., his letter to Gian Rinaldo Carli of 3 February 1762: 'an eloquent man with a lively imagination . . . a head for figures that is sublime . . . a man of singular gifts . . . extraordinary power of imagination coupled with an intense understanding of the human heart . . . a deep knowledge of algebra, an accomplished poet, a mind equipped to lay down new pathways'. He goes on to point to his 'inertia' and tendency to discouragement ('avvilimento'), which might put a brake on his endeavours. See Francioni, ed. 1984, 226.

30. Alessandro Verri had composed thirty-four petitions in defence of men facing judicial proceedings. See Francioni, ed. 1984, 224, referring to a letter of Alessandro to Pietro of 7 November 1766. See further Capra 2016, 94–95. Pietro Verri had himself once held the post of protector of criminals.

31. See n. 27 above.

32. Francioni, ed. 1984, 223–24: letter to Pietro's biographer, Isidoro Bianchi, dated 16 April 1803.

33. See Francioni, ed. 1984, 135–99 for the first version of the text; also Capra 2016, 97–99. It should be noted that a case has been made for Pietro Verri (perhaps together with his brother Alessandro) as author of the preface 'To the Reader', which appeared for the first time in the definitive edition of Beccaria's treatise of 1766. See Francioni 1985–86, 274; also 'Nota introduttiva' (to section IV, 'Scritti relativi a *Dei delitti e delle pene*'), in Francioni, ed. 2014, 781–94. This position has recently been endorsed by Audegean: 2019, 33–34.

34. Beccaria, *Carteggio II*, 320.

35. The comments are from Luigi Cremani, a colleague on the Commission for the Penal Code, and councillor Emanuele Khevenhüller, cited in Capra 2017, 182–83.

36. Note, e.g., his (over-)reaction to the criticism that he received from his superiors for his report on the institution of a new market for cereals (in 1779). See Beccaria, *Carteggio II*, 544–48.

37. Beccaria, *Carteggio I*, 221, 26 January 1766. Of the three, Galileo Galilei (1564–1642), Niccolò Machiavelli (1469–1527) and Pietro Giannone (1676–1748), the last named, a philosopher and jurist, was the most recent victim. He died in prison in Turin for his heterodox views, in the lifetime of Beccaria.

38. See Capra 2002, 233–42.

39. Cited by Woolf 1979, 96, from Valsecchi 1934, 147n.

40. Venturi 1958, 19. Italics are mine.

ARGUMENT AGAINST THE DEATH PENALTY

1. The bibliography is extensive. An excellent starting-point is Audegean 2010, 37–170; and see notes below. A recent comprehensive bibliographical survey is now available in Audegean and Delia, eds 2018.

2. My discussion of the chapters preceding ch. 28 is necessarily selective.

3. Beccaria was familiar with, and in dialogue with, contractarians such as Grotius, Hobbes, Locke, Pufendorf and Vattel, not to mention Rousseau, whose *Social Contract* (of 1762) was published at precisely the time when Beccaria was launching his project.

4. The attack continues, with additional detail, in the 'Introduction', where reference is made to the savagery, barbarity, atrocity, severity and uncertainty of punishments. See the previous chapter at n. 33 for the argument that the 'Note to the Reader', which appears first in the fifth edition of 1766, was composed by Pietro Verri. The tone in the note is defensive. Beccaria/Verri? is hitting back at criticisms of the first editions, in the first instance the polemic of the monk Facchinei—which produced a lengthy (and anonymous) rebuttal from the Verri brothers. In addition to defending himself against the charge that he was anti-religious, on the political front Beccaria/Verri? was anxious to stress that the manifold 'errors' and 'abuses' in the law of his day were not to be attributed to current rulers, but to legislators and jurisconsults of the past, from Justinian in the sixth century to the evil trio of Carpzov, Claro and Farinacci (sixteenth and early seventeenth centuries).

5. This position, and the accompanying separation in Beccaria's account between crime and sin, predictably antagonised ecclesiastical (and monastic) opinion.

6. Note that in ch. 2 he writes, 'No man has made a gift of part of his freedom with the common good in mind; that kind of fantasy exists only in novels'; cf. in ch. 40, 'It is a false idea of utility to sacrifice the thing to the name and to separate the public good from the good of each individual.'

7. See Verri, *Meditazioni sulla felicità*, ed. Francioni (1996), 81, with n. 66.

8. Beccaria, *Carteggio I*, no. 28, 219–27. The case for Francis Hutcheson's *Inquiry into the Original of our Ideas of Beauty and Virtue* as a source for the idea is put by Shackleton 1972, 1,466–73. It seems that Hutcheson's work was read by the 'Fisticuffs' in the French translation of 1749. It is not unlikely that Beccaria in his letter to Morellet was selective as to whom to mention and to praise.

9. See Francioni 2017, 23–44. In his *Commonplace Book*, Bentham acknowledged his debt to Beccaria: 'Priestley was the first (unless it was Beccaria) who taught my lips to pronounce this sacred truth', cited in Shackleton 1972, 1,463. See also the letter to Voltaire of 1776: 'I have built solely on the foundation of utility, laid down as it was by Helvétius; Becarria [*sic*] has been *lucerna pedibus*, or if you please, *manibus meis*.' See Sprigge, ed. 1968, vol. 1. See now Schofield 2019, 65–74.

10. Cf. ch. 7: 'Necessity alone, from the confrontation of emotions and the opposition of interests, has given rise to the idea of common utility, which is the foundation of human justice.' Also ch. 19: 'a society cannot be called legitimate where it is not an unfailing principle that men should be subjected to the fewest possible ills' (a negative form of the greatest happiness principle). References to the Social Contract (or compact, or pact) are passim. The concept is central to Beccaria's whole argument, and not only to his critique of the death penalty.

11. For a powerful discussion of this principle, see Audegean 2017. (For an Italian version of this paper, Audegean 2014).

12. Beccaria comments in passing on 'the lack of any express sanction' in the State of Nature.

13. See 'To the Reader' for the reference to Hobbes. Otherwise only Montesquieu is cited by name, three times.

14. Described elsewhere as 'the physical despotism of every individual' (ch. 9).

15. Cf. ch. 4: 'a tacit or express oath which the united wills of the subjects have made to the sovereign, as the bonds necessary to curb and control the domestic turbulence of particular interests'; cf. ch. 22, on theft, which is characterised as 'unjust despotism against the Social Contract'.

16. In ch. 25, Beccaria writes, 'a punishment is just not simply because it produces some good, but because it is necessary'; cf. the statement in ch. 3 that 'extreme

severity' is 'useless', and *also* 'contrary to justice'; the sentence continues, 'and to the very nature of the Social Contract'.

17. Beccaria's argument at this point reflects Plato, *Laws* 11.934A (cf. 9.854D), as transmitted via Seneca (*De ira* 1.19.5ff; cf. 2.31) and Grotius (*De iure belli* 2.20.4. See also Plato, *Protag.* 324B. Characteristically, Beccaria doesn't identify his sources, unlike Pelli, who uses (and cites) Seneca. Seneca writes, 'For, as Plato says, a sensible person does not punish a man because he has sinned, but in order to keep him from sin; for while the past cannot be recalled, the future may be forestalled.' (transl. Basore). Beccaria also asserts that retribution clashes with a central raison d'être of the state, to bring peace to the community, because of the example it gives of useless and gratuitous anger. This argument will recur and be developed further in ch. 28.

18. See chs 4 and 14.

19. For the meaning of 'in the cause of virtue', see ch. 3, where the argument is that extreme severity of punishments might be, (a) 'directly contrary the public good and the aim of discouraging crimes'; if not this, then it will be at least (b), 'useless'; and in any case (c), 'contrary not only to those beneficent virtues that arise from an enlightened reason which prefers to govern happy men than a herd of slaves among whom timorous cruelty is rife'; but also (d), 'contrary to justice and to the very nature of the Social Contract'.

20. The first two concepts are joined in paragraph two by the third, and the three members of the trilogy will be shuffled thereafter.

21. It needs to be emphasised that when Beccaria talks of making people better ('migliori') he does not have in mind here (or anywhere else) the reform or correction of the criminal as an end of punishment. He is single-mindedly pressing the case for deterrence and prevention as the end of punishment. The earliest advocate of the reformative view of punishment is Plato: see *Protag.* 324B; *Gorgias* 525B; *Republic* 2.380A–B; *Laws* 854D–E.

22. Audegean (2017) credits L. Ferrajoli with this perception.

23. This might be considered a case of Beccaria throwing back at his critics, more particularly those of a religious persuasion, a weapon from their own armoury. See Ippolito 2017, 165. But note that Rousseau, by no means a member of the ecclesiastical establishment, had made use of it, without apparent irony, in his own argument. See *Social Contract* 2.5: 'on demande comment les particuliers, n'ayant point droit de disposer de leur propre vie, peuvent transmettre au souverain ce même droit qu'ils n'ont pas?'

24. For comprehensive accounts of earlier contractualist writers, see Francioni, ed. 1984, 20 n. 1, 26 n. 1; Ippolito 2017.

25. Hobbes, *Leviathan* Pt 1, ch. 14, p. 214.

26. The reference is to *Leviathan* Pt 1, ch. 14, p. 202: 'A man cannot lay down the right of resisting them, that assault him by force, to take away his life; because he cannot be understood to ayme thereby, at any Good to himself'. See also, in Hobbes's ch. 28, on punishment, p. 482.

27. Ippolito 2017, 163: 'On ne trouve . . . ni la netteté conceptuelle, ni l'architecture linéaire des grandes théories contractualistes de la politique moderne. Beccaria laisse le contenu du pacte dans l'indétermination . . . .'

28. Rousseau's general position on the death penalty is set out in *Social Contract* 2.5.3, immediately before the passage quoted above (2.5.4): 'It is in order not to become the victim of an assassin that one consents to die if one becomes an assassin oneself. Under this treaty, far from disposing of one's own life, one thinks only of guaranteeing it'. For discussion, see Ippolito 2017, 167ff.

29. Note that Rousseau holds that 'any evil-doer' ('tout malfaiteur') against the 'social right' is 'a rebel and traitor to the fatherland'. This is not the position that Beccaria is here considering.

30. I follow here Philippe Audegean's reading of the passage (pers. comm).

31. For Hobbes, the word is 'terrour': see *Leviathan* Pt 1, ch. 28, p. 486.

32. See James 1997.

33. Beccaria asks whether perpetual servitude was more likely than death to deter potential criminals, and answers, 'I would say that it is more likely to'.

34. The argument impressed Albert Camus. See his 'Reflections on the Guillotine', at 194; cited in Reinert 2018, 143.

35. Modern commentators have noted that in practice hard labour, in several of its forms, was itself an effective killer. See, e.g., Blanning 1994, 81–82, citing the high death rate of pullers of barges on the Danube in 1784.

36. One such was published in 1766, its appearance roughly coinciding with the fifth (and definitive) edition of Beccaria's work: Paolo Risi, *Animadversiones ad criminalem jurisprudentiam pertinentes*, Milan 1766.

37. Retribution is quickly dismissed in ch. 12.

38. Montesquieu, *Esprit des lois* 15.2. See Ippolito 2017, 169–70.

39. See also ch. 14: a judge's opinions and moods have led to the suffering of innocent people. A much more extended and elaborate discussion of the issue is to be found in Paolo Risi's *Animadversiones* (see n. 36 above).

40. The source of this argument is elusive. It is not to be found in Risi's *Animadversiones*, although the author emphasises the responsibility of judges to ensure that innocent people are not condemned on evidence that is not 'as clear as the air'. I have not found the argument presented in a text earlier than, intriguingly, a speech of Robespierre 'sur la peine de mort', to the National Assembly on 30 May 1791. See Robespierre, *Oeuvres*, vol. 7, 432–33, 437 (two slightly different versions).

41. See Straumann 2015, 192–93. Beccaria was also drawn to Grotius's neo-Stoic discussion of the distinction between punishment and vengeance, penal sanction and anger.

42. See McClintock 2010. Grotius's work received a new lease of life when Jean Babeyrac published a revised edition with translation and elaborate notation in 1724.

43. See esp. Heineccius, *Antiquitatum Romanarum iurisprudentiam illustrantium syntagma* (1719).

44. Heineccius, against Grotius and Pufendorf, held that the law of nature was derived entirely from the will of God. Heineccius also thought that punishment should be both deterrent and reformatory. Beccaria omitted the latter point.

45. See Beccaria, *Carteggio I*, 219–28.

46. Venturi 1969, 705–6; cited at Audegean 2017, n. 15.

Postscript: From Forced Labour to Penal Servitude

1. For reaction to *On Crimes and Punishments* in the short term, see Venturi, ed. 1965; Pasta 2016; Audegean and Delia, eds 2018. For data on executions in Milan itself in the Beccarian period, see Mereu 1988. The numbers of executions actually rose in the years immediately following the publication of Beccaria's work.

2. There is no shortage of such volumes. See, e.g., Hood and Hoyle 2015; Costa, ed. 2010; Garland 2010; Garland, McGowen and Meranze, eds 2011. For a succinct summary and evaluation of the arguments, see Ferrajoli 2010 and, in more detail, Ferrajoli 1989. The principal arguments for retention of the death penalty have not changed significantly since the time of Pelli and Beccaria: they are *quia peccatum* (i.e., retribution) and *ne peccetur* (i.e., prevention and deterrence), and they are just as indecisive and unconvincing now as then. The argument on the other side from the absolute value of the human being—which had its germ in Hobbes's perception that the raison d'être of the state and the positive law was to protect and defend human life—has never been universally persuasive, even among progressive and reformist thinkers, from Hobbes on. The argument from human rights has become more prominent since the end of World War 2, under the sponsorship of the United Nations, but the UN has never been able to impose the abolition of the death penalty on its member states. See Hood and Hoyle 2015, 14–22.

3. Cf. Esposito and Wood 1982, 36: 'Cesare Beccaria, Father of Prison Slavery'.

4. See McClintock 2010, for the Roman origins of this concept and later juristic commentary. I single out Salvius Julianus as the most prominent of the jurists who advised the emperor, Antoninus Pius (AD 138–61), from whose office issued the earliest rescripts concerning *servus poenae*. On Julianus, see, briefly and succinctly, Buckland 1968, 29–30.

5. Hard labour in the mines became increasingly prominent in late antiquity as various forms of the death penalty were gradually phased out under Christian emperors. The penalty would have involved confinement, but a custodial sentence per se was not a formal punishment in Roman antiquity. See Millar 1984, 128–47; Hillner 2015.

6. It is interesting that a work of 1770 in this line of commentators on *servitus poenae* refers back in complimentary fashion to Beccaria's treatise: N. Ypey, *Specimen juris universalis juxta atque civilis inaugurale exhibens quaedam de servitute tum in genere tum in specie de servitute poenae*, Frankfurt 1770.

7. 'A Student in Politics', *Proposals to the Legislature*. The anonymous author was well read, and shows considerable familiarity with the Fen country of East Anglia: I would like to think he was an academic in Cambridge. We can safely assume that Beccaria did not know of his existence.

8. At the same time, he recognised that enslavement of an Englishman was regarded as problematic at the time, as Bentham did later on. See here pp. 157–59.

9. See the important discussion of Audegean 2015, 47–68.

10. See ch. 33 of the treatise, and the discussion of Beccaria's treatment of smuggling in Reinert 2018, 163–67.

11. Gallarati Scotti, Beccaria Bonesana, Risi, 'Voto degli infrascritti individui'. For the text, see Romagnoli, ed. 1958, 735–41; my translation here at pp. 115–21.

12. See n. 4 above.

13. See, e.g., Spierenburg, ed. 1984; Spierenburg 1991. The classic work of Foucault (1975) has recently come under criticism, from Spierenburg and others, for its assumption that there was a relatively fast transition from the gallows and corporal punishment to imprisonment at the turn of the eighteenth century.

14. Gallarati Scotti, Beccaria Bonesana, Risi, 'Voto' (see n. 11 above).

15. The earliest English translations of Beccaria (Exshaw 1767; Newbery 1775) do not employ the term 'penal servitude', in contrast with the translation of R. Davies in R. Bellamy's edition of 1995, and that of Thomas of 2008.

16. Hansard 16 & 17 Vict. Cap. 99.

17. Italics mine. Hansard gives a version that I suspect is less accurate, but carries the same implication, that the speaker thought he was coining the phrase 'penal servitude'.

18. The first occurrence I have found is in Bigge 1822. See also Lang 1837, 18.

19. Colonial secretaries did not employ the term. Nor does it make an appearance in the various reports to Parliament of Lieutenant-Colonel Joshua Jebb, surveyor general of prisons, which culminated in his report of 1852. Yet Jebb was in effect the chief architect of the penal servitude regime. It was of course open to private individuals to innovate. One anonymous writer wrote a short tract advocating 'penal state servitude' (or 'state servitude'), under the title, *What is to be done with our convicts. Sketch of a system of penal state servitude. An efficient, reformatory and economic substitute for Transportation and Imprisonment* (Edinburgh 1851).

20. In the course of the debate of 11 July 1853 anxiety surfaced about the likely behaviour of ex-convicts after the abolition of convict transportation. The home secretary, Viscount Palmerston, was trying to convince members of Parliament that the system of ticket-of-leave, or conditional pardon, could be transplanted from the colonies to home. Palmerston described the condition of such people as 'qualified servitude'. Up jumped J. G. Phillimore, who represented Leominster in Herefordshire. He is reported as saying that 'he would be sorry to see any person in this country in a state . . . of qualified servitude. That was an expression that he would regret to hear applied to persons who walked the soil of England.'

21. Italics mine.

22. Venturi 1964, 707–19. See now McClintock: 2018, 206–36.

23. Ch. 22, on theft.

24. Ch. 27, on leniency in punishing; cf. ch. 28, on the death penalty. Beccaria's background in mathematics was being brought into service here; later Bentham would appreciate this and take the methodology a step further with his 'felicific calculus'.

25. See chs 22 (theft); 27 (leniency in punishing); 28 (the death penalty).

26. See ch. 33, on smuggling: 'prigione e servitù'.

27. See ch. 22 (theft), end.

28. Ch. 33 (smuggling): 'travaglio e servigio'; cf. ch. 20, on violence.

29. Ch. 20 (violence).

30. Cf. Rousseau, *Contrat social* 1.7.8: even those who do not obey the laws are protected by them. They are 'forced to be free'.

31. In this section I deal exclusively with what I see as the reception of Beccaria's substitute penalty in Bentham. For Bentham's well-known acknowledgement of his debt as a utilitarian philosopher to Beccaria, see here p. 182n9; 188n41.

32. On transportation, see, e.g., Shaw 1966; Atkinson 1994, 88–115; Devereaux 1999, 52–76; Kercher 2003, 527–84. On the death penalty in Britain, see, e.g., Beattie 1986; Devereaux 2015, 839–85; Devereaux 2016, 1–36.

33. See esp. Beattie 1986, 520–618 on 'the emergence of imprisonment'; also Innes 1987; Innes 2009.

34. Morieux 2019.

35. Enter, in the first instance, the hulks. These were condemned or unseaworthy ships on which convicts were stacked in grim conditions and from which they did hard labour on the Thames for from three to ten years or for as long as they lived. Originally an interim measure, the hulks survived down to the 1850s.

36. For the abortive and short-lived attempt to found penal colonies in West Africa from 1780, see Christopher 2011.

37. See Evans 1982.

38. See Prest 2010.

39. The closest Blackstone gets to Beccaria's 'schiavitù' is in the following passage: 'Sir Thomas More and the Marquis Beccaria at the distance of more than two centuries have very sensibly proposed that kind of corporal punishment which approaches the nearest to pecuniary satisfaction, viz, a temporary imprisonment with an obligation to labour . . . in works of the most slavish kind' (p. 237). This needs to be put alongside a problematic passage in Book 4.1.2, where Blackstone appears to designate both imprisonment and slavery as possible punishments.

40. See, e.g., Blackburn 1988; Oldfield 1988.

41. On Beccaria and Bentham, see Hart 1966, 19–29; Béal 2018, 61–64; Schofield 2019. For the influence of Beccaria on British jurists and philosophers in general, see, in addition to Béal 2018, Blamires 1997; Draper 2000; Dunthorpe 1999; Stern 2014; Duthille 2017. *Diciottesimo Secolo* 4 (2019) is devoted entirely to Beccaria and Britain. I have not seen any discussion in the literature of the points that I am raising.

42. See Bentham Papers, Box cxli, fols 88 and 120, University College London Library.

43. 'Servitude' was of course a common alternative to 'service', in the eighteenth and nineteenth centuries, of the kind that domestic servants, apprentices and sailors performed. In the context of the penal law, however, it is an equivalent of slavery.

44. Bentham Papers 1750–1885, Mss 4 = AJB037: 147–087 and 147–088 = Smith 2.10.5, p. 163: penal servitude versus voluntary labour. The sub-heading and favoured term is 'laborious punishment'; in Dumont's edition, 'travail pénal' opposes 'travail volontaire'. For 'public servitude', see Mss 5 = AJB393a: 141–087, Smith 2.10.8, p. 165. The expression is omitted in Dumont: again, the sub-heading and favoured term in his passage is 'laborious punishment'. The Mss show that Bentham actually wrote this. I am most grateful to Philip Schofield of

the Bentham Project of University College London for making this material available to me.

45. See n. 44 above. C. B. Adderley MP, who identifies himself as 'a plain country gentleman', in his pamphlet *Transportation not necessary* (London 1851) refers directly (on p. 61) to the relevant work of Bentham, but to the French version. He goes on to speak of the punishment of 'perpetual *incarceration*' (italics mine).

46. Smith, ed. 1.10, 'Popularity', p. 70.

47. There is a parallel discussion in Bentham Papers, AJB115: 159–37, under the heading 'Popularity' and the sub-heading 'Liberty'. Beccaria is cited directly for his assertion that no man has ever consented to subject himself to the death penalty. This, according to Bentham, is a part of his general argument that the principle of utility should be the basis of a penal system. See Mss 5 and 9, p. 3. The anonymous author who styled himself 'A Student in Politics' (see here pp. 163–64n6) also recognised the sensitivity of the British on the matter of slavery 'at home', and suggested a punishment of de facto slavery, slavery in all but name: he writes (in 1754; pp. 36–38 of his tract), 'But I find, where the shoe pinches, change the word SLAVERY into a term that has not so harsh a sound to the British ear, and all is easy. Let it then be carefully observed, not once to mention the name of SLAVE through this act of parliament; but in proportion to the offences, let the punishment be nominated short or long labour . . . At least let a state of BONDAGE be introduced here, on the same footing it now stands in our American Colonies.' Beattie 1986 cites p. 20 of this work on disproportionality, but makes no comment on the author's advocacy of slavery.

48. As to the death penalty, Bentham says that he agrees with Beccaria. See *Traité de législation civile et pénale* (1802). See too the fuller discussion in *Théorie des peines et des récompenses* (1829), where he declares himself against it in all but exceptional circumstances. These include the most atrocious cases of homicide; otherwise his exceptions are similar to those contemplated by Beccaria, but see esp. Trimaille 2012.

49. On the history of imprisonment in America, see esp. Meranze 1996; McLennan 2008; Manion 2015. For a comprehensive treatment of the reception of Beccaria in America, see Bessler 2014. Bessler, in some passing references to involuntary servitude, the Northwest Ordinance and the Thirteenth Amendment, does not make the connection with Jefferson.

50. R. Vaux, *Notices of the original and successive effects to improve the discipline of the prison and successive effects to improve the discipline of the prison at Philadelphia and to reform the criminal code of Pennsylvania, with a few observations of the penitentiary system* (Philadelphia 1826), 10. On the death penalty in America, see Banner 2002; Garland 2010; Garland, Meranze and McGowen 2011.

51. *Minutes of the Supreme Executive Council of Pennsylvania, from its Organization to the Termination of the Revolution, vol. XVI.* (Harrisburg 1853); see also *Pennsylvania Archives, ninth series, Vol. II, Part I, 1794–1796* (ed. MacKinney, Rule and Hood).

52. Stroud 1827, 108–12. There are three columns. The first is a list of crimes, the second the punishment of slaves and the third the punishment of white persons. In every single case, the punishment for the slave is death, and the punishment for white persons almost without exception 'imprisonment' for a period of time; a footnote states, 'imprisonment simply, means *at hard labour in the penitentiary*' (italics mine). On p. 110, we are informed that the death penalty is applied for numerous crimes in Virginia and Mississippi, even in the case of free white persons. Benjamin Rush, a pioneer of penal reform in Pennsylvania, in his attack on the death penalty of 1794, calls his preferred alternative penalty 'confinement and hard labour'. See Teeters, ed. 1954. Once contractual hard labour became the norm, this is reflected in the terminology of the sentence.

53. So in pardons issued by Governor Mifflin of Pennsylvania, evidence is produced in the form of a 'certificate from the Jailor' attesting that the 'term of servitude' of a particular offender 'is expired'. For examples, see works cited in n. 51 above.

54. Onuf 1987; Finkelman 1986; Edward Coles, *History of the Ordinance of 1787* (1856), 376–98.

55. Italics mine.

56. On the Thirteenth Amendment, see, e.g., Hamilton 1951; Kares 1994–95, 372ff.; Balkin and Levinson 2012.

57. *The Congressional Globe*, Thirty-Eighth Congress, first session, Saturday 9 April 1864.

58. See especially Blackmon 2008.

59. Similarly, Jefferson, a member of the small committee set up by Congress to produce a new code of laws in 1776, took responsibility for the law of descents and the criminal law, which 'fell of course within my portion'. See Ford, ed. 1914, 67–69.

60. Jefferson's draft of the article in question which failed to pass the Congress read, 'That after the year 1800 of the Christian era there shall be neither slavery nor involuntary servitude in any of the said States, otherwise than in the punishment of crimes whereof the party shall have been duly convicted to have been personally guilty.'

61. Note that Charles Sumner refers to the formulation of Article 6 in the Northwest Ordinance as 'the old Jefferson ordinance', while suggesting that it be superseded (because the reason for its creation 'no longer exists').

62. Jefferson writes on penalties, 'On the subject of the criminal law, all were agreed that the punishment of death should be abolished, except for treason and mur-

der; and that for other felonies should be substituted hard labor in the public works, and in some cases the *lex talionis*. How this last revolting penalty came to obtain our probation I do not remember.' See Ford, ed. 1914, 69.

63. 6 Haw.25; 21 Gratt.790; 55 Mo.101; 49 Cal.463. See United States Caselaw.

64. 38 N.J.Eq.128. It should be noted that the sentence of 'penal servitude' following the Fenian revolt of 1866, as recorded in the documents from the Fortieth Congress, was a British judgement passed on American citizens.

65. 'Peonage is a form of involuntary servitude that is distinguished from other forms by the fact that the servant is indebted to the master'. See Cook 1984, 353ff. For Webster's speech, see the version revised by himself in *Congressional Globe*, Thirty-first Congress, first session, Appendix, pp. 269–76.

66. See n. 4 above.

SELECT BIBLIOGRAPHY

Sources

Pelli

Pelli, Giuseppe, *Contre la peine di mort, précédé de Correspondance avec Beccaria* (1760), P. Audegean, ed. and transl., Paris 2016.

Pelli, Giuseppe, *Contro la pena di morte* (1760), P. Audegean, ed., Padua 2014.

Pelli, Giuseppe, *Efemeridi*, Series 1.1–30 and 2.1–18, R. Pasta, ed., online: http://pelli.bncf .firenze.sbn.it/it/progetto.html

Pelli, Giuseppe, *Efemeridi*, Series 2.19–50, Biblioteca Nazionale Centrale di Firenze, segnatura: NA 1050 I–II.

Beccaria

Beccaria, Cesare, *Carteggio, parte I (1758–1768)*, C. Capra, R. Pasta, F. Pino Pongolini, eds, in *Edizione Nazionale delle Opere di Cesare Beccaria*, vol. 4, L. Firpo and G. Francioni, eds, Milan 1996.

Beccaria, Cesare, *Carteggio, parte II (1769–1794)*, C. Capra, R. Pasta, F. Pino Pongolini, eds, in *Edizione Nazionale delle Opere di Cesare Beccaria*, vol. 5, L. Firpo and G. Francioni, eds, Milan 1996.

Beccaria, Cesare, *Consulte Amministrative e Giuridiche*, in *Opere*, S. Romagnoli, ed., vol. 2, Florence 1958.

Beccaria, Cesare, *Dei delitti e delle pene*, G. Francioni, ed., in *Edizione Nazionale delle Opere di Cesare Beccaria*, vol. 1, L. Firpo and G. Francioni, eds, Milan 1984.

Beccaria, Cesare, *Dei delitti e delle pene*, R. Bellamy, ed., R. Davies, transl., Cambridge 1995.

Beccaria, Cesare, *Dei delitti e delle pene, con una raccolta di lettere e documenti relativi alla nascita dell'opera e alla sua fortuna nell' Europa del Settecento*, F. Venturi, ed., Turin 1965.

Beccaria, Cesare, *Edizione Nazionale delle Opere di Cesare Beccaria*, L. Firpo and G. Francioni, eds, 16 vols, Milan 1984–2014.

Beccaria, Cesare, *On Crimes and Punishments and Other Writings*, A. Thomas, ed., A. Thomas and J. Parzen, transl., Toronto 2008; online edition: https://www-degruyter-com.ezp.lib .cam.ac.uk/viewbooktoc/product/471824

Beccaria, Cesare, *Opere*, S. Romagnoli, ed., 2 vols, Florence 1958.

OTHER SOURCES

A hearty lover of his country, *Solon Secundus: or Some defects in the English laws: with their proper remedies*, London 1695.

A Student in Politics, *Proposals to the Legislature, For preventing the frequent executions and exportations of Convicts, in a Letter to the Right Honourable Henry Pelham, Esq.*, London 1754.

Adderley, Charles Bowyer, *Transportation not necessary*, 2 vols, London 1851.

Alembert, Jean d', *Mémoires et réflexions sur Christine, reine de Suède* (1753), in *Mélanges de littérature, d'histoire et de philosophie*, vol. 2, 2nd edn, Amsterdam 1759: 227–300.

Anonymous, *What is to be done with our convicts. Sketch of a system of penal state servitude. An efficient, reformatory and economic substitute for Transportation and Imprisonment*, Edinburgh 1851.

Aristotle, *On the Soul* (*De anima*), transl. W. S. Hett, Loeb Classical Library, Cambridge, Mass. 1957.

Aulus Gellius, *Attic Nights*, 3 vols, transl. J. C. Rolfe, Loeb Classical Library, Cambridge, Mass., 1927–28.

Bellers, John, *Essays about the Poor: Manufactures, Trade, Plantations and Immorality* (1699), in G. Clarke, ed., *John Bellers. His Life, Times and Writings*, London and New York, 1987: 102–4.

Bentham, Jeremy, *Commonplace Book*, in *The Works of Jeremy Bentham, Published under the Superintendence of his Executor, John Bowring*, 11 vols, vol. 10: *Memoirs Part I and Correspondence*, Edinburgh 1843; online: https://oll.libertyfund.org/titles/bentham-the-works -of-jeremy-bentham-vol-10-memoirs-part-i-and-correspondence

Bentham, Jeremy, *The Correspondence of Jeremy Bentham*, vol. 1: *1752–1776*, T.L.S. Sprigge, ed., London 1968.

Bentham, Jeremy, *Oeuvres de Jérémie Bentham*, vol. 2: *Théorie des peines et des récompenses*, É. Dumont, ed., Brussels 1829.

Bentham, Jeremy, *The Rationale of Punishment*, R. Smith, ed., London 1830.

Bentham, Jeremy, *Traité de législation civile et pénale*, É. Dumont, ed., 1st edn, 3 vols, Paris 1802.

Bentham Papers 1750–1885, University College London Library, Box cxli, fols 88 and 120; Mss 4 (=AJB037: 147–087 and 147–088); Mss 5 (=AJB393a: 141–087); Mss 9 (=AJB115: 159–137).

Bigge, John Thomas, *Report of the Commissioner of Inquiry into the state of the colony of New South Wales*, London 1822.

Blackstone, William, *The Letters of William Blackstone 1844–1780*, W. R. Prest, ed., London 2010.

Boccaccio, Giovanni, *The Decameron*, G. H. McWilliam, transl., 2nd edn, Penguin Classics, London 1995.

Buondelmonte, Giuseppe, *Ragionamento sul diritto della guerra giusta*, in *Magazzino toscano d'instruzione e di piacere, tomo secondo*, Livorno 1755: 521–39; 2nd edn (repr.) Florence 1757.

Camus, Albert, 'Reflections on the Guillotine', in *Resistance, Rebellion, and Death: Essays*, J. O'Brien, transl., New York 1960: 173–234.

Cassius Dio, *Roman History*, E. Cary, transl., 9 vols, Loeb Classical Library, Cambridge, Mass. 1914–70.

Cicero, *De oratore*, E. W. Sutton and H. Rackham, eds and transl., 2 vols, Loeb Classical Library, Cambridge, Mass. 1942.

Cocceji, Heinrich von, *De sacro-sancto talionis iure* (1705), in *Exercitationum curiosarum Palatinarum, Traiectinarum et Viadrinarum*, vol. 2, Lemgoviae (Lemgo) 1722: 733–48.

Cocceji, Heinrich and Samuel von, 'Commentary on Grotius, *De iure belli ac pacis*: see Grotius, *De iure belli*.

Coles, Edward, *History of the Ordinance of 1787* (1856), in C. W. Alvord, ed., *Governor Edward Coles*, Springfield, Ill. 1920: 376–98.

Digest: The Digest of Justinian, T. Mommsen and P. Krüger, eds, A. Watson, transl. and ed., 4 vols, Philadelphia 1985.

Diogenes Laertius, *Solon*, in *Lives of Eminent Philosophers*, R. D. Hicks, transl., vol. 1, Loeb Classical Library, Cambridge, Mass. 1980.

Gallarati Scotti, Beccaria Bonesana, Risi, 'Voto degli infrascritti individui della giunta delegata per la riforma del sistema criminale nella Lombardia Austriaca riguardante la pena di morte, 1792', in Beccaria, *Opere*, S. Romagnoli, ed., vol. 2, Florence 1958: 735–41.

Grotius, Hugo, *De iure belli ac pacis* (1625), with notes of Johann Friedrich Gronovius and Jean Barbeyrac, ed. and commentary by Heinrich and Samuel von Cocceji [1744–47], 5 vols, Lausanne 1751–52.

Grotius, Hugo, *The Rights of War and Peace* (1625), R. Tuck, ed., from the edition of Jean Barbeyrac, 3 vols, Indianapolis 2005; online: https://oll.libertyfund.org/titles/grotius-the-rights-of-war-and-peace-2005-ed-3-vols

Hansard online: https://api.parliament.uk/historic-hansard/index.html

Heineccius, Johann Gottlieb, *Antiquitatum Romanarum iurisprudentiam illustrantium syntagma*, 2 vols, Halle 1719.

Heineccius, Johann Gottlieb, *Elementa juris Germanici, tum veteris, tum hodierni*, 2 vols, (1735–36), 3rd edn, Geneva 1748.

Heineccius, Johann Gottlieb, *Elementa juris naturae et gentium commoda auditoribus methodo adornata* (1738), 3rd edn, Halle 1749.

Heineccius, Johann Gottlieb, *Praelectiones academicae in Hugonis Grotii de jure belli et pacis, libros tres*, Roboretum (Rovereto) 1746; online: https://reader.digitale-sammlungen.de/de/fs1/object/display/bsb11300697_00005.html

Herodotus, A. D. Godley, ed. and transl., 4 vols, Loeb Classical Library, Cambridge, Mass. 1975–97.

Hobbes, Thomas, *Leviathan*, N. Malcolm, ed., 3 vols, Oxford 2012–14.

Hugo, Victor, *Écrits sur la peine de mort*, R. Jean, ed., Le Paradou 1979.

Hutcheson, Francis, *An Inquiry into the Original of our Ideas of Beauty and Virtue, in Two Treatises*, London 1725.

Jefferson, Thomas, *Autobiography of Thomas Jefferson, 1743–1790*, P. L. Ford, ed., New York 1914.

Julius Capitolinus, *Gordiani*: see Scriptores Historiae Augustae.

Lampredi, Giovanni Maria, *De licentia in hostem liber singularis in quo Samuelis Cocceii sententia de infinita licentia in hostem exponitur et confutatur. Accessit (ejusdem) De maiestate principis ad legem constituendam omnino necessaria oratio quam habuit in sacra Florentina academia postridie kal. martias ann. 1759*, Florence 1761.

Lang, John Dunmore, *Transportation and Colonisation, or the Causes of Comparative Failure of the Transportation System in the Australian Colonies*, London 1837.

Leibniz, Gottfried Wilhelm, *Theodicy, Essays on the Goodness of God, the Freedom of Man and the Origin or Evil* (1710 original in French), H. M. Huggard, Eng. transl., New Haven, Conn. 1952; online: https://www.gutenberg.org/files/17147/17147-h/17147-h.htm

Leopold, grand duke of Tuscany (Pietro Leopoldo I), *Riforma della legislazione criminale* (30 November 1786), in Venturi, ed. 1965: 258–300.

Livy, 14 vols, Loeb Classical Library, Cambridge, Mass. 1919–59.

Livy, *Summaries, Fragments and Julius Obsequens*, A. C. Schlesinger, transl., General index by R. M. Geer, vol. 14, Loeb Classical Library, Cambridge, Mass. 1959 (1967 repr.).

Maximus of Tyre, *The Philosophical Orations*, M. B. Trapp, transl., Oxford 1997.

Minutes of the Supreme Executive Council of Pennsylvania, from its Organization to the Termination of the Revolution, vol. XVI. Containing the proceedings of the Supreme Executive Council from February 7th, 1789, to December 20th, 1790, both days inclusive, Harrisburg 1853.

Montesquieu, *De l'esprit des lois*, Geneva 1748; online edn, Nourse 1772: https://fr.wikisource.org/wiki/De_l'esprit_des_lois_(éd._Nourse)

Montesquieu, *The Spirit of the Laws*, A. M. Cohler, B .C. Miller and H. S. Stone, transl., Cambridge 1989.

Natale, Tommaso, *Rifessioni politiche intorno all'efficacia e necessità delle pene*, Palermo 1772.

Pausanias, *Description of Greece*, Book 2: *Corinth*, W.H.S. Jones, transl., Loeb Classical Library, Cambridge, Mass. 1998 (repr.); Book 4: *Messenia*, W.H.S. Jones and H. A. Ormerod, transl., Loeb Classical Library, Cambridge, Mass. 1989 (repr.).

Pennsylvania Archives, ninth series, Volume II, Part I, 1794–1796, G. MacKinney, ed., directed by J. N. Rule and J. R. Hood, 1931.

Plato, *Euthyphro, Apology, Crito, Phaedo*, C. Emlyn-Jones and W. Preddy, eds and transl., Loeb Classical Library, Cambridge, Mass. 2017.

Plato, *Laches, Protagoras, Meno, Euthydemus*, W.R.M. Lamb, transl., Loeb Classical Library, Cambridge, Mass. 1999 (repr.).

Plato, *Laws*, R. G. Bury, transl., 2 vols, Loeb Classical Library, Cambridge, Mass. 1926.

Plato, *Lysis, Symposium, Gorgias*, W.R.M. Lamb, transl., Loeb Classical Library, Cambridge, Mass. 2001 (repr.).

Plutarch, *Lycurgus*, in Plutarch, *Lives*, vol. 1: *Theseus and Romulus, Lycurgus and Numa, Solon and Publicola*, B. Perrin, ed. and transl., Loeb Classical Library, Cambridge, Mass. 1967.

Plutarch, *Solon*, in Plutarch, *Lives*, vol. 1: *Theseus and Romulus, Lycurgus and Numa, Solon and Publicola*, B. Perrin, ed. and transl., Loeb Classical Library, Cambridge, Mass. 1967.

Pseudo-Quintilian, *Declamationes XIX maiores*, L. Håkanson, ed., Stuttgart 1982.

Pufendorf, Samuel von, *De iure naturae et gentium, libri octo* (1672), F. Böhling, ed., vol. 4 (1998) in *Gesammelte Werke*, W. Schmidt-Biggemann, ed., Berlin 1998–; online: https://archive.org/details/samuelispufendor1672pufe/page/n5

Pufendorf, Samuel von, *De officio hominis et civis secundum legem naturalem libri duo* (1673), transl. from Latin into French by Jean Barbeyrac, 4ᵗʰ edn, revised and augmented, Amsterdam 1718.

Pufendorf, Samuel von, *On the Duty of Man and Citizen according to the Natural Law* (1673), F. G. Moore, Eng. transl., New York 1927; online: http://fama2.us.es/fde/ocr/2010/deOfficioHominisT2.pdf

Risi, Paul, *Animadversiones ad criminalem jurisprudentiam pertinentes*, Milan 1796.

Robespierre, Maximilien de, *Oeuvres de Maximilien Robespierre*, M. Bouloiseau et al., eds, vol. 7: *Discours. Deuxième partie (janvier–septembre 1791)*, Paris 1952.

Rousseau, Jean-Jacques, *Discours sur les sciences et les arts*, Geneva 1750; online: https://www.rousseauonline.ch/pdf/rousseauonline-0034.pdf

Rousseau, Jean-Jacques, *Discours sur l'origine et les fondements de l'inégalité parmi les hommes*, Amsterdam 1755; online: https://www.rousseauonline.ch/pdf/rousseauonline-0002.pdf

Rousseau, Jean-Jacques, *Du contrat social, ou principes du droit politique*, Amsterdam 1762; online: http://www.rousseauonline.ch/Text/du-contrat-social-ou-principes-du-droit-politique.php

Rousseau, Jean-Jacques, *Émile ou De l'Éducation*, La Haye 1762; online: https://www.rousseauonline.ch/pdf/rousseauonline-0022.pdf

Rush, Benjamin, M. D., *A Plan for the Punishment of Crime: Two Essays* (1787), N. K. Teeters, ed., Philadelphia 1954.

Scriptores Historiae Augustae, *The Three Gordians*, D. Magie, ed. and transl., in vol. 2 of 3 vols, Loeb Classical Library, Cambridge, Mass. 1993.

Seneca, *Moral Essays*, vol. 1: *De ira*, J. W. Basore, ed. and transl, Loeb Classical Library, Cambridge, Mass. 1970.

Sigonio, Carlo, *M. Tullii Ciceronis consolatio, vel De luctu minuendo*, in *Opera omnia edita et inedita*, F. Argelati and L.A. Muratori, eds, vol. 6, Milan 1737: 837–78.

Solon Secundus: see A hearty lover of his country.

Smith, Richard, ed., *Jeremy Bentham. The Rationale of Punishment*, London 1830.

Stobaeus, *Florilegium*, A. Meineke, ed., 4 vols, Leipzig 1855–57.

Stroud, George M., *Sketch of the Laws relating to Slavery in the Several States of the United States of America*, Philadelphia 1827.

Suetonius, *The Lives of the Caesars*, Book 1: *The Deified Julius*, J. C. Rolfe, transl., in vol. 1 of 2 vols, Loeb Classical Library, Cambridge, Mass. 1970.

Tertullian, *Adversus Judaeos*, H. Tränkle, ed., Wiesbaden 1964.

The Congressional Globe, Washington 1834–73; Thirty-first Congress, first session, Appendix: 269–76; Thirty-eighth Congress, first session, Saturday 9 April 1864. Online: https://memory.loc.gov/ammem/amlaw/lwcglink.html#anchor31

United States Caselaw Access Project: https://case.law

Vattel, Emer de, *Le droit des gens ou Principes de la loi naturelle appliqués à la conduite et aux affaires des nations et des souverains*, 2 vols, London 1758.

Vaux, Robert, *Notices of the original and successive effects to improve the discipline of the prison at Philadelphia and to reform the criminal code of Pennsylvania, with a few observations of the penitentiary system*, Philadelphia 1826.

Verri, P. *Meditazioni sulla felicità*, G. Francioni, ed., Pavia 1996.

Voltaire, *Histoire de Charles XII, roi de Suède* (1731), in *Oeuvres complètes*, vol. 4, G. von Proschwitz, ed., Oxford 1996.

Voltaire, *Oeuvres complètes*, N. Cronk et al., eds, Voltaire Foundation, Oxford 1968– ; online: http://www.voltaire.ox.ac.uk

Voltaire, *Oeuvres de 1762 (I)*, in *Oeuvres complètes*, vol. 56A, D. Guiragossian Carr et al., eds, Oxford 2001.

Voltaire, *Traité sur la tolérance à l'occasion de la mort de Jean Calas*, Toulouse 1763.

Winstanley, Gerrard, *The Law of Freedom in a Platform: Or True Magistracy Restored* (1652), in *The Complete Works of Gerrard Winstanley*, T. N. Corns, A. Hughes and D. Loewenstein, eds, vol. 2, Oxford 2009.

Winstanley, Gerrard, *The New Law of Righteousness* (1649), in *The Complete Works of Gerrard Winstanley*, T. N. Corns, A. Hughes and D. Loewenstein, eds, vol. 1, Oxford 2009.

Xenophon, *Constitution of the Lacedaemonians*, in *Scripta minora*, E. C. Marchant, ed. and transl., Loeb Classical Library, Cambridge, Mass. 1968.

Ypey, Nicolai, *Specimen juris universalis juxta atque civilis inaugurale exhibens quaedam de servitute tum in genere tum in specie de servitute poenae*, Frankfurt 1770.

GENERAL BIBLIOGRAPHY

Atkinson, A. 1994, 'The free-born Englishman transported: convict rights as a measure of eighteenth-century empire', *Past & Present* 144: 88–115.

Audegean, P. 2010, *La philosophie de Beccaria: savoir punir, savoir écrire, savoir produire*, Paris.

Audegean, P. 2012, 'Le plus ancien programme de l'abolitionisme italien: le "Discorso della pena di morte" de Giuseppe Pelli (1760–1761)', in L. Delia and F. Hoarau, eds, *La peine de mort*, in *CORPUS, revue de philosophie* 62: 135–56.

Audegean, P. 2014, '*Dei delitti e delle pene*: significato e genesi di un pamphlet giuspolitico', in Ippolito, ed., *La libertà attraverso il diritto*: 71–92.

Audegean, P. 2015, 'Beccaria et la naissance de la Prison', *L'Irascible. Revue de l'Institut Rhône-Alpin de Sciences Criminelles* 5: 47–68.

Audegean, P. 2017, 'Cesare Beccaria's *On Crimes and Punishments*: the meaning and genesis of a jurispolitical pamphlet', *History of European Ideas* 43: 884–97.

Audegean, P. 2019, 'Droit naturel et droit à la vie. Beccaria lecteur de Hobbes', *Diciottesimo Secolo* 4: 33–45.

Audegean, P., ed. 2014, *Giuseppe Pelli. Contro la pena di morte*, Padua.

Audegean, P., ed. and transl. 2016, *Giuseppe Pelli. Contre la peine di mort, précédé de Correspondance avec Beccaria*, Paris.

Audegean, P., transl. 2019, *Dario Ippolito. L'esprit des droits: Montesquieu et le pouvoir de punir*, Lyon.

Audegean, P. and Delia, L. 2018, 'Introduction: les deux sources de la modernité pénale', in Audegean and Delia, eds, *Le moment Beccaria*: 1–12.

Audegean, P. and Delia, L., eds 2018, *Le moment Beccaria: naissance du droit pénal moderne (1764–1810)*, Liverpool.

Audegean, P., Campanini, M. and Carnevali, B., eds 2017, *Rousseau et l'Italie: Littérature, morale et politique*, Paris: 147–76.

Balkin, J. M. and Levinson, S. 2012, 'The dangerous Thirteenth Amendment', *Columbia Law Review* 112: 1459–500.

Banner, S. 2002, *The Death Penalty: An American History*, Cambridge, Mass.

Béal, C. 2018, 'Beccaria et le réformisme pénal en Angleterre (1764–1790)', in Audegean and Delia, eds, *Le moment Beccaria*: 45–64.

Beales, D. 1987–2009, *Joseph II*, vol. 1: *In the Shadow of Maria Theresa, 1741–1780*, Cambridge 1987; vol. 2: *Against the World, 1780–1790*, Cambridge 2009.

Beattie, J. M. 1986, *Crime and the Courts in England 1600–1800*, Oxford.

Berti, F. 2003, *La ragione prudente: Gaetano Filangieri e la religione delle riforme*, Florence.

Berti, F. 2014, 'Diritto penale e diritti dell'uomo : il garantismo di Gaetano Filangieri', in Ippolito, ed., *La libertà attraverso il diritto*: 115–47.

Berti, F. 2018, 'Un "beccarien" avant la lettre? La philosophie pénale de Tommaso Natale', in Audegean and Delia, eds, *Le moment Beccaria*: 205–22.

Bessler, J. D. 2014, *The Birth of American Law: An Italian philosopher and the American Revolution*, Durham, N.C.

Betri, M. L. and Maldini Chiarito, D. 2002, *Scritture di desiderio e di ricordo-autobiografie, diari, memorie, tra Settecento e Novecento*, Milan.

Blackburn, R. 1988, *The Overthrow of Colonial Slavery, 1776–1848*, London.

Blackmon, D. A. 2008, *Slavery by Another Name: The Re-Enslavement of Black Americans from the Civil War to World War II*, New York.

Blamires, C. 1997, 'Beccaria et l'Angleterre', in M. Porret, ed., *Beccaria et la culture juridique des Lumières*, Geneva: 69–81.

Blanning, T.C.W. 1994, *Joseph II*, London.

Buckland, W. W. 1968, *A Text-Book of Roman Law from Augustus to Justinian*, 3rd edn, revised by P. Stein, Cambridge.

Cantarella, E. 2007, *Il ritorno della vendetta. Pena di morte: giustizia o assassinio*, Milan.

Capecchi, S. 2002, 'Scrivere all'ordine del giorno: le "efemeridi" di Giuseppe Pelli e la letteratura periodica', *Studi Italiani* 1–2: 47–93.

Capecchi, S. 2006, *Scrittura e coscienza autobiografica nel diario di Giuseppe Pelli*, Rome.

Capra, C. 2002, *I progressi della ragione. Vita di Pietro Verri*, Bologna.

Capra, C. 2016, 'Beccaria e i Verri negli anni dei Pugni e del *Caffè*', in V. Ferrone and G. Ricuperati, eds, *Il caso Beccaria. A 250 anni dalla pubblicazione del Dei delitti e delle pene*, Bologna: 87–110.

Capra, C. 2017, 'Beccaria fonctionaire et l'évolution de ses idées', in P. Audegean et al., eds, *Le bonheur du plus grand nombre: Beccaria et les Lumières*, Lyon: 177–93.

Caracciolo, A. 1968, *Domenico Passionei tra Roma e la repubblica delle lettere*, Rome.

Christopher, E. 2011, *A Merciless Place: The Lost Story of Britain's Convict Disaster in Africa*, Oxford.

Clarke, G., ed. 1987, *John Bellers. His Life, Times and Writings*, London.

Comanducci, P. 1981, *Settecento Conservatore: Lampredi e il diritto naturale*, Milan.

Cook, J. M. 1984, 'Involuntary servitude: modern conditions addressed in United States v. Mussry', *Catholic University Law Review* 34: 153–80.

Corns, T. N., Hughes, A. and Loewenstein, D., eds 2009, *The Complete Works of Gerrard Winstanley*, 2 vols, Oxford.

Costa, P., ed. 2010, *Il diritto di uccidere: l'enigma della pena di morte*, Milan.

Cronk, N. et al., eds 1968–, *Les Oeuvres complètes de Voltaire*, Voltaire Foundation, Oxford; online: http://www.voltaire.ox.ac.uk

Devereaux, S. 1999, 'In place of death: transportation, penal practices and the English state, 1770–1830", in C. Strange, ed., *Qualities of Mercy: Justice, Punishment, and Discretion*, Vancouver: 52–76.

Devereaux, S. 2015, 'Inexperienced humanitarians? William Wilberforce, William Pitt, and the executions crisis of the 1780s', *Law and History Review* 33: 839–85.

Devereaux, S. 2016, 'The bloodiest code: counting executions and pardons at the Old Bailey, 1730–1837', *Law, Crime and History* 6: 1–36.

Diciottesimo Secolo 2019: *Diciottesimo Secolo, Rivista della Società Italiana di Studi sul Secolo XVIII* 4 (on Beccaria and Britain).

Draper, A. J. 2000, 'Cesare Beccaria's influence on English discussion of punishment, 1764– 1789', *History of European Ideas* 26: 177–99.

Dunthorpe, H. 1999, 'Beccaria and Britain', in D. W. Howell and K. O. Morgan, eds, *Crime, Protest and Police in Modern British Society*, Cardiff: 73–96.

Duthille, R. 2017, 'Les radicaux anglais lecteurs de Beccaria (1767–1795)', in P. Audegean et al., eds, *Le bonheur du plus grand nombre: Beccaria et les Lumières*, Lyon: 287–99.

Esposito, B. and Wood, L. 1982, *Prison Slavery*, Washington, D.C.

Evans, R. 1982, *The Fabrication of Virtue: English Prison Architecture, 1750–1840*, Cambridge.

Ferrajoli, L. 1989, *Diritto e ragione. Teoria del garantismo penale*, Rome.

Ferrajoli, L. 2010, 'Il fondamento del rifiuto della pena capitale', in Costa, ed., *Il diritto di uccidere*: 57–58

Ferrajoli, L. 2019, 'Beccaria e Bentham', *Diciottesimo Secolo* 4: 75–84.

Finkelman, P. 1986, 'Slavery and the Northwest Ordinance: a study in ambiguity', *Journal of the Early Republic* 6: 343–69.

Firpo, L. and Francioni, G., eds 1984–2014, *Edizione Nazionale delle Opere di Cesare Beccaria*, 16 vols, Milan; vol. 1, 1984: *Dei delitti e delle pene*, G. Francioni and L. Firpo, eds; vol. 4, 1994: *Carteggio, Parte I (1758–1768); Carteggio, Parte II (1769–1794)*, C. Capra, R. Pasta and F. Pino Pongolini, eds.

Ford, P. L., ed. 1914, *Autobiography of Thomas Jefferson, 1743–1790*, New York.

Foucault, M. 1975, *Surveiller et punir: naissance de la prison*, Paris.

Francioni, G. 1985–1986, 'Notizia sul manoscritto della seconda redazione del *Dei delitti e delle pene* (con una appendice di inediti di Pietro Verri relativi all'opera di Beccaria)', *Studi settecenteschi* 5: 229–96.

Francioni, G. 2017, 'Beccaria, philosophe utilitariste', in P. Audegean et al., eds, *Le bonheur du plus grand nombre: Beccaria et les Lumières*, Lyon: 23–44.

Francioni, G., ed. 1984, *Cesare Beccaria, Dei delitti e delle pene*, in Firpo and Francioni, eds, *Edizione Nazionale*, vol. 1: 17–129.

Francioni, G., ed. 2014, *Edizione Nazionale delle opere di Pietro Verri*, vol. 1: *Scritti letterari filosofici e satirici*, Rome.

Fratoianni, A. and Verga, M., eds 1992, *Pompeo Nero: atti del colloquio di studi di Castelfiorentino 6–7 maggio 1988*, Castelfiorentino.

Garland, D. 2010, *Peculiar Institution: America's Death Penalty in an Age of Abolition*, Oxford.

Garland, D., McGowen, R. and Meranze, M., eds 2011, *America's Death Penalty: Between Past and Present*, New York.

Hamilton, H. D. 1951, 'The legislative and judicial history of the Thirteenth Amendment', *National Bar Journal* 9: 26–134.

Hart, H.L.A. 1966, 'Beccaria and Bentham', *Atti del Convegno internazionale su Cesare Beccaria, Torino 4–6 ottobre 1964*, Turin: 19–29.

Hillner, J. 2015, *Prison, Punishment and Penance in Late Antiquity*, Cambridge.

Hood, R. and Hoyle, C. 2015, *The Death Penalty: A Worldwide Perspective*, 5th edn, revised and updated, Oxford.

Innes, J. 1987, 'Prisons for the poor: English bridewells, 1555–1800', in F. Snyder and D. Hay, eds, *Labour, Law and Crime: An Historical Perspective*, London: 42–122.

Innes, J. 2009, 'The King's Bench prison in the later eighteenth century: law, authority and order in a London debtor's prison', in *Inferior Politics: Social Problems and Social Politics in Eighteenth-Century Britain*, Oxford: 227–78.

Ippolito, D. 2008, *Mario Pagano: il pensiero giuspolitico di un illuminista*, Turin.

Ippolito, D. 2012, *Diritti e potere: indagini sull'illuminismo penale*, Rome.

Ippolito, D. 2016, *Lo spirito del garantismo. Montesquieu e il potere di punire*, Rome.

Ippolito, D. 2017, 'Contrat social et peine capitale. Beccaria contre Rousseau', in P. Audegean, M. Campanini and B. Carnevali, eds, *Rousseau et l'Italie: Littérature, morale et politique*, Paris: 147–76.

Ippolito, D., ed. 2014, *La libertà attraverso il diritto: Illuminismo giuridico e questione penale*, Naples.

James, S. 1997, *Passion and Action: The Emotions in Seventeenth Century Philosophy*, Oxford.

Jean, R., ed. 1979, *Écrits de Victor Hugo sur la peine de mort*, Le Paradou.

Kares, L. 1994–95, 'Unlucky Thirteenth: a constitutional amendment in search of a doctrine', *Cornell Law Review* 80: 372–412.

Kercher, B. 2003, '"Perish or prosper: the law and convict transportation in the British empire, 1700–1850', *Law and History Review* 21: 527–84.

Manion, J. 2015, *Liberty's Prisoners: Carceral Culture in Early America*, Philadelphia.

Mazza, M. F. and Tomasello, B. M. 2005, *Gli scritti di Giuseppe Pelli Bencivenni: anagrafe storica*, Florence.

McClintock, A. 2010, *Servi della pena: condannati a morte nella Roma imperiale*, Naples.

McClintock, A. 2018, 'L'allegoria della giustizia sul frontespizio di *Dei delitti e delle pene*', *Quaderni di Storia* 88: 206–36.

McLennan, R. M. 2008, *The Crisis of Imprisonment: Protest, Politics and the Making of the American Penal State, 1776–1941*, Cambridge.

Meranze, M. 1996, *Laboratories of Virtue: Punishment, Revolution, and Authority in Philadelphia, 1760–1835*, Chapel Hill, N.C.

Merback, M. B. 1999, *The Thief, the Cross and the Wheel: Pain and the Spectacle of Punishment in Medieval and Renaissance Europe*, Chicago.

Mereu, I. 1982, *La morte come pena: saggio sulla violenza legale*, 3rd edn, Rome.

Mereu, I. 1988, *La pena di morte a Milano nel secolo di Beccaria*, Vicenza.

Millar, F. 1984, 'Condemnation to hard labour in the Roman empire, from the Julio-Claudians to Constantine', *Papers of the British School of Rome* 52: 128–47.

Morieux, R. 2019, *The Society of Prisoners: Anglo-French Wars and Incarceration in the 18th Century*, Oxford.

Oldfield, J. 1988, *Popular Politics and British Anti-Slavery: The Mobilisation of Public Opinion against the Slave Trade 1787–1807*, Manchester.

Onuf, P. S. 1987, *Statehood and Union: A History of the Northwest Ordinance*, Bloomington, Ind.

Pasta, R. 1990, 'Beccaria tra giuristi e filosofi: aspetti della fortuna in Toscana e nell'Italia centro-settentrionale', in S. Romagnoli and G. D. Pisapia, eds, *Cesare Beccaria tra Milano e l'Europa: Convegno di studi per il 250° Anniversario della Nascita Promosso dal Comune di Milano*, Milan: 512–33.

Pasta, R. 1997, 'Dalla carte di Giuseppe Pelli: lettura e censura a Firenze', in M. G. Tavoni and F. Waquet, eds, *Lo spazio del libro nell'Europa del Settecento. Atti del Convegno di Ravenna (15–16 dicembre 1995)*, Bologna: 153–80.

Pasta, R. 2002, '"Ego ipse . . . non alius". Esperienze e memorie di un lettore del Settecento e Novecento', in M. L. Betri and D. Maldini Chiarito, eds, *Scritture di desiderio e di ricordo. Autobiografie, diari, memorie tra Settecento e Novecento*, Milan: 187–206.

Pasta, R. 2009, 'Introduzione. Sguardi sul mondo e testimonianze di se', in R. Pasta, ed., *Scritture dell'io fra pubblico e privato*, Rome.

Pasta, R. 2016, 'Contro la pena di morte: Beccaria, Giuseppe Pelli e il codice leopoldino', in V. Ferrone and G. Ricuperati, eds, *Il Caso Beccaria. A 250 anni dalla pubblicazione del Dei delitti e delle pene*, Bologna: 191–207.

Prest, W. R., ed. 2010, *The Letters of William Blackstone 1744–1780*, London.

Reinert, S. 2018, *The Academy of Fisticuffs: Political Economy and Commercial Society in Enlightenment Italy*, Cambridge, Mass.

Reungoat, S. 2012, 'La peine de mort et ses alternatives dans la pensée économique et sociale anglaise, 1660–1720', *CORPUS, revue de philosophie* 62: 37–52.

Rogers, M. 1996, 'Gerard Winstanley on crime and punishment', *Sixteenth Century Journal* 27/3: 735–47.

Romagnoli, S., ed. 1958, *Cesare Beccaria, Opere*, 2 vols, Florence.

Rosa, M. 1992, 'La revisione della legge di ammortizzazione (1751): il confronto fra Pompeo Neri e Giulio Rucellai', in Fratoianni and Verga, eds, *Pompeo Nero*: 87–102.

Rosa, M. 1999, *Settecento religioso. Politica della ragione e religione del cuore*, Venice.

Schofield, P. 2019, '"The first steps rightly directed in the track of legislation": Jeremy Bentham on Cesare Beccaria's *Essay On Crimes and Punishments*', *Diciottesimo Secolo* 4: 65–74.

Shackleton, R. 1972, 'The greatest happiness of the greatest number: the history of Bentham's phrase', *Studies on Voltaire and the Eighteenth Century* 90: 1466–73.

Shaw, A.G.L. 1966, *Convicts and the Colonies: A Study of Penal Transportation from Great Britain and Ireland to Australia and Other Parts of the British Empire*, London.

Spierenburg, P. 1991, *The Prison Experience: Disciplinary Institutions and Their Inmates in Early Modern Europe*, New Brunswick.

Spierenburg, P., ed. 1984, *The Emergence of Carceral Institutions: Prisons, Galleys and Lunatic Asylums 1550–1900*, Rotterdam.

Sprigge, T.L.S., ed. 1968, *The Correspondence of Jeremy Bentham*, vol. 1: 1752–1776, London.

Stern, S. 2014, 'Blackstone's Criminal Law: Common-Law Harmonization and Legislative Reform', in M. D. Dubber, ed., *Foundational Texts in Modern Criminal Law*, Oxford: 61–78.

Straumann, B. 2015, *Roman Law in the State of Nature*, Cambridge.

Teeters, N. K., ed. 1954, *A Plan for the Punishment of Crime by Benjamin Rush, M.D., 1746–1813 or 1815*, Philadelphia.

Timpanaro Morelli, M. A. 1978, 'A proposito di un recente biografia di Giovanni Maria Lampredi', *Rassegna Storica Toscana* 24: 153–98.

Timpanaro Morelli, M. A., ed. 1976, *Lettere a Giuseppe Pelli Bencivenni, 1747–1808*, Rome.

Tribe, K. 2006, 'Cameralism and the science of the state', in M. Goldie and M. Wokler, eds, *The Cambridge History of Eighteenth-Century Political Thought*, Cambridge: 525–46.

Trimaille, G. 2012, 'La peine de mort dans la doctrine utilitariste de Jeremy Bentham', *CORPUS, revue de philosophie* 62: 215–30.

Tuck, R. 1999. *The Rights of War and Peace: Political Thought and the International Order from Grotius to Kant*, Oxford.

Valsecchi, F. 1934, *L'assolutismo illuminato in Austria e Lombardia*, vol. 2.1: *La Lombardia. La politica interna*, Bologna.

Venturi, F. 1958, *Illuministi italiani*, vol. 3: *Riformatori Lombardi piemontesi e toscani*, Milan.

Venturi, F. 1964, 'L'immagine della Giustizia', *Rivista Storica Italiana* 76: 707–19.

Venturi, F. 1969, *Settecento riformatore*, vol. 1: *Da Muratori a Beccaria*, Turin.

Venturi, F., ed. 1965, *Cesare Beccaria, Dei Delitti e delle pene: Con una raccolta di lettere e documenti relative alla nascita dell'opera e alla sua fortuna nell'Europa del Settecento*, Turin.

Woolf, S. 1979, *A History of Italy 1700–1860*, London.

INDEX